W9-BRY-528

Micrographic Systems

Micrographic Systems

THIRD EDITION

William Saffady

Association for Information and Image Management
1100 Wayne Avenue, Suite 1100
Silver Spring, MD 20910

AIIM Catalog No. R052

©1990 by the Association for Information and Image Management
1100 Wayne Avenue, Suite 1100
Silver Spring, MD 20910
Tel: 301/587-8202
Fax: 301/587-2711

Printed in the United States of America

Saffady, William
Micrographic Systems, Third Edition

(Image technology consumer handbook).
1. Image Technology 2. Title 3. Series

ISBN O-89258-190-5

Contents

Foreword

Preface

1 Micrographic Systems: An Introduction 1

Archival Microfilming 3 / Active Records Management 7 /
Managing Computer Output 9 / Micropublishing 11 / Library
Applications 13 / Micrographics Systems Analysis 15 /
Micrographics Standards 17 / The Concept of Reduction 20

2 Types of Microforms and Their Characteristics 23

Reel Microfilm 24 / Microfilm Cartridges 28 / Microfiche 30 /
Updatable Microfiche 37 / Microfilm Jackets 39 / Card
Jackets 43 / Aperture Cards 44 / Ultra High Reduction
Microforms 47 / Opaque Microforms 49

3 Source Document Microfilming 51

Recording Technologies 54 / Microfilm Cameras 58 / Microfilm
Processing 69 / Microfilm Inspection 73 / Microform
Duplication 77 / Production Support Equipment 83 /
Microfilm Service Bureaus 84

4 Computer Output Microfilm   85

COM Recorders 87 / Recording Technology 90 / Forms
Recording 93 / COM Software 95 / COM-Generated
Microforms 98 / Image Characteristics 100 / Processing
and Duplication 103 / COM as a Computer Output
Alternative 104

5 Display and Printing Equipment   109

Reader Design 111 / Optical Characteristics 114 / Application
Characteristics 116 / Human Factors 120 / Reader-Printer
Design 121 / Printing Technology 124 / Enlarger-Printers 127

6 Retrieval Concepts and Systems   129

Flash Targets 130 / Odometer Indexing 132 / Sequential Frame
Numbering 133 / Blip Encoding 135 / Microfiche Titling and
Indexing 138 / The CAR Concept 141 / CAR System
Components 143 / CAR Software 148 / Microform Storage
Equipment 150

7 Micrographic Cost Analysis   155

Example 1: Microfilming Inactive Records 156 / Example 2:
Microfilming Active Records 166 / COM vs. Paper Printers 172

8 Interfaces With Other Technologies   177

Microfacsimile 179 / Micrographics and Electronic Document
Imaging 183 / Computer-Input Microfilm 188 / Microform
Storage of Digital Data 190 / COM and Word Processing 191

Suggested Additional Readings   193

Micrographic Standards   207

Glossary of Micrographic Terms   211

Index   231

Foreword

ONE OF THE best selling and enduring books published by AIIM is *Micrographics Systems.* The first edition by Daniel M. Costigan was printed in 1975. Five years later, AIIM persuaded him to write the second edition. Now AIIM is able to provide a third edition, but this time with a new author—William Saffady, Professor, School of Information Science and Policy at the State University of New York, Albany.

This revision exists by popular demand. Even though the second edition was removed from the AIIM publications catalog in 1987, the association continued to receive numerous requests for it. *Micrographic Systems,* has been considered a classic in the field and has been used as a text in library science, records management, and information management courses. Much of its popularity is due to the clear presentation of the material and excellent introduction to the subject of micrographics.

Author William Saffady has taken a fresh approach to the text, reflecting his style of presentation. Like his predecessor, he addresses the technology, processes, equipment, retrieval techniques, and the relationship of micrographics to other information management technologies. The latter brings the book into the final decade of the twentieth century with a discussion of integrated information systems which incorporate micrographics.

I predict that this third edition will also become a classic.

MARILYN COURTOT
Director, Standards and Technology

Preface

THIS BOOK IS intended for micrographics specialists, information systems analysts, office automation specialists, records managers, archivists, and other information management professionals who want a systematic introduction to micrographics technology and applications. It is divided into eight chapters:

Chapter One introduces basic micrographic concepts, defines essential terminology, surveys the history and current status of micrographic applications, and reviews the most important principles of micrographic systems analysis. The chapter concludes with a discussion of micrographic standards and the concept of reduction.

Chapter Two describes the basic types of microforms and reviews their system characteristics, emphasizing their strengths and limitations for particular types of information management applications.

Chapter Three deals with source document microfilming. It begins with a discussion of micrographic recording technology, followed by a survey of production equipment and methodologies. Various types of cameras, processors, and duplicators are described and categorized. The chapter also includes a discussion of archival processing and storage requirements.

Chapter Four provides a similar treatment of computer-output microfilm production. It begins with a survey of the functional characteristics of COM recorders, followed by a discussion of COM input requirements and output capabilities. The chapter concludes with an evaluation of COM's role as a computer output technology.

Chapter Five surveys microform display and printing equipment, particularly readers and reader/printers. The discussion emphasizes capabilities and features that influence the selection of such devices in particular information management situations.

Chapter Six discusses micrographic storage and retrieval concepts, systems, and techniques. It begins with a survey of straightforward manual and semi-automated retrieval methodologies, followed by a detailed discussion of computer-assisted retrieval (CAR) systems. The chapter concludes with a survey of microform storage equipment.

Chapter Seven deals with micrographic cost analysis, emphasizing the preparation of cost estimates and cost justification statements. It presents detailed discussions of three hypothetical but realistic information management applications that illustrate basic cost analysis concepts and indicate the cost saving potential of micrographic technology.

Chapter Eight discusses the relationship of micrographics to other information management technologies, including facsimile, electronic document imaging, optical character recognition, machine-readable data storage, and word processing.

Three appendixes provide suggestions for additional reading, a list of micrographic standards, and a glossary of important micrographic-related terms and acronyms.

A word of thanks must be given to those who have contributed to this work: Marilyn Courtot and AIIM's Non-Serial Publications Commitee for their guidance during the development stage of this project; Shawn Marshall and Ann Lancaster for their excellent work editing the manuscript; and Cheryl Butler for her patience while compiling the index.

Micrographic Systems

1 Micrographic Systems: An Introduction

An INFORMATION SYSTEM is an interrelated group of procedures and components designed to accomplish a particular information management task, such as the processing of insurance claims, the long-term storage of bank checks, the dissemination of technical reports, or the retrieval and reproduction of engineering drawings. While they may rely entirely on manual procedures, information systems often utilize computers and other technologies. As the name suggests, a micrographic system is an information system based on micrographics technology.

Broadly defined, micrographics is a specialized information management technology that is concerned with the production and use of microforms—optical information storage media that contain photographically-reduced images that are too small to be read with the unaided eye. The images—which require magnification to be viewed, printed, or otherwise utilized—are properly termed *microimages*. They may be produced from paper documents or from data generated by computer programs.

In source document microphotography, the oldest and most easily understood approach to microform production, cameras equipped with reduction lenses record images of paper documents on special, high-resolution photographic film. Computer-output microfilm (COM), a variant form of computer printing technology, converts computer-generated data to human-readable information on microfilm, microfiche, or other microforms without creating an intervening paper copy.

While microforms may contain machine-readable, binary-coded data, micrographics is primarily a document storage and retrieval

1

technology. As such, it can accommodate both textual and graphic information. Microforms can be created from textual source documents, such as office correspondence, financial records, technical reports, library materials, legal case files, client files, patient records, insurance claims files, and student records. Microforms can also contain images of engineering drawings, maps, charts, x-rays, and other graphic documents.

Depending on the type of equipment used, COM-generated microimages may be created from data, text, or graphic files. Data and text files contain alphanumeric information. Graphic files can include engineering drawings and other design documentation created by CAD/CAM systems. They may also contain graphic images generated by computer-controlled scientific or medical instrumentation.

Although it is spelled with an "s," the word *micrographics* is treated grammatically as a singular noun. As an adjective, it may be spelled with or without an "s." This book will use the latter adjectival form. Micrographics was introduced in the 1970s as an alternative to the older term *microfilm*. The term micrographics avoids confusion with that of microfilm as it indicates a particular type of microform, more accurately one where microimages may reside on paper substrates or other non-film media. It further reflects the fact that film, where used, is only one component in a micrographic system. The definition of micrographics presented here should not be confused with a newer, completely different use of the term to denote graphics generated by microcomputer systems.

The intentionally broad definitions given above encompass document storage and retrieval systems of varying complexity. On the one hand, a straightforward micrographic implementation can provide compact, long-term storage for inactive records in a variety of work environments. At the other extreme, a sophisticated micrographic system, possibly augmented by computer hardware and software, can address the complex document storage and retrieval requirements of high-volume transaction processing applications. Regardless of scope, a micrographic system encompasses the hardware, software, supplies, personnel, and other components and resources required to implement micrographic technology in a particular information management situation. It includes microforms, production equipment and supplies, retrieval devices, and storage facilities, as well as the procedures that specify how those components will be utilized.

Although micrographic systems have been successfully implemented in all types of work environments, they are best suited to information processing applications that can benefit from one or more of the advantages of micrographic technology. While conversions from computerized information systems to micrographics are possible, most micrographic implementations are designed to replace paper-based document management systems. In such situations, the advantages of micrographics include storage space savings, faster document retrieval to improve productivity or responsiveness, enhanced file integrity and security, simplified document distribution, reduced mailing costs, and greater media stability.

As an introduction to micrographic systems, the following sections survey information management applications in which these benefits are important. The application survey is followed by a brief discussion of micrographic systems analysis. The chapter concludes with sections on reduction and micrographic standards. These two topics are critical to an understanding of microform selection, production, and retrieval concepts.

Archival Microfilming

As a variant form of photography, micrographic technology has been used in novelty applications since the nineteenth century. At that time miniaturized images, accompanied by magnifying lenses, were mounted in rings, pendants, penholders, and other objects. The forerunner of the V-mail and Airgraph microfilming services implemented during World War II, were microfilmed messages carried by pigeons to and from a besieged Paris during the Franco-Prussian War. While the use of microfilm to create security copies of business records was proposed and demonstrated in the mid-nineteenth century, the first viable commercial applications of micrographic technology date from the late 1920s when George McCarthy developed a 16 mm microfilm camera for bank checks. McCarthy's invention was the ancestor of the modern rotary cameras (to be described in Chapter Three). McCarthy's Check-O-Graph microfilmer was subsequently acquired by the Eastman Kodak Company which marketed it and its successors under the Recordak trade name.

By the mid-1930s, banking applications were widely implemented, and interest in micrographic technology had spread to other financial and non-financial business activities. Since that time records management applications in corporations, government agencies, and other work environments have dominated micrographic system implementations. The earliest examples were limited to long-term storage of files that were closed and seldom referenced. While no longer the focal point of industry attention, the compact storage of inactive records—sometimes described as archival microfilming—remains a significant micrographic application.

Records managers have long recognized that many documents undergo brief periods of active reference, followed by longer periods of relative inactivity. Office correspondence and memoranda, for example, are usually referenced once or twice shortly after they are written or received but after that may never be consulted again. Similarly, legal case records, insurance claim files, medical history files, technical project files, and similar documents may remain unused for months or years following the termination of a given transaction or activity. However, if matters to which they refer require future activity, they may later be referenced frequently. Although they are not needed to support daily operations and may seldom be consulted, many inactive records must be retained for some period of time to meet legal requirements, in anticipation of possible future reference, or—in some cases—for their historical or research significance. Too often, inactive records accumulate in office work areas or central file rooms where they are stored, along with active documents, in expensive file cabinets that occupy valuable floor space.

While sometimes ignored by department managers and other administrators, the economic implications of such practices are clear: at the time this book was written, prices for a conventional, four-drawer, vertical-style, letter-size file cabinet ranged from about $250 to $400. Prices for larger cabinets, lateral-style cabinets, and special models were much higher, exceeding $1,000 for fire resistant cabinets and safe-type files. A typical letter-size, vertical-style cabinet requires seven to eight square feet of installation area, including space for extended drawers. Larger cabinets require proportionally greater amounts of floor space. In early 1990, annual floor space costs ranged from about $15 to $60 per square foot, depending on office type and geographic location. Amortizing the purchase price of a filing equipment over ten-years of useful life and adding the cost of required installation space, results in an annual cost of between $130 and $460 for maintaining a single vertical-style, letter-size file cabinet in office floor space. These figures are exclusive of filing supplies and labor.

As their most obvious advantage, micrographic systems can significantly reduce the number of file cabinets and amount of floor space required for inactive records storage. As described more fully in Chapter Two, a 100-foot reel or cartridge of 16 mm microfilm can store 2,500 to 3,000 letter-size pages—the approximate contents of one vertical-style file drawer. One drawer-type microfilm filing cabinet measuring 23 inches wide by 30 inches deep by 54 inches high requires about 12 square feet of installation space and can store almost 1,500 reels or cartridges of 16 mm microfilm—the equivalent of about 375 four-drawer, vertical-style file cabinets for paper documents. Such cabinets would require over 2,200 square feet of installation space. In this example, microfilm reduces floor space requirements by over 99 percent.

As additional advantages for inactive records, microforms are stable, legally acceptable storage media. As discussed more fully in later chapters, microforms offer stability appropriate to lengthy record retention requirements. When properly processed and stored, silver gelatin microfilm—the type most widely used in source document cameras—will retain its original information-bearing characteristics indefinitely. The most widely used duplicating films, to be described in Chapter Three, will remain stable for up to 100 years.

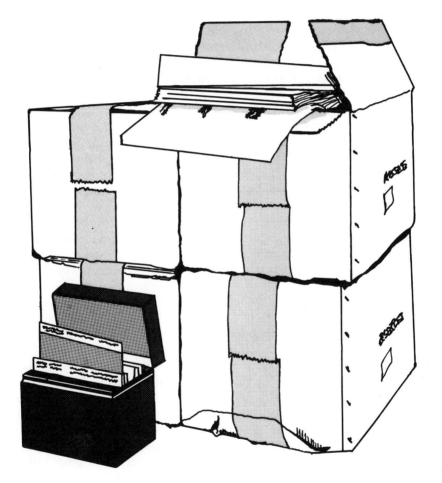

FIGURE 1.   Comparative space requirements of microfiche versus paper for a given quantity of information.

Because microform copies are legally acceptable substitutes for paper documents, the latter can be discarded following filming. In the United States, the legal status of microform copies is recognized by both common law and statutory law. If the absence of original documents can be satisfactorily explained, the "best evidence" principle of common law permits the substitution of duplicate copies in evidence. The destruction of such documents after they have been microfilmed in conformity with an organization's formal business practices presumably constitutes a satisfactory explanation for using duplicate copies.

Among statutory provisions, the Uniform Photographic Copies of Business and Public Records in Evidence Act (Title 28, Section 1732 of the U.S. Code) permits the destruction of paper documents and substitution of microform copies produced in the regular course of business, except where retention of the original documents is specifically required by law. It addresses the use of microform copies to satisfy legally-mandated retention requirements as well as the admissibility of microform copies as evidence. Applying only to judicial proceedings, the Uniform Rules of Evidence (Title 28, Rule 1003 of the Appendix to the U.S. Code) states that duplicate records, including microform copies, are admissible in evidence as substitutes for original documents unless serious questions are raised about the authenticity of the original records or of copies made from them. Less prescriptive than the Uniform Photographic Copies of Business and Public Records in Evidence Act, the Uniform Rules of Evidence Act neither authorizes nor prohibits the destruction of paper documents following microfilming.

The Uniform Photographic Copies of Business and Public Records in Evidence Act and the Uniform Rules of Evidence Act have been adopted by the U.S. federal government and by many states. The legal status of microform copies is most firmly established in jurisdictions where both statutes have been adopted. In other situations, specific state statutes may permit or restrict the admissibility of microform copies or their acceptability as substitutes for paper documents in records management applications with legally-mandated retention requirements. As an additional limitation, the statutes cited above apply only to source document microfilming. Microforms produced by the computer-output microfilm recorders are considered original rather than duplicate records (to be described in Chapter Three).

While compactness, stability, and legal acceptability are significant advantages, micrographic systems cannot offer all-encompassing solutions to storage space problems posed by inactive records. They represent, instead, one of several approaches to effective space utilization. In well planned records management programs, the microfilming of inactive records is combined with selective destruction and off-site storage. As discussed later in this book, the conversion of large quantities of paper documents to microforms can involve considerable expense. Microfilming only inactive records to be held over a long period of time permits recovery of microfilming costs through accumulated savings in storage space and filing equipment purchases. Compared to the storage of inactive paper documents in office work areas, the time to recover microfilming costs typically ranges from two to five years. Compared to the storage of inactive records in off-site warehouse facilities, however, the time to recover microfilming costs may range between seven and twelve years. To increase the likelihood of cost-effective applications, micrographic systems should be implemented in the context of formal record retention and disposal schedules. When specific periods of time are established for particular groups of records to be retained microfilming occurs within these set schedules.

Active Records Management

The primitive nature of retrieval equipment available in the 1930s and 1940s necessitated the early emphasis on inactive records by micrographics systems analysts. By the late 1950s and early 1960s, however, the quality and convenience of micrographic display and printing devices had improved significantly. While archival applications still dominated micrographic system implementations, a number of product developments facilitated the transition to active records management. The current focal point of industry and user attention still remains on active record management. Among the most important examples are self-threading microfilm cartridges which successfully addressed problems of inconvenient media handling associated with microfilm reels, and aperture cards which simplified the filing and printing of engineering drawings and other large documents. Cartridges and aperture cards demonstrated the superior performance of microforms when compared to paper documents. Thus, they encouraged the use of micrographics in applications where convenient retrieval was as important as storage space savings. Microfilm jackets that served as updatable carriers for strips of 16 mm film cut from rolls, permitted the application of micrographic technology to growing files. Originally developed for the insurance industry where policy files may remain open for decades, jacket systems were subsequently implemented in a variety of work environments. Schools, hospitals, law offices, and police departments became jacket system users. During the late 1950s and early 1960s, a variety of experimental products and customized implementations demonstrated the technical feasibility of automated microform retrieval. By the mid-1960s, automated microfilm retrieval devices were commercially available. Computer-assisted retrieval systems, demonstrated in concept in the 1960s, were introduced as turnkey products in the early 1970s.

For some records managers and other information specialists, a discussion of active micrographic applications that facilitate document retrieval may seem contradictory, since micrographic systems are sometimes criticized for being difficult to use. As with any information management technology, however, such difficulties are invariably the result of poor system planning and operation. Properly designed and implemented, micrographic systems offer a number of significant advantages for active records management:

TABLE 1   Some Advantages of Micrographics for Active Records Management.

- Conserve space required for office operations
- Reduce walking time to record storage areas
- Improve information retrieval
- Simplify browsing through documents
- Minimize file maintenance routines
- Enhance file integrity
- Facilitate distribution of documents to satellite files
- Reduce mailing or other document delivery costs
- Enhance portability of files
- Simplify management of computer-output records
- Complement or supplement computer and other information management technologies

1.   Space is an important resource in active records management applications. Few work areas offer enough space to comfortably accommodate the personnel and equipment essential to office operations. The space savings associated with micrographics are as significant for active documents as they are for inactive records. By reducing space requirements, micrographic systems can permit the consolidation of otherwise scattered office operations, thereby simplifying management and enhancing productivity.

2.   Micrographic systems also enhance managerial and clerical productivity through the rapid retrieval of information essential to work performance. When documents are miniaturized, large quantities of records can be stored at or near workers' desks. Because physical distances between records and the workers who use them are reduced, time-consuming trips to remote file areas are eliminated.

3.   Individual microforms, to be described more fully in Chapter Two, can contain hundreds or thousands of pages—the equivalent of many file folders. A variety of automated and semiautomated indexing methodologies and retrieval devices facilitate document display and printing. Once a given microform is loaded into a retrieval device, large quantities of records are available for browsing. Hundreds of pages can be traversed in just a few seconds.

4.   Micrographic systems can simplify file maintenance by minimizing or eliminating much filing and refiling activity. Computer-

assisted retrieval systems, to be described in Chapter Six, record documents on microfilm as they are received, eliminating time-consuming sorting procedures.

5. As a related advantage, microforms enhance file integrity. Once documents are recorded on microfilm or other microforms, their sequence is fixed. Removal or misfiling of individual pages becomes impossible, although individual microforms can, of course, be misfiled or misplaced. As a related advantage, documents recorded on microfilm cannot be altered.

6. Utilizing equipment and methodologies to be described in Chapter Three, microforms are easily, quickly, and inexpensively duplicated. Backup copies can consequently be produced for vital records protection or other purposes. Microforms can also be copied to create satellite files for branch offices, geographically dispersed departments, or off-premises reference. As will be discussed in Chapter Eight, available technology also permits the electronic transmission of microimages to remote locations.

7. Microforms can drastically reduce mailing costs, because when documents are miniaturized, hundreds of pages can be mailed for the price of a first-class stamp. As an example, a business envelope that contains five sheets of paper can hold six microfiche containing almost 600 letter-size pages. Microforms can usually be mailed first class for less than the cost of mailing an equivalent number of paper documents at third- or fourth-class rates. Microforms offer comparable economies to users of overnight package delivery services.

8. Microforms are well suited to applications where large quantities of documents must be transported from one work area to another or from offices to field locations. Where a need exists to carry large numbers of files, engineering drawings, or other records on a business trip, the same microfilmed documents can be carried in a briefcase. Portable microform display devices, with integral storage space, are available for such situations.

9. Microforms are well suited to the "paperless" office concepts advocated by some information management specialists. As will be discussed in later chapters, micrographic technology can be effectively integrated with computers, word processing, electronic mail, and other automated office systems to address a broad range of information management requirements. Computer-assisted indexing systems can support elaborate retrieval capabilities based on complex combinations of search terms. As a less obvious advantage for data processing installations, computer-assisted retrieval and computer-output microfilm systems can conserve valuable computer resources—notably, processing time and online storage facilities.

Managing Computer Output

Although online computer implementations have efficiently replaced many paper-based records management systems, computers are an increasingly important source of paper records. Some computer applications, such as word processing, are specifically designed to produce paper output; others generate documents—such as purchase orders, invoices, and exception reports—as by-products of online transaction processing. Even computing applications that rely on online processing for all operations typically produce one or more paper reports for backup purposes.

Since the 1960s, improvements in computer printing technology have permitted the production of increasing numbers of documents in ever shorter periods of time. Aided by computer technologies, word and data processing applications have the ability to overwhelm offices with large quantities of paper records that must be filed, retrieved, and otherwise managed. For example, so-called page printers of the type encountered in many mainframe and minicomputer installations use combinations of lasers and xerography to produce documents at speeds ranging from two to five pages per second. Operating fourteen hours per day for 250 days per year, one such printer can generate over 25 million pages per year. Optimistically, one can assume that half of those pages are either sent to other organizations or replace existing documents which are then discarded. The remaining 12.5 million pages will fill the equivalent of about 1,000 file cabinets, each occupying seven to eight square feet of floor space.

Computer-generated records can, of course, be microfilmed like any other source documents, and several of the cameras (to be described in Chapter Three) can be equipped with continuous-form feeders to simplify filming of unbursted computer printouts. Computer-output microfilm (COM) technology is one of the most important records management tools of the last quarter century. It addresses the problem of computer-produced documents at its source by circumventing the production of paper records entirely.

As noted at the beginning of this chapter, a computer-output microfilmer or COM recorder is a variant form of computer printer that produces microform rather than paper output. A COM recorder converts the machine-readable data generated by computer programs to human-readable information on microfilm, microfiche, or other microforms, just as if it had been printed onto paper and subsequently filmed. Graphic-type COM recorders were introduced in the 1950s as high-speed alternatives to mechanical plotters in scientific and technical applications. They are best suited for applications requiring high-volume, high-resolution printing of engineering drawings, maps, contour plots, circuit diagrams, and similar computer-generated graphics. (See Chapter Four for a more detailed description.) COM recorders offer an important output alternative in computer-aided design installations. Business-oriented COM recorders, designed as alternatives to paper printers, were likewise introduced in the late 1950s when a custom-designed device was installed at the U.S. Social Security Administration. With the proliferation of mainframe and minicomputer installations, they gained popularity in the 1960s and 1970s and are today widely installed in centralized data processing installations. Many more organizations use data processing or microfilm service bureaus to satisfy their COM production requirements.

Compared to paper output, the classically cost-effective COM application is a long, frequently updated report that is produced in multiple copies. Produced in paper form, such reports can require considerable printer time and storage space. In terms of production speed, COM recorders are as fast as page printers and much faster than line printers. Compared to paper output, COM-generated microforms offer significant advantages in storage space. A tray-type microfiche container that occupies less than one square foot of desk space can contain the equivalent of over 400,000 computer printout pages, while a microfiche storage cabinet can contain the equivalent of almost twenty million computer printout pages. Easier to handle than bulky paper reports, COM-generated microforms facilitate retrieval of desired information. Although paper printouts are required in some cases, COM can eliminate much needless paper output, thereby preventing records management problems before they start.

Micropublishing

While information specialists currently emphasize the role of micrographic systems in records management applications, microforms have also been widely and successfully used as publishing media. Although the first public discussions of micro-editions of reference works date from the mid-nineteenth century, actual micropublishing began in the 1930s when Eastman Kodak microfilmed the retrospective file of the *New York Times* for sale to libraries. Broadly defined, micropublishing is the publication of information in multicopy microforms for sale or distribution to the public or specifically-defined user groups. The term encompasses both original micropublications, which contain information published for the first time in any form, and retrospective micropublications, which contain material previously published in paper form. Simultaneous micropublications, a third category, are issued at the same time as their paper counterparts. Usually, the microform edition is created after the paper version by filming printed pages.

Compared to conventional publishing, micropublishing offers potentially significant economic advantages in certain situations. Ideally, copies of books and other publications should be printed as orders are received. Despite recent technological advances, however, current printing methodologies do not permit the economical production of single paper copies on demand. As a result, conventional publishers must make a decision about edition size prior to the actual printing of a book or other publication. For every work, there is a minimum edition size necessary to recover editorial, design, advertising, printing, binding, and other production costs. Large editions permit lower unit prices, but unsold copies must be warehoused, thereby incurring storage costs. Money invested in unsold stock cannot be used for other purposes, and recent changes in tax laws have placed unfavorable limitations on tax deductions associated with large printings. If unsold copies must be liquidated, additional advertising and distribution costs will be incurred. While various formulas and computer programs can help publishers determine an appropriate edition size for a particular work, some risk is unavoidable.

Micropublishing, by way of contrast, is a demand publishing process. Master microforms are created in anticipation of sales, but duplicates are not produced until orders are received. To establish a price, the cost of producing the microform is typically prorated over the sale of a relatively small number of duplicates. Warehousing, unsold stock, and related expenses are eliminated. As an additional advantage, the required capital investment in microform production equipment is often much lower than the cost of print shop equipment and supplies. Thus, micropublishing is well suited to items in limited demand for which the cost of a full paper edition cannot be justified. Micropublications can also be produced more quickly than their paper counterparts, making them a good choice for information that must be published in a timely manner.

Micropublishing contains information that is being published for the first time in any form. Original micropublications may be created by microphotography or computer-output microfilming of the source document. An important category of original micropublications are intended for controlled distribution to closed user groups that are identified in advance of publication. Widely cited examples include microform editions of technical documentation intended for aircraft service personnel, repair manuals designed for reference by appliance technicians, COM-generated parts lists distributed to automobile dealers, and collections of computer hardware and software documentation distributed to mainframe and minicomputer customers.

Original micropublications intended for public sale include specialized reference works, monographs, journals, reports, conference proceedings, and manuscript collections with limited audiences. The National Technical Information Service (NTIS), for example, publishes microfiche versions of scientific and technical reports resulting from federally-sponsored research. The Educational Resources Information Clearinghouse (ERIC) performs a similar function for reports dealing with educational subjects. The U.S. Government Printing Office has issued microform versions of various publications since the late 1970s. Several university presses use microforms for the original publication of highly specialized monographs and scholarly journals in such fields as literary criticism, classics, art, philosophy, philology, and regional history.

Retrospective micropublishing, a form of reprinting, is primarily intended for research materials. The earliest retrospective micropublishing programs—which, as noted above, concentrated on newspaper backfiles—grew out of concern for the ephemeral nature of information in newsprint. Today, thousands of newspapers are available in microform versions. Since the 1930s, publishers have offered microform reprints of out-of-print books, especially those that are in limited demand. University Microfilms International, for example, maintains a backlist of over 120,000 out-of-print titles which are available in microform. A number of smaller micropublishers specialize in out-of-print titles in specialized subject areas, such as history and literature. As discussed below, several publishers offer microform versions of back issues of magazines, journals, and other periodicals. A popular category of retrospective micropublications includes vendor catalogs, engineering and construction specifications, industrial standards, and similar reference materials that contain information essential to technical projects. Other retrospective micropublishers offer microform editions of college catalogs, corporate reports, and company prospectuses.

Library Applications

Many users have their first experience with microforms in a college or public library. Since the late 1920s, libraries have used microforms to develop and manage their collections, to reproduce and preserve library materials, and to reduce storage and binding costs. Microforms are also employed as a component in information storage and retrieval systems. In the United States, the earliest library applications of micrographics involved the filming of archives, manuscripts, and rare books contained in foreign repositories. In the 1920s and 1930s, even the largest American research libraries lacked the primary source materials required to support scholarly work. In some cases, libraries or individual researchers were able to obtain hand-transcribed or photostatic copies of needed materials. However, the slowness and high unit cost of such copying techniques effectively prohibited the acquisition of entire collections of important books or documents. As a result, historians, literary scholars, and other researchers specializing in foreign studies were forced to travel to European libraries, archives, and manuscript repositories.

To address this situation, a number of American libraries implemented microfilming programs that were designed to copy large quantities of research materials from European collections. The Library of Congress, for example, microfilmed over three million pages of books and manuscripts from the British Museum. This project demonstrated the feasibility of micrographics as a major acquisitions tool. During the 1930s and 1940s, similar projects were undertaken by Harvard University, Brown University, St. Louis University, the University of

Texas, the Bancroft Library, the American Council of Learned Societies, the Modern Language Association, and other organizations.

Although some libraries still maintain microfilming operations, most library microforms are now purchased from micropublishers. Following the lead of library-administered projects, the earliest micropublishers emphasized rare research materials from foreign repositories. The rapid expansion of higher education during the 1960s, however, produced a second collection development crisis in American libraries. While the microfilming projects described above significantly improved the availability of advanced research materials, many small and newly established colleges faced the difficult task of building library collections to support undergraduate instruction, while the rapid development of community colleges created a market for dynamic, subject-oriented information packages in microform.

To address these needs, a number of micropublishers produced especially prepared microform collections containing important out-of-print books essential for undergraduate background reading and term papers. Others created microform collections dealing with specific historical, literary, or sociological topics. The most ambitious projects included thousands of titles. They have been compared to huge anthologies containing not merely selections but complete books and other works.

Since the 1960s, a number of technical libraries have implemented specialized information systems utilizing microforms as a preferred substitute for conventional printed materials. The availability of government-sponsored technical reports in microform has spurred the development of complementary microfilm and microfiche systems for proprietary research reports, laboratory notebooks, patent files, and similar documents.

Like their business counterparts, librarians have long recognized the space-saving potential of microforms. Reference books, subject indexes, legal compendia, and other publications that require hundreds of linear feet of shelving can be reduced to desktop files. A number of libraries leave paper copies of scholarly journals and other periodicals unbound at the end of each volume year and acquire microform shelf copies from micropublishers. Libraries follow a predetermined schedule covering the period of most active reference—typically one or two years after receipt of the last volume issue—then they discard the paper issues, leaving the microform backfile to satisfy continuing reference requirements. This approach offers both economy and backfile integrity. Binding costs are avoided and storage expenses significantly reduced. Microform backfiles also protect files by offering some defense against theft or mutilation of paper issues.

While xerography is the preferred reprographic technology for personal research and interlibrary loan applications, microforms remain a viable alternative to the full-size reproduction of entire books, archival record series, manuscript collections, and similar voluminous materials. Where large quantities of documents are involved, microforms can simplify copy handling and significantly reduce reproduction time and mailing costs. Libraries have also used microforms to preserve the information content of fragile materials. Microforms prevent deterioration by eliminating handling.

Micrographic Systems Analysis

As broadly defined earlier in this chapter, an information system is a combination of operations and resources that accomplishes a particular information management task. Information systems analysis is a set of methodologies and work steps for the evaluation, planning, design, and implementation of information systems. A systems analysis typically begins with a detailed study of an existing information system. Its purpose is to gather the information necessary to understand and evaluate the system, improve it, or replace it with a new one. The systems analyst must determine what information processing tasks are being performed by an existing system; whether, and to what extent, the system is deficient; and what alternatives for improvement or replacement exist. While some information processing operations can be analyzed by a single person, complex systems often require a team of analysts working under the direction of a project leader.

Information systems analysts often specialize in the application of particular technologies. Computer systems analysts obviously exemplify this tendency. Similarly, micrographic systems analysts specialize in the planning, design, and implementation of micrographic systems. Micrographics systems analysis requires careful attention to information gathering procedures, a thorough understanding of micrographics' advantages and limitations as an information management technology, and a good working knowledge of micrographic systems concepts and products. As an information management methodology, micrographic systems analysis encompasses, but is not necessarily limited to, the following tasks:

1. Identification of candidate applications;

2. Examination of documents or data files that will serve as input to the micrographic system;

TABLE 2   Steps in Micrographic Systems Analysis.

- Identify candidate applications
- Examine documents or data files
- Select appropriate microform
- Plan and specify microform production capabilities
- Plan and specify microform retrieval system
- Prepare cost estimates and justifications

3. Selection of an appropriate microform from among possibilities, to be discussed in Chapter Two;

4. Planning and implementation of microform production capabilities, including the preparation of specifications, the selection of equipment and training of personnel for work steps to be performed in-house, and the evaluation of capabilities, qualifications, and rates for work steps to be performed by microfilm service bureaus;

5. Planning and implementation of microform storage and retrieval capabilities, including the design of retrieval procedures and/or software, the evaluation of display and printing devices, and the selection of microform storage equipment; and

6. Preparation of system cost estimates and cost justification analyses.

TABLE 3   Inventory of Document Characteristics for Micrographics Systems Analysis.

- File series name, form number, or report number
- Brief description and statement of business purpose
- Storage location
- Inclusive dates
- Physical attributes

size	condition
color	texture
thickness	double-sided printing

- Arrangement
- Number of pages
- Anticipated annual file growth
- Number and type of storage containers
- Nature and frequency of reference activity
- Retention requirements

While the training and experience of individual analysts may differ, micrographic systems analysis is invariably based on straightforward investigative and evaluative techniques. Following one or more preliminary meetings that establish major objectives and specify the constraints within which the analyst must work, the systems analysis begins with an intensive data gathering phase, including a detailed inventory of the documents or data files associated with candidate applications. The accompanying table lists typical items of information to be collected during an inventory of potential source document microfilming applications. The micrographic systems analyst must determine the type and number of source documents to be microfilmed. He or she must identify special document characteristics that influence reproducibility, including size, condition, color, and texture, and determine the frequency and nature of reference activity, including document distribution requirements; and ascertain retention periods.

Where a COM implementation will replace a computer-generated paper printout, the analyst must determine the printout's length, page format, distribution list, frequency of production, and reference characteristics.

The micrographic systems analyst will invariably inspect procedures manuals, organization charts, job descriptions, and other written documents pertinent to the system being studied. In most cases, information gathering efforts rely heavily on personal interviews as a means of identifying application requirements and determining the strengths and limitations of existing and proposed systems. In a well-planned systems analysis, interviews will involve a representative cross-section of managerial and clerical workers. In studies of large systems or where personnel are geographically scattered, questionnaires often serve as a supplement or alternative to personal interviews.

If careful study of system operations and application requirements confirms the advantages of a micrographic implementation, the analyst presents a design plan, including hardware, software, and procedural specifications. As discussed in subsequent chapters, the design plan typically specifies the type of microform to be utilized and recommends equipment and procedures for microform production, storage, and retrieval. Estimates for implementation and operating costs are included along with a cost justification analysis. Although customarily embodied in a detailed narrative report, the analyst's design recommendations are often accompanied by flowcharts that make use of special micrographic symbols to depict production and retrieval procedures. A template designed specifically for micrographic flowcharts is available from the Association for Information and Image Management (AIIM). It is described in the ANSI/AIIM MS4 standard, *Flowchart Symbols and their Use in Micrographics.*

Micrographic Standards

As micrographic technology has matured, early tendencies toward customized product design have given way to standardization. Micrographic standards provide guidelines for the production and use of microforms and related equipment. Except when mandated by procurement documents or an organization's internal operating procedures, adherence to micrographic standards is voluntary. Standards benefit both users and vendors, however, by facilitating the selection of micrographic products appropriate to particular applications, lowering equipment costs, shortening product development cycles, promoting compatibility and interchangeability of supplies and components, simplifying system implementation and training, and generally increasing user confidence in and acceptance of micrographic technology.

Existing micrographic standards can be divided into two broad groups: proprietary and nonproprietary. Proprietary standards, as the name suggests, are developed by specific organizations and institutions

EXPLANATION OF TEMPLATE SYMBOLS. For instructions on "Flowchart Symbols and their Use in Micrographics" see ANSI/AIIM MS4.

Symbol	Description
	ALL MICROFORMS Represents any microform used in a micrographic systems flow.
	MICROFORM RECORDING Represents the recording function of transferring information to an original microform master.
	**MICROFORM PROCESSING** Represents the processing function for making information or a medium permanent and/or readable by man or machine.
	DUPLICATING Represents the making of a single or multiple copies of a document or microform, usually with the aid of a master or intermediate.
	STORAGE/RETRIEVAL—ON-LINE Represents the processing function for making information or a medium permanent and/or readable by man or machine.
	STORAGE/RETRIEVAL — OFF-LINE Represents the storing of information off-line, regardless of the medium on which the information is recorded.
	INPUT/OUTPUT Making information available for processing (input) or the recording of processed information (output). The abbreviation of input/output in I/O.
	DOCUMENT A medium for conveying information usually in paper form.
	PREDEFINED PROCESS A process consisting of one or more operations that are specified elsewhere.
	PROCESSING Any operation on data where the operation is the execution of a defined action.
	DECISION A determination of direction to follow when given a number of alternative paths.
	MANUAL INPUT The entry of data into a computer or system by direct manual manipulation of a device.
	AUXILIARY OPERATION An off-line operation performed on equipment not under direct control of the central processing unit.
v > ^ <	**INFORMATION FLOW** Indicates the direction in which information is transmitted from one location to another. Used most often with the Communication Link symbol.
	COMMUNICATION LINK The automatic transmission of information from one location to another.
o	**CONNECTOR** A means of representing on a flowchart the junction of two lines of flow or a break in a single line of flow.
	PUNCHED CARD A card that is punched with a combination of holes to represent letters, digits, or special characters.
	MANUAL OPERATION Offline process using human techniques and associated speeds.
	TERMINAL A point in a system or communication network at which data can enter or leave, e.g. start, stop, delay, or interrupt.
	MAGNETIC TAPE Representation of a medium on which data is recorded.
	DISPLAY A device on which visual representation of data is shown, e.g. online indicators, video devices, console printers, and plotters.

FIGURE 2. Standard flowchart symbols for micrographic system planning.

for their own use. A number of government agencies, corporations, and nonprofit institutions have developed standards which govern microform production and micrographic equipment procurement within their own organizations. Perhaps the best known examples are the various micrographic standards developed by the U.S. Department of Defense.

Nonproprietary standards are intended for a wide audience of micrographic vendors and users. In the United States, the various standing and ad hoc standards committees of the Association for Information and Image Management prepare proposed standards that are distributed for comment and vote by all interested AIIM members. These standards concern micrographic terminology, characteristics of the various types of microforms, micrographic production and use equipment, and quality control procedures. Recommendations for micrographic standards, submitted by individuals or groups, are reviewed by the AIIM Standards Board and assigned to an appropriate committee composed of vendor and user representatives. The committee develops a draft standard that is forwarded to AIIM. The Director of Standards and Technology makes any necessary stylistic modifications and prepares a ballot for the Standards Board. If the Standards Board approves the draft standard, a ballot is prepared for the AIIM membership. While AIIM has historically emphasized micrographics-related standards, it has recently broadened its standardization activities to include other information- and image-oriented technologies, including electronic document imaging systems.

The American National Standards Institute (ANSI) is responsible for the development and dissemination of national standards for a wide range of products and services. As a federation of trade associations, technical societies, professional organizations, consumer groups, and private companies, ANSI functions as a clearinghouse and coordinating body for national standardization activities. Like AIIM, it operates through a series of committees whose members represent the varied interests of vendors and users. AIIM is an ANSI-accredited standards developer. AIIM standards conform to ANSI guidelines, and, to save time, they are typically balloted through AIIM and ANSI simultaneously. To facilitate evaluation by interested parties, ANSI requires the announcement of proposed standards in the *ANSI Reporter*. Approval results in a new ANSI/AIIM standard. Only standards approved by the AIIM membership are termed industry standards. ANSI standards relevant to micrographic technology have also been developed by other organizations. Such standards typically deal with the characteristics of photographic materials, including microfilms.

International standards, based on the prevailing practices of over seventy nations, are developed by the International Standardization Organization (ISO). Micrographic standards approved by AIIM and ANSI are submitted to the appropriate ISO technical committee. The approval, which can take several years to complete, follows steps similar to those discussed above.

ANSI represents U.S. standards interests at the international level and credentials U.S. delegates to ISO committees. AIIM serves as the administrator of the Technical Advisory Group (TAG) to the ISO TC 171 committee on Micrographics and Optical Memories for Document and Image Recording, Storage, and Standardization. The TAG represents ANSI in the development of international micrographic standards. Individual sections of this book will cite ANSI/AIIM, ISO, and other standards pertinent to specific aspects of micrographic systems analysis.

The Concept of Reduction

By definition, microforms present information in reduced size. Used in this context, reduction is a measure of the number of times a given linear dimension of a document or other object is reduced through microphotography. This measure is expressed as $24\times$, $42\times$, $48\times$, and so on, where the reduced linear dimension is 1/24, 1/42, or 1/48 the length of its full-size counterpart. Alternatively, reduction can be expressed as a ratio which reflects the relationship between a given linear dimension of a document and the corresponding linear dimension of a microimage made from that document—for example, 24:1, 42:1, or 48:1.

As the accompanying table indicates, the micrographics industry has historically divided reductions into five broad categories, ranging from low to ultra high. Micrographics increases the image storage capacity of individual microforms and correspondingly reduces the number of microforms that must be stored, handled, or duplicated in a given application. Their storage capacity makes high, very high, and ultra high reductions conceptually more attractive than low and medium ones. The choice of reduction for a specific application, however, is based on a number of factors, including the nature of the documents being microfilmed, the type of microform used, and the characteristics of available production and retrieval equipment. The reduction selected must be suitable for microfilming a given document or group of documents without loss of information. The reduction must also support legible duplication of microforms through the required number of generations. Characteristics that influence the reproducibility of source documents are described in the ANSI/AIIM MS35 standard, *Requirements and Characteristics of Original Black-and-White Documents That May Be Microfilmed*. Drafting practices that affect the microfilmability of engineering drawings are discussed in the ISO 3098 standard, *Technical Drawings—Lettering—Part 1: Currently Used Characters*, and the ANSI Y14.2M standard, *Engineering Drawing and Related Documentation Practices—Line Conventions and Lettering*.

TABLE 4   Micrographic Reductions.

Designation	Range	Typical Applications
low	through 1:15	Microfilming manuscripts, rare books, old newspapers, and other documents in too poor condition to be legibly reproduced at higher reductions.
medium	1:15-1:30	Source document microfilming; common reductions include 1:24 for letter-size pages, 1:29 for legal-size pages.
high	1:30-1:60	Computer-output microfilming at 1:42 or 1:48; source document filming of computer printout pages at 1:32.
very high	1:60-1:90	Computer-output microfilming at 1:72.
ultra high	1:90 and above	Ultrafiche and ultrastrip production; 1:90, 1:120, 1:150, and higher reductions possible.

As linear measurements, stated reductions and reduction ratios do not reflect the total reduction in document area achieved through microphotography. For example, a microimage of letter-size document reduced 1:24 occupies just 1/576 of the area of the original. With conventional silver gelatin microphotographic materials—the type used by most source document cameras— individual characters are defined and shaped by silver grains. As reductions increase, fewer silver grains are available in any given area of film and the legible reproduction of characters becomes more difficult.

Low reductions (1:15 and below) are typically reserved for badly faded or otherwise deteriorating documents printed in very small type faces. This is the case with some library collections which may include old manuscripts, newspapers, and books of varied typography and condition. Medium reductions (1:15 to 1:30) are most widely utilized for source document microphotography in the broad spectrum of business-oriented applications. U.S. letter-size and international A4-size pages are typically microfilmed at 1:24. U.S. legal-size pages, which have no international size counterpart, are usually filmed at 1:27. While it falls just outside of the medium range, 1:32 is sometimes used for computer printout-size (international B4-size) pages. As a related point, it is important to note that reduction specifications contained in product brochures and in microfilm production specifications are typically nominal rather than exact. They may vary by as much as +1:1.5.

Because computer-output microfilming begins with machine-readable data rather than source documents, type fonts, character sizes, and other image characteristics can be optimized for micro-reproduction. As a result, high (1:30 to 1:60) and very high (1:60 to 1:90) reductions are the norm in COM applications. As discussed in the next chapter, ultra high reductions (1:90 and above) require special photographic materials and production methodologies.

2 Types of Microforms and Their Characteristics

As DEFINED IN the preceding chapter, *microform* is a generic term for any optical information storage medium that contains photographically reduced images. These images require magnifications to be read. This definition intentionally excludes eye-legible paper reproductions made by photocopiers equipped with modest reduction capabilities, but it does encompass a variety of film-based media created by source document microphotography or COM technology. As previously noted, the selection of a microform appropriate to specific application requirements is an important step in micrographic systems analysis. Microform selection is guided by the general systems design principle that form follows function. Available microforms differ in physical shape, image capacities, production requirements, retrieval characteristics, and cost. The micrographic systems analyst must understand these differences and find the best match between microform characteristics and an application's functional requirements.

While available microforms can be categorized in various ways, a division by physical shape into roll and flat formats facilitates discussion of their distinctive system characteristics. The roll microforms consist of thin ribbons of 16 mm or 35 mm microfilm that are wound on a reel or loaded into a cartridge. Flat microforms are sheets of film. Examples include microfiche, microfilm jackets, and aperture cards. A now-defunct group of flat microforms, collectively termed *micro-opaques*, consists of microimages on paper substrates. This chapter surveys the most important microforms. It describes their physical characteristics and emphasizes the advantages and limitations

FIGURE 3.   Typical roll microforms: 16 and 35 mm.

that promote or constrain their use in specific information management applications.

Reel Microfilm

Roll microform, as noted above, is a generic designation for reel microfilm and microfilm cartridges. Like motion picture film, most microfilm is supplied in rolls for use in cameras and COM recorders. Following its exposure and processing, roll microfilm may be converted to other formats. However, much of it is simply wound onto plastic or metal reels for viewing and storage. The characteristics of such reels are described in the ANSI/AIIM MS34 standard, *Dimensions for 100 Ft Reels for Manually Threaded Processed 16 mm and 35 mm Microfilm*. With the exception of 105 mm rolls that are occasionally used in automated microform retrieval systems, reel microfilm measures 16 mm or 35 mm wide. While length may vary, 100 feet and 215 feet are most common. An 8 mm microfilm format, developed in the early 1970s specifically for low-volume applications in small offices, was discontinued shortly after its introduction. Its phase-out was largely because the 8 mm film width necessitated reductions that proved impractically high for many source documents.

For most business-oriented applications of reel microfilm, 16 mm is the film width of choice. While exact microimage capacity depends on document size, reduction, camera characteristics, and other factors, a 100-foot reel of 16 mm microfilm typically contains 2,500 to 3,000 letter-size pages reduced 1:24—the approximate contents of one vertical-style file drawer. A 215-foot reel can store approximately 5,400 letter-size pages. In COM applications, a 100-foot reel of 16 mm microfilm can contain 1,800 computer printout pages reduced 1:24—the equivalent of over 3.5 reams of paper.

With its larger image area, 35 mm microfilm is typically reserved for applications that involve large documents or require low reductions. When a D-size (24 inches by 36 inches) engineering drawing is reduced 1:24, for example, the resulting microimage will not fit on 16 mm film. A wider film is required. As discussed in Chapter One, the typographic characteristics and physical condition of many library materials often necessitates reductions lower than 1:15.

Rare books and manuscripts may be filmed at reductions as low as 1:9, while 1:14 is widely used for newspapers. In such cases, microimage size exceeds 16 mm on its shortest dimension. Since their applications involve larger documents or lower reductions, 35 mm reels contain fewer microimages than their 16 mm counterparts. A 100-foot reel can store about 700 D-size engineering drawings reduced 1:24 or about 1,300 letter-size manuscript pages reduced 1:10. Critics of 35 mm reel microfilm often cite the limited selection of display and printing devices. They note that the cost/performance characteristics of available models seldom compare favorably with those of other micrographic products. For that reason, engineering drawings intended for active reference are often converted from 35 mm reels to aperture cards, as discussed later in this chapter.

Regardless of width, reel microfilm offers several potentially significant advantages:

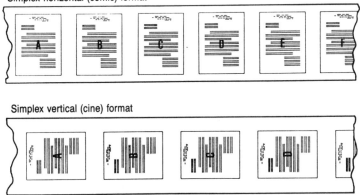

Simplex horizontal (comic) format

Simplex vertical (cine) format

FIGURE 4.   Horizontal and vertical image orientations.

TABLE 5 Capacity of 100 foot Roll of Microfilm for Source Documents of Various Sizes Recorded at Various Reductions.

Document Size*	Reduction									
	14x	16x	18x	20x	22x	24x	26x	28x	30x	32x
6.0	2,510	2,820								
8.0	1,930	2,180	2,430	2,670	2,820					
8.5	1,820	2,070	2,290	2,530	2,750	2,980				
10.0	1,570	1,780	1,980	2,180	2,380	2,570	2,760	2,820		
12.0	1,320	1,500	1,670	1,850	2,020	2,180	2,350	2,510	2,670	2,820
14.0	1,140	1,300	1,450	1,600	1,750	1,900	2,040	2,180	2,320	2,460
16.0	1,010	1,140	1,280	1,410	1,540	1,670	1,800	1,930	2,060	2,180
18.0	900	1,020	1,140	1,260	1,380	1,500	1,620	1,730	1,850	1,960
20.0	810	920	1,030	1,140	1,250	1,360	1,470	1,570	1,670	1,780
22.0	740	840	940	1,040	1,140	1,240	1,340	1,440	1,530	1,630
24.0	680	770	870	960	1,050	1,140	1,230	1,320	1,410	1,500
26.0		720	800	890	970	1,060	1,140	1,230	1,310	1,390
28.0		670	750	830	910	990	1,070	1,140	1,220	1,300
30.0			700	770	850	920	1,000	1,070	1,140	1,220
32.0				730	800	870	940	1,010	1,080	1,140
34.0				690	750	820	880	950	1,010	1,080
36.0					710	770	840	900	960	1,020
38.0					680	740	790	850	910	970
40.0						700	760	810	870	920
42.0						670	720	770	830	880
44.0							690	740	790	840
46.0								710	760	810
48.0								680	730	770

*In inches for dimension parallel to edges of film

1. In source document applications, it is the least expensive type of microform to create, in terms of both equipment and labor. A good selection of reasonably priced cameras is available for 16 mm reel microfilm, although cameras that can produce 35 mm microfilm are more expensive and limited in availability.

2. The ANSI/AIIM MS14 standard, *Specifications for 16 and 35 mm Microfilms in Roll Form*, offers considerable flexibility in image positioning. To address the broadest range of application requirements, microimages can be recorded on 16 mm or 35 mm microfilm with the text of documents parallel or perpendicular to the film edges. The parallel format is popularly termed the comic mode because the image orientation resembles the panels of a comic book. Because it emulates motion picture film, the perpendicular image orientation is sometimes termed the cine mode. In either orientation, a frame may contain one or more pages. Multipage frames conserve film and increase storage capacity. Its applications involve checks, credit card slips, signature cards, and other small documents.

3. If application requirements change, reel microfilm can be converted to one or more of the other microforms, to be discussed in later sections of this chapter. For example, 16 mm reel microfilm can be converted to cartridges, microfiche, or microfilm jackets; 35 mm microfilm can be converted to aperture cards or microfilm jackets.

Despite these strengths, reel microfilm suffers serious, long recognized limitations in applications that require the rapid retrieval of microimages. To view or print a desired document image, a reel must be removed from its container and mounted with more or less difficulty on a reader or reader-printer. The operator then threads the film through a lens assembly, typically lifting a small glass film holder in the process. The film's leading edge is inserted into a take-up spool and advanced using a manual or motorized control. When viewing or printing is completed, the film must be rewound and the reel returned to its container. This procedure is inconvenient, time-consuming, and potentially troublesome. Occasional users, unable to thread the film and reluctant to ask for help, may simply give up. Following use, reels may be returned to the wrong containers. In the worst case, an entire reel of microfilm, inadvertently wound onto the reader's take-up spool, may be replaced in the container, backwards, for the next unfortunate user to find.

Reel microfilm further limits the user to serial access. Once the appropriate reel has been correctly mounted and the film threaded, users seeking a particular microimage must pass through all preceding images. To speed things along, readers and reader-printers equipped with motorized controls can advance film at ten feet per second, supporting an average image retrieval time of five seconds with 100-foot reels and eleven seconds with 215-foot reels. These speeds — which do not include the potentially considerable time required for film loading—compare very favorably with retrieval times in many paper filing installations, but office workers are increasingly accustomed to online computer systems that provide nearly instantaneous response.

As will be discussed in Chapter Five, reel microfilm readers cost more than flat microform readers. At the time this book was written, a high quality microfiche reader could be purchased for less than $200. Reel microfilm readers of comparable quality cost three to five times as much.

Apart from cutting and splicing, there is no way to add or remove microimages from reel microfilm. This restricts applications to closed files, and makes reel microfilm unacceptable in applications—such as criminal history records—where court-ordered expungements may require the removal, without a trace, of documents pertaining to dismissed cases. Reel microfilm can be duplicated, but relatively expensive equipment is required, and the selective duplication of microimages is difficult.

Limited by inconvenient handling and serial access, 16 mm and 35 mm reel microfilm is never the microform of choice in active micrographic systems. It is well suited, however, to compact, long-term storage in applications where economy of production is a paramount consideration and little or no reference activity is anticipated. It is also an excellent microform for vital records protection, again assuming little or no reference activity, and as an effective backup medium for microfilm jacket and aperture card systems. In micropublishing and library applications, reel microfilm is an acceptable microform for newspaper backfiles, manuscript collections, and similar voluminous materials. In such cases, a 16 mm or 35 mm microfilm reel may be mounted at the beginning of a work session and individual documents studied sequentially for many hours. Because film loading is infrequent and each image is examined, inconvenience is minimized.

Microfilm Cartridges

The system characteristics of other microforms are, to a great extent, responses to one or more of the previously discussed disadvantages of reel microfilm. This is clearly the case with microfilm cartridges which offer the advantages of reel microfilm. These cartridges afford special high image capacity, flexible image positioning that can accommodate various sizes of documents, and reasonable production costs—without the inconvenience of manual film threading. A cartridge is a plastic single-core container for 16 mm microfilm in 100- or 215-foot lengths. When mounted on an appropriate reader or reader-printer, microfilm from the cartridge is automatically threaded onto a take-up spool built into the reader or reader-printer. The film passes out of the cartridge during use and must be rewound into the cartridge prior to removal from the reader or reader-printer.

As noted in Chapter One, microfilm cartridges were introduced in the late 1950s as one of the first microforms intended specifically for active records management applications. Through the 1970s, however, the lack of standards and consequent compatibility problems deterred the development of cartridge applications, while competition among the major suppliers complicated the development of standards. In the late 1960s, over thirty proprietary styles of microfilm cartridges were available for sale, all of them incompatible with one another. The two most popular products—the 3M Cartridge and the Recordak (Kodak) Film Magazine—each measured four inches by four inches by one inch in size but differed in design and could not be used interchangeably in readers and reader/printers. By choosing the proprietary-style cartridges of one supplier, micrographic systems analysts necessarily limited the selection of display and printing devices suitable for use in particular applications. Problems of equipment selection were further aggravated by the availability of several different cartridges within individual vendors' product lines. In the 1970s, for example, Eastman Kodak and the 3M Company each offered several different types of cartridges, none of which were interchangeable.

To address the incompatibility problem, several companies have introduced special cartridges that can be used interchangeably in readers and reader/printers designed for either the 3M Film Cartridge or Recordak Film Magazine. The most important step in the direction of compatibility, however, was the development of the ANSI/AIIM MS15 standard, *Dimensions and Operational Constraints for Single Core*

FIGURE 5. Microfilm cartridge.

Cartridge for 16mm Processed Microfilm. Based on specifications first developed in 1975, the so-called ANSI/AIIM standard cartridge differs from previous proprietary designs. While seeming to contribute to the incompatibility problem, this precaution was necessary to avoid giving any one manufacturer an advantage during the time required to develop and test new display and printing equipment.

Unlike earlier models that required the transfer of microfilm from reels, the ANSI standard cartridge is a simple collar-like enclosure for a reel of microfilm. It is less expensive than most other cartridges and does not require special loading equipment. If desired, a reel of microfilm can simply be inserted into an ANSI standard cartridge immediately prior to use. While some micrographic installations may continue to use proprietary-type cartridges, the ANSI standard cartridge is the microform of choice in active records management applications utilizing 16 mm microfilm. As a significant advantage for micrographic systems analysts, the ANSI standard cartridge is supported by a wide selection of readers and reader-printers.

As previously noted, microfilm cartridges retain the advantages of 16 mm reels while eliminating manual film threading as an obstacle to convenient retrieval of desired document images. As will be discussed in Chapter Seven, cartridges are widely and successfully utilized in automated microfilm retrieval systems, where they are often the microform of choice. As a potential disadvantage, readers and reader-printers that use cartridges are more complex and expensive than the reel microfilm devices. Furthermore, cartridges retain the serial access limitations of reel microfilm, and certain tasks—such as the addition, removal, or selective duplication microimages—will prove more difficult when 16 mm reels are converted to cartridges.

A related microform, the 16 mm cassette, encloses both the film supply and take-up spools in a single container, eliminating the need to rewind film prior to removal from a reader or reader-printer. They are described in the ANSI/AIIM MS16 standard, *Dimensions and Operational Constraints for Double Core (Bi-Axial) Cassette for 16 mm Processed Microfilm.* Though conceptually attractive, microfilm cassettes never experienced the market acceptance enjoyed by 16 mm cartridges, and relatively few micrographic equipment manufacturers have offered them. In the United States, the last examples were discontinued in the mid-1980s.

Microfiche

A microfiche is a sheet of microfilm containing multiple images in a two-dimensional grid pattern of rows and columns. In America, the term is considered both a single and plural noun and is often simply abbreviated as *fiche.* Outside of the United States, the plural form is sometimes spelled with an ''s.'' Sheet microforms have been used extensively in Europe since the 1950s. The earliest American applications date from the 1960s when several government agencies adopted microfiche as a publishing medium for scientific and technical reports. Other document storage and retrieval applications were slow to follow. As late as 1970, articles about micrographics in business periodicals described microfiche as an innovation, although the growth of COM installations and micropublishing have led to a rapid expansion of microfiche applications since that time. Today, microfiche are widely utilized in a variety of source document applications, and they are the microform of choice for most COM applications.

Although microfiche are available in several different sizes, American and international standards specify external dimensions of 105 mm by 148 mm (approximately four by six inches), the international A6 size. Government agencies, multinational corporations, libraries, research institutions, and other organizations can thus purchase or exchange microfiche worldwide with reasonable assurance of size compatibility. As described in the next chapter, individual microfiche may be created from sheets of film precut to 105 by 148 mm or from 105 mm rolls that are cut into 148 mm lengths following exposure and development. In Europe, a few business installations and micropublications employ microfiche in nonstandard sizes ranging from 76 mm by 127 mm (approximately three by five inches) to 210 mm by 297 mm (approximately, nine by twelve inches). In the United States, departures from the standard size are rare but have occurred. IBM, for example, selected tabulating card-size (3.25 by 7.375 inches) microfiche as the publishing medium for its technical reports and computer system documentation. The discontinued 3M Library Processing System, a collection of microfilmed cataloging records, utilized five-by-eight inch microfiche. During the 1960s, the Atomic Energy Commission and National Aeronautics and Space Administration issued technical reports on both three-by-five inch and five-by-eight inch microfiche.

Regardless of external dimensions, most microfiche produced in the United States employ a uniform-division internal format based on a fixed grid pattern for microimages and a maximum practical reduction. Rows are identified by letters and columns by numbers. Any given image can be identified by its row and column coordinates. Microfiche produced from source documents are typically paginated horizontally, successive pages being recorded across individual rows from left to right. COM-generated microfiche are typically paginated vertically, successive pages being recorded down individual columns from top to bottom.

Reflecting changes in application requirements and equipment capabilities, microimage grid patterns and reductions have changed over time, and are likely to continue to do so. Consolidating previously separate specifications for source document and COM applications, the most recent revision of the ANSI/AIIM MS5 standard, *Microfiche,* recognizes four internal formats for 105 mm by 148 mm microfiche.

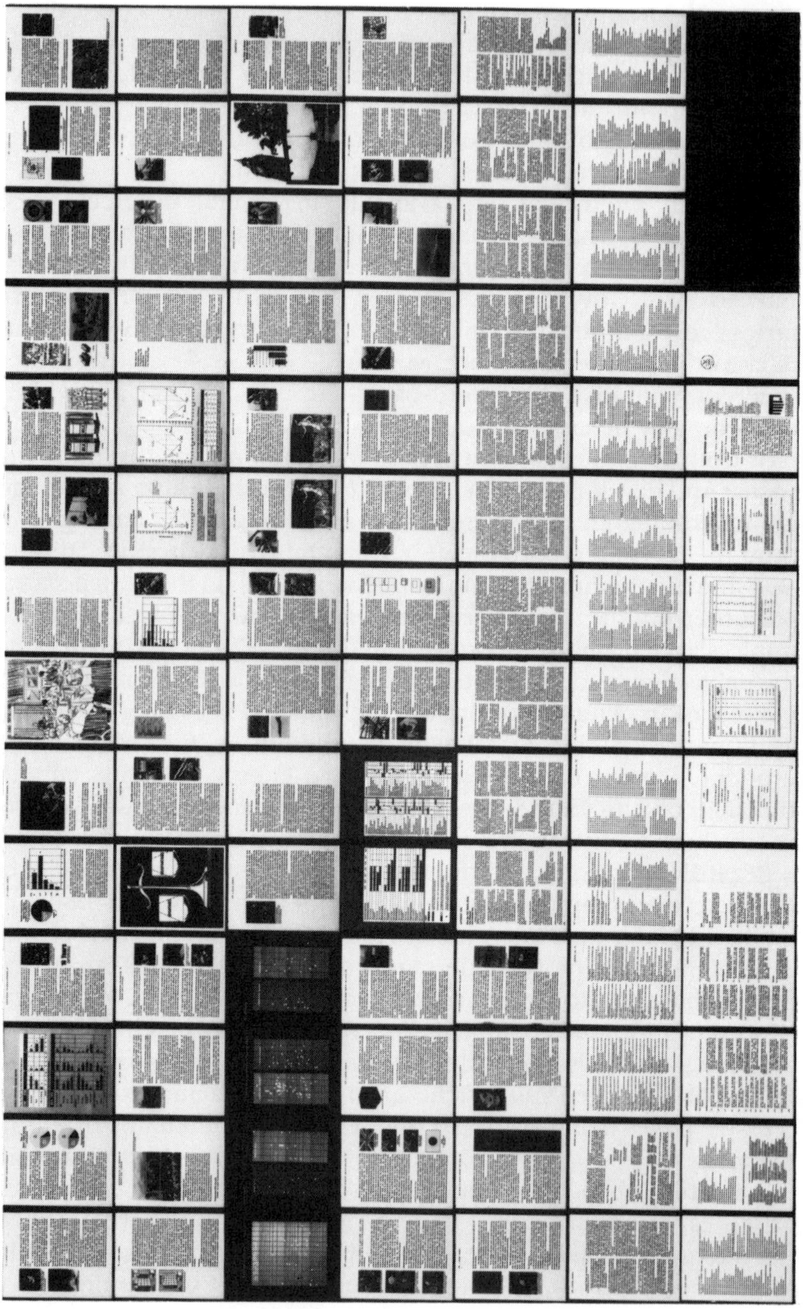

FIGURE 6. Microfiche.

TABLE 6   Microfiche Formats.

Format	Number of Frames	Frame Size	Rows and Columns	Page Size	Reduction Range
24/63*	63	15.5 × 12.5 mm	7 × 9	11 × 14 in. 279 × 356 mm	1:19–1:26
24/98*	98	10 × 12.5 mm	7 × 14	8.5 × 11 in. 216 × 279 mm	1:12–1:29** 1:23–1:26†
48/270*	270	7.75 × 6.25 mm	15 × 18	11 × 14 in. 279 × 356 mm	1:47–1:50
48/420*	420	5 × 6.5 mm	15 × 28	8.5 × 11 in. 216 × 279 mm	1:47–1:50
20/60	60	11.75 × 16.5 mm	5 × 12	8.5 × 11 in. 216 × 279 mm	1:12–1:26
42/208	208	7 × 8.75 mm	13 × 16	11 × 14 in. 279 × 356 mm	1:41–1:44
42/325	325	5.5 × 7 mm	13 × 25	8.5 × 11 in. 216 × 279 mm	1:30–1:46** 1:41–1:44†

*ANSI/AIIM standard
**Source document microfilming
† COM

With capacities ranging from 98 to 420 pages, each format is identified by its preferred reduction and the number of images per microfiche:

1. The 24/98 format —the most popular image layout for source document microfiche—provides seven rows and fourteen columns for a total of 98 images. If letter-size pages are filmed, the recommended reduction is 1:24. Since a fixed image area is allotted to each film frame, lower reductions are possible for smaller documents. Five by seven inch book pages, for example, can be filmed at 1:16, while seven by nine inch book pages can be recorded at 1:19. Alternatively, several small documents may be combined in a single frame. Larger documents must be microfilmed at higher reductions or in sections occupying several frames. A4-size documents, for example, are reduced 1:26, while legal size pages are typically recorded at 1:29.

2. The 24/63 format specifies an image grid pattern of seven rows and nine columns with a preferred reduction of 1:24 for 11-by-14-inch, computer printout-size pages. Originally developed for COM applications, it is no longer supported by newer COM recorders which invariably favor the high-reduction formats described below. The 24/63 format is used, however, in source document applications involving computer printouts.

3. The 48/270 format is the most popular microfiche layout for COM applications. Based on computer printout-size (eleven by fourteen inch) pages, it specifies a grid pattern of fifteen rows and eighteen columns. The preferred reduction is 1:48.

4. The 48/420 format is based on letter-size (8.5 by eleven inch) pages. It specifies a grid pattern of fifteen rows and twenty-eight

columns with a preferred reduction of 1:48. It is well suited to COM applications involving word processing documents. The 48/420 format can also be used for source document recording, although such high reductions—as noted in Chapter One—require documents with appropriate typographic and physical characteristics.

An appendix to the latest ANSI/AIIM microfiche standard notes the existence and continued use of three other formats recognized by previous standards.

1. The 20/60 format is based on a microfiche grid pattern developed in the 1960s by the federal Committee on Scientific and Technical Information (COSATI) for the micropublication of government reports. Sometimes described as the COSATI format, it was subsequently adopted by other American and European micropublishers, although the 24/98 format ultimately supplanted it. As its name suggests, the 20/60 layout provides five rows and twelve columns for a total of sixty frames per microfiche. If letter-size pages are filmed, the recommended reduction is 1:18 to 1:20. Reductions for other page sizes can range from 1:12 to 1:26. At a time when many scientific and technical reports existed only as marginally legible carbon copies produced by manual typewriters, the 20/60 format's modest reduction increased the likelihood of legible microreproduction. While such precautionary measures are seldom required today, many libraries maintain backfiles of government-produced reports and other micropublications in the 20/60 format.

2. Originally developed for COM applications, the 42/208 format is based on computer printout-size pages. Widely used through the mid-1970s, it specifies a grid pattern of thirteen rows and sixteen columns with a preferred reduction of 1:42. While it continues to be supported by some COM recorders, the standard 48/270 format is preferred.

3. The 42/325 format specifies a grid pattern of thirteen rows and twenty-five columns with a preferred reduction of 1:42 for letter-size pages. Smaller and larger documents can be recorded at reductions ranging from 1:30 to 1:46. Though seldom used, the 42/325 format is compatible with both source document and COM applications. The standard 48/420 format is preferred.

Other nonstandard microfiche formats have been used in special situations. Available microfiche cameras, for example, have optionally supported 20/72, 24/49, 24/63, 30/98, 40/144, 42/160, 42/200, 42/338, 48/252, and other combinations of reduction and page capacity for source documents of various sizes. Several COM recorders support a 1:72 reduction with over 600 printout-size pages per microfiche.

Sometimes encountered in engineering and scientific applications, the 105 mm full-frame format uses an entire microfiche to record a single microimage, typically of an engineering drawing, architectural rendering, or other large document. As such, it offers an alternative to 35 mm reel microfilm and to the aperture card and 35 mm jacket formats described below. The images may be created from source documents or by computer-output microfilm from computer-generated graphic files. Because reductions as low as 1:5 can be used, the 105 mm full-frame format is well suited to drawings that are in such poor condition that they cannot be legibly recorded at the higher reductions required by 35 mm microfilm. The low reductions also permit visual inspection without magnification. Where drawing modifications are required, 105 mm full-frame microfiche can be retouched like full-size contact negatives. As a further advantage, they can be interfiled with conventional microfiche, thus eliminating the need to maintain separate files of drawings and textual documents pertaining to engineering, architectural, and construction projects. As a potentially significant disadvantage, however, there is a very limited selection of production and retrieval equipment for 105 mm full-frame microfiche.

Since the 1960s, micrographic systems analysts have been particularly attracted by microfiche's suitability as a unit record for documents less than a few hundred pages in length and by the development of microfiche standards that have facilitated the introduction of inexpensive, high-quality readers and reader-printers. Because of their high image capacity, microfilm reels and cartridges are considered *non-unitized* microforms. In a medical records application, for example, a single 16 mm reel or cartridge can store fifty patient files containing an average fifty letter-size pages each. Because the files stored on a given reel or cartridge will typically pertain to different patients, a user interested in one patient's file must consult a microform that contains the records of forty-nine other patients. During the time that one file is being consulted, the other forty-nine files are unavailable for use. As a further complication where microfilmed records contain sensitive or proprietary information, a user may not be authorized to view all documents recorded on a given reel or cartridge.

Microfiche, by way of contrast, are generally considered a *unitized* microform. In most applications, the images recorded on a given microfiche are related to one another. With their much lower storage capacity, microfiche can more readily establish a one-to-one correspondence between a physical microform and a logical record, such as a folder of related documents, a computer-generated report, a technical manual, a laboratory notebook, or an issue of a periodical publication. This distinction between unitized and non-unitized microforms is subject to exceptions, of course. Roll microforms, for example, can effectively unitize long documents or large document collections, such as newspaper and periodical backfiles, engineering project files, litigation files, or clinical records associated with pharmaceutical product testing. On the other hand, individual microfiche may sometimes contain several short reports or other documents.

Because of the rapid development of American and international microfiche standards, manufacturers have been able to build relatively inexpensive display and printing devices. As will be discussed in Chapter Five, highly functional microfiche readers and reader-printers are widely available at reasonable prices, and even the least costly models have features associated with considerably more expensive reel and cartridge microfilm devices. Portable units are available for travel or field use.

Among their other advantages, microfiche can be quickly and easily duplicated by equipment that will be described in Chapter Three. To prevent the loss of valuable documents and permit the simultaneous use of microfilmed information by two or more persons, reference copies can be made on demand and the master microfiche returned to the file immediately following duplication. Depending on application requirements and the nature of the information, duplicate microfiche may be retained or discarded at the user's discretion. In most cases, the cost of microfiche duplication will compare very favorably with that of photocopying an equivalent number of paper documents.

Unlike roll microforms, which are limited to serial access, microfiche permit semidirect image retrieval. With an appropriate manual or automated filing system, individual microfiche can be accessed directly. An area at the top of each microfiche is usually reserved for an eye-legible title or other identifying information. Once a given microfiche is inserted into a reader or reader-printer, access to specific information may require the sequential examination of microimages. Rather than traversing each image from the beginning to the end of the microfiche, however, users can move horizontally, vertically, and diagonally across rows and columns.

Like all microforms, microfiche have limitations. While they are easily and economically duplicated, source document microfiche can be expensive to create, often costing three to five times as much as roll microforms. As noted in the next chapter, much of this cost differential is attributable to the high price of microfiche cameras which are more complex than their roll film counterparts. In COM applications, by way of contrast, microfiche are typically the least expensive microform to create.

Whether produced from source documents or by computer-output microfilm, their compact size renders microfiche vulnerable to loss or theft, while the uniformity associated with standardization can promote misfiling. As a preventive measure, microfiche heading areas can be color-coded, and the microfiche themselves can be corner-cut or edge-notched. As a final point, the micrographic industry supports microfiche so effectively with high-quality, relatively inexpensive display, printing, and duplicating equipment. On that basis alone, microfiche may be selected for a given application in preference to other, potentially more suitable, microforms. This is the case with some micropublications produced from long documents, periodical backfiles, or large manuscript collections that might be more effectively handled with microfilm reels or cartridges.

Updatable Microfiche

While they offer space savings, convenient retrieval, file integrity, and other advantages discussed in Chapter One, conventional microfilm and microfiche systems cannot conveniently accommodate files to which documents must be added following filming. The need to control storage space and facilitate retrieval for such files is a commonly encountered records management requirement in such diverse fields as insurance, banking, medicine, law enforcement, court administration, education, engineering, and libraries. In insurance applications, for example, policy files often remain open for decades with new documents being added at regular intervals. Files created at the time a student is admitted to college will continue to accumulate documents through the student's graduation. Similarly, documents are continually added to files for ongoing construction or engineering projects. Such additions may continue for months or even years after the projects are completed.

As discussed more fully in the next chapter, most microfilm and microfiche systems employ silver halide microphotographic materials which lose their sensitivity following exposure and development. Even though empty spaces may remain on a given roll or microfiche, additional images cannot be recorded in them. Addressing this limitation, updatable microfiche systems use unconventional photographic technologies that permit the addition of images to previously exposed microfiche. They are primarily designed for active records management applications where spacing savings and other advantages of microforms are desired but where interfiling requirements prevent the use of conventional micrographic technology.

At the time this chapter was written, updatable microfiche systems were offered by A.B. Dick Record Systems, Bell and Howell, and Memcom International. Introduced in the 1970s, all three systems employ precut, 105 mm by 148 mm sheets of unexposed film that are inserted into a camera. The operator uses an exposure button in combination with a cluster of row and column keys to record documents in particular microfiche locations. Images are developed inside the camera and can be viewed or duplicated immediately. With all three updatable systems, previously exposed microfiche can be reinserted into the camera to add new images to blank spaces. The three systems differ, however, in the type of recording technology they use and in their ability to modify previously recorded images.

The updatable microfiche system marketed by A.B. Dick resembles a photocopier in appearance, technology, and operation. It uses a variant form of xerographic recording called transparent electro-photography in which a specially designed sheet of microfilm is electro-statically charged and exposed to light reflected from a source document. As in conventional electrophotography, charges are dissipated in areas of the film corresponding to light (background) areas of the document. The remaining electrostatic charges form a latent image of the document's dark (information) areas. The latent image is made visible by applying a toner that contains carbon particles.

Unlike conventional silver gelatin microfilm, the transparent elec-trophotographic film utilized by the A.B. Dick system retains its sensitivity through repeated exposures. Consequently a previously exposed microfiche can be reinserted into the camera and new microimages added to blank spaces. If desired, obsolete images can be double-exposed with a mask reading "void" or "superseded". In addition, an area at the top of each frame is provided for the insertion of special annotation cards. One of these cards typically includes the camera operator's name, date, and other information about the circumstances of the original filming. The other can be used for later cross-referencing to supplementary or replacement documents. The A.B. Dick microfiche are shaped like miniature file folders with a center tab protruding above the top row. Self-adhesive labels, containing eye-legible identifying information, can be attached to the protruding tab. The remainder of the microfiche measures 105 mm by 148 mm and includes a heading area for eye-legible titling. Cameras are available for several different microfiche formats.

The Bell and Howell Microx updatable microfiche system uses a photoplastic film on which a latent image is formed from a pattern of electrostatic charges. The image is developed by deforming the film through the application of heat and is subsequently fixed by cooling. The system's camera is integrated with a film processor and display device located in a single housing. Document images are developed immediately after recording and displayed for operator inspection. Conforming to the American national standard, Microx microfiche measure 105 mm by 148 mm. As with the A.B. Dick system, new images can be added to blank areas of previously exposed microfiche, and previously recorded images can be annotated through double exposure. The Microx system is unique, however, permitting the erasure of previously recorded images and their replacement with new ones. Erasure is performed by deforming the photoplastic film. A locking mechanism minimizes the likelihood of inadvertent erasure.

Memcom International markets an updatable microfiche system that is based on the MicrOvonics microrecording technology developed by Energy Conversion Devices. Using energy-induced changes, it records document images on a metallic-coated film that is covered with a photoplastic material. The images are actually created in two steps. Source documents are first exposed to a roll of dry silver microfilm which serves as a printing intermediate for the updatable microfiche. Operations are performed automatically and sequentially inside the camera and are transparent to the operator. New images can be added to previously exposed microfiche. While document images cannot be erased, double exposure permits the addition of information to blank spaces within previously recorded frames. A special reader is required unless the user has created vesicular duplicates.

Regardless of the technology employed, the microfiche created by updatable systems are duplicated to create one or more working copies for use in readers and reader-printers. Special duplicators are available for that purpose.

Microfilm Jackets

Like updatable microfiche systems, microfilm jackets are designed for applications requiring the addition of documents to previously filmed files. Broadly defined, a microfilm jacket is a transparent acetate or polyester carrier with one or more sleeves or channels designed to hold flat strips of 16 mm or 35 mm microfilm. In most cases, the microfilm strips are cut from rolls, although several companies have developed cameras that produce fully processed, precut strips of 16 mm microfilm. While the film strips can be inserted into jackets by hand, a motorized viewer-inserter is customarily used. Most microfilm jackets also feature a translucent, matte-finished heading area for eye-

FIGURE 7. Microfilm jacket.

TABLE 7 Typical Microfilm Jacket Formats.

Size	Number of Channels	Channel Size	Document Type	Number of Pages	Heading Size
76 × 127 mm	3	16 mm	letter	27	17.5 mm
86 × 127 mm	4	16 mm	letter	36	8.5 mm
102 × 152 mm	5	16 mm	letter	60	8.5 mm
103 × 152 mm	4	16 mm	letter	48	26.2 mm
103 × 152 mm	2	16 mm	letter	24	66.6 mm
105 × 148 mm	4	16 mm	letter	48	25.4 mm
105 × 148 mm	5	16 mm	letter	60	10 mm
86 × 187 mm	4	16 mm	letter	60	9.5 mm
129 × 203 mm	6	16 mm	letter	96	12.7 mm
102 × 129 mm	6	16 mm	printout	30	15.8 mm
148 × 105 mm	7	16 mm	printout	35	12.7 mm
86 × 127 mm	2	35 mm	drawings	4	8 mm
103 × 152 mm	2	35 mm	drawings	6	23.8 mm
86 × 187 mm	2	35 mm	drawings	8	8 mm
129 × 203 mm	3	35 mm	drawings	12	12.7 mm
105 × 152 mm	1	35 mm	drawings	3	8.7 mm
	3	16 mm	letter	36	
86 × 187 mm	1	35 mm	drawings	3	9.5 mm
	2	16 mm	letter	30	
129 × 203 mm	1	35 mm	drawings	4	12.7 mm
	4	16 mm	letter	64	

legible identifying information that can be handwritten, typewritten, printed out by computer, or entered by other methods.

Microfilm jackets are updatable microforms in the sense that new document images can be added to a given jacket, as long as space remains in the sleeves. Similarly, film strips containing obsolete images can be removed. Jackets resemble microfiche but are available in a much wider range of external sizes and image capacities. The ANSI/AIIM MS11 standard, *Microfilm Jackets*, describes their basic characteristics. The most commonly encountered jackets are designed for 16 mm microfilm strips. In the United States, the most popular jacket configuration measures four by six inches wide (approximately 102 mm by 152 mm). It features five 16 mm channels with a heading area measuring one-third of an inch (8 mm to 9 mm) high—sufficient for one line of identifying information. The exact image capacity is determined by the size of the documents being filmed, the reduction ratio, and the frame spacing observed by the microfilm camera. Typically, this most popular jacket size can contain sixty or seventy letter-size pages (five strips of 12 or 14 images each) reduced 1:24 and filmed in the comic mode. A variant configuration provides just four sleeves for 16 mm film strips but increases the height of the heading area to

27 mm for information that is extra eye-legible. Jackets with as few as two sleeves and very wide heading areas are available for applications where a substantial amount of identifying information accompanies a small number of documents. Such applications may be better served by the card jackets described in a later section.

While the four by six inch jacket is often described as microfiche-size because it can be used in ordinary microfiche display, printing, and duplicating equipment, it is actually slightly larger than a standard microfiche. If size compatibility with microfiche is required for interfiling or other reasons, several vendors offer a jacket which measures exactly 105 mm by 148 mm. Like its slightly larger counter-part, the microfiche-sized jacket is available in several different configurations. The most common features five 16 mm channels and a 10 mm heading area. That configuration is the most popular jacket size outside of the United States. Variant configurations offer fewer channels and larger heading areas.

It is important to note that the 105 mm by 148 mm microfilm jacket is only compatible with national and international microfiche standards in its external dimensions. As previously discussed, the popular ANSI Type-1 format for microfiche of documents provides for a total of ninety-eight images arranged in seven rows and fourteen columns, each row being just 11 mm wide. The most popular jacket formats more closely resemble the sixty-image ANSI Type-2 (COSATI) format, but image spacing within each 16 mm film strips seldom conforms to specifications set forth in the American National Standard for microfiche. Where compatibility with the ANSI Type-1 standard is required, 105 by 148 mm jackets are available with seven channels, each measuring 11 mm wide and designed for the insertion of 16 mm microfilm strips created by any of the several available cameras that support standard microfiche image spacing. Such jackets require that the edges of 16 mm film strips be trimmed to 11 mm.

Three-by-five-inch (76 mm by 127 mm) jackets are available for smaller files. The most popular configuration features three 16 mm channels for a maximum image capacity of twenty-seven letter-size documents reduced 1:24. The heading area, which measures 18 mm high, can hold two lines of eye-legible, typewritten information. A slightly larger jacket measures three and three-eighths inches by five inches (86 mm by 127 mm) and features four 16 mm channels for a total image capacity of thirty-six letter-size pages reduced 1:24. While these smaller jackets are about 30 percent less expensive than the 4 inch by 6 inch configurations, they can prove inconvenient when used in microfiche readers, reader-printers, and duplicators. In large-scale applications, however, supply cost savings may outweight such inconvenience. For larger files, a few manufacturers offer a 5 inch by 8 inch (127 by 203 mm) jacket with six 16 mm channels capable of storing up to ninety document images. As with the 3 inch by 5 inch configurations, such large jackets may prove inconvenient to display, print, or duplicate in equipment designed for 105 mm by 148 mm microfiche.

Thirty-five millimeter microfilm jackets are designed for applications involving engineering drawings, architectural renderings, maps, x-rays, and other large documents. In the 4 inch by 6 inch size, two 35 mm channels can store a total of six D-size (24 by 36 inch) engineering drawings or eight x-rays. A 25 mm heading area provides ample space for eye-legible information. A 3 inch by 5 inch configuration provides two 35 mm channels for a total capacity of four D-size drawings. A 5 inch by 8 inch jacket offers three 35 mm channels for a total capacity of 12 D-size drawings.

Several vendors also offer a tabulating-size jacket with two 35 mm channels and a total capacity of eight drawings. Because they are size-compatible with the aperture cards described later in this chapter, tabulating size jackets can be easily integrated into existing manual or automated storage and retrieval systems for engineering drawings. Since conventional aperture cards are limited to a single frame of 35 mm film, tabulating-size 35 mm microfilm jackets can more effectively unitize multidrawing sets. Tabulating-size jackets are also available with four 16 mm channels and sufficient image capacity for sixty letter-size documents reduced 1:24.

Jackets that combine 16 mm and 35 mm channels permit unitization of the two microfilm sizes in a single carrier. They can prove useful, for example, in engineering, architectural, and construction applications where letter-size project reports are recorded on 16 mm microfilm and engineering drawings or architectural renderings are recorded on 35 mm microfilm. Similarly, in medical applications, textual records can be combined with x-rays—the former being recorded on 16 mm microfilm, the latter on 35 mm microfilm. In 4 inch by 6 inch and tabulating sizes, a typical combination jacket features a single channel for 35 mm microfilm plus two or three channels for 16 mm film strips.

Because microfilm jackets closely resemble miniaturized paper files, they seldom require extensive modifications of long-established filing procedures or other work patterns. Only the file size changes. As an additional advantage, jackets can protect microimages from scratching or other damage. Like microfiche, jackets can be color-striped, edge-notched, or otherwise coded for misfile protection. Using equipment to be described in the next chapter, jackets can be duplicated to create microfiche-like distribution copies. As a potential disadvantage, jacket production can prove time-consuming, labor-intensive, and expensive, especially in high volume file conversions. Unlike updatable microfiche systems, multiple work steps involving several different pieces of equipment are required. As compact storage media, jackets are vulnerable to theft or loss. Prior to creating strips for insertion into jackets, duplicate rolls are often made for security purposes.

Card Jackets

As their name implies, card jackets combine the attributes of an index card and a microfilm jacket. Like conventional jackets, they contain sleeves or channels for strips of 16 mm or 35 mm microfilm. As their unique feature, card jackets offer considerable card space for handwritten, typed, or computer-printed information. Card jackets are consequently well suited to personnel records, credit history files, patient files, student records, and similar applications where the information contained in microfilmed documents can be summarized or updated by eye-legible notations. In library and information center applications, card jackets can combine microfilmed technical reports with abstracts or other eye-legible document summaries.

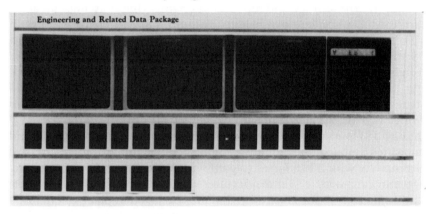

FIGURE 8. Aperture card jacket.

Card jackets measure 105 mm by 148 mm and are available in several different configurations. The most common features two or three 16 mm sleeves with a total capacity of 15 to twenty letter-size pages reduced 1:24. Card jackets with larger image capacities or 35 mm sleeves are available, but any increase in the number or width of the film sleeves will correspondingly reduce the amount of paper space available for eye-legible information. Like conventional microfilm jackets, card jackets are an updatable microform. Provided that space remains in a given sleeve, additional images can be inserted. Obsolete film strips can be removed at any time. Card jackets are manufactured from opaque card stock in a variety of colors or with color striping for simplified misfile detection. Edge-notching is also possible. The front and back of the card can be custom printed with special formats or logos. For the simplified dissemination of microform copies, card jackets are also available in a translucent stock which can be duplicated in its entirety, including eye-legible information, by ordinary microfiche duplicating equipment.

Card jackets are available in a tabulating-size variant that is designed for applications where size-compatibility with aperture cards or tabulating-size microfilm jackets is desired. It combines card space for eye-legible information with two or three sleeves for the insertion of 16 mm microfilm strips. The tabulating-size card jackets are available in either opaque or translucent card stock. The latter is intended for use with aperture card duplicators. As with card jackets, a choice of colors and color striping is offered. Cards can also be printed in custom formats.

Aperture Cards

Aperture cards are the oldest and most famous of those microforms. They combine the space-saving advantages of microimages with eye-legible information in paper form. Introduced in the 1950s to simplify the storage and retrieval of engineering drawings, an aperture card is a conventional eighty-column, tabulating-size card with a hole or aperture that is designed for the insertion of one frame of 35 mm microfilm. As with microfilm jackets, individual frames are usually cut from rolls, although special cameras can accept unexposed film premounted in aperture cards. As described in the ANSI/AIIM MS41 standard, *Unitized Microfilm Carriers (Aperture, Camera, Copy, and Image Cards)*, an aperture card measures 3.25 by 7.375 inches (85.7 mm by 187.3 mm). The aperture spans columns 53 through 77 and measures 1.304 inches high by 1.908 inches wide. A microfiche-size alternative, which has failed to gain wide acceptance, is a 105 mm by 148 mm card with a 35 mm aperture. Regardless of card size, the aperture contains a 35 mm film chip that may be glued in place or enclosed between pieces of polyester in a transparent pocket.

Like card jackets, the front and back of an aperture card can be custom-printed to accommodate special application requirements. To distinguish different sets of drawings or other documents, aperture cards can be ordered in various colors. Color striping and edge notching can be used for misfile protection. To minimize the wear and tear associated with frequent reference, cards can be ordered in a heavy-duty stock and with rounded corners.

Most aperture cards contain eye-legible handwritten or typed information that identifies and describes the microfilmed material. Aperture cards can also be purchased on fan-folded supports for computer printing. Like their tab card counterparts, aperture cards can be keypunched with drawing numbers or other identifying information for machine sorting and selection. Several vendors offer keypunch equipment that is specifically designed for aperture card preparation. The newest devices are microprocessor-controlled and combine a card punch, a typewriter-like keyboard, and a microform display. They can also print human-readable characters at the top of each card column and record copying instructions for use by certain card duplicating systems. Aperture card sorters and collators can quickly arrange stacks of punched cards in alphabetic or numeric sequence without damage

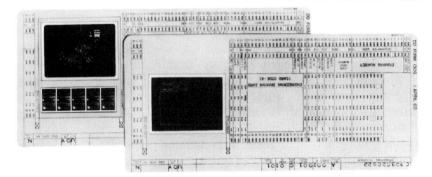

FIGURE 9. Aperture cards.

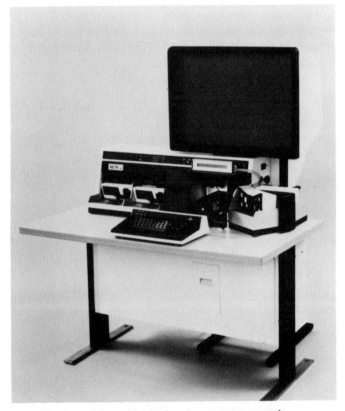

FIGURE 10. Keypunch device for aperture cards.
Courtesy Alos Micrographics.

to microimages. They can also assemble sets of master cards and copy cards to meet specific distribution requirements. Where selective retrieval of individual cards is desired, automated systems, to be described in Chapter Seven, offer an effective alternative to sorting.

The aperture card is an excellent unitized microform for large, single-page documents. Since their introduction, they have been the microform of choice for engineering drawings. They can also be used for maps, charts, and x-rays. While 35 mm microfilm jackets and 105 mm full-frame microfiche address the same applications, a much wider selection of production, display, printing, and retrieval equipment is available for aperture cards. Aperture card reductions vary with the document size. D-size (24 by 36 inch) or international A1-size (594 mm by 841 mm) drawings are usually microfilmed at 1:24. E-size (34 by 44 inch) or international A0-size (841 mm by 1,189 mm) are typically reduced 1:30. Larger drawings may be filmed in segments at 1:24. Aperture cards can also contain up to four letter-size pages reduced 1:16 or eight letter-size pages reduced 1:24. These two formats are described as four-up and eight-up, respectively.

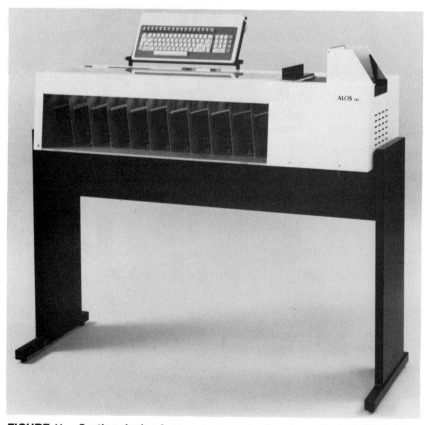

FIGURE 11. Sorting device for aperture cards. *Courtesy Alos Micrographics.*

Ultra High Reduction Microforms

Utilizing reductions in excess of 1:90, ultrafiche and ultrastrips combine the ease of handling of flat microforms with the image capacity of roll microforms. While 3 by 5 inch media have been produced, the typical ultrafiche is a 4 by 6 inch transparency that can store 3,000 or more letter-size pages. Ultrastrips measure 35 mm wide by 8 inches long. Images are typically recorded in five segments, each containing 25 rows and twenty columns for a total strip capacity of 2,500 letter-size pages. Other configurations are possible for larger documents. Produced at reductions ranging from 1:150 to 1:250, ultrastrips have been used in telephone directory assistance, signature verification, credit card account management, and similar applications requiring the rapid retrieval of a few lines of information from very large data bases.

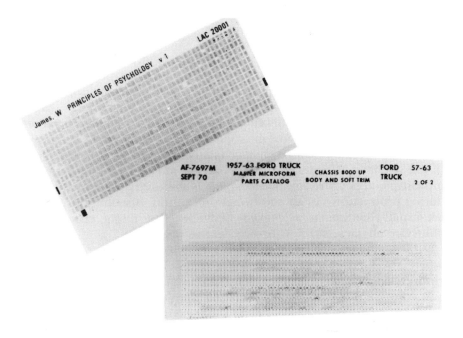

FIGURE 12.   Ultrafiche.

FIGURE 13.   Ultrastrip.

Although ultra high reductions were used in the earliest novelty applications of microphotography, modern ultrafiche and ultrastrip technology developed out of research in computer memories. The creation of ultra high reduction microimages is a complex, relatively expensive process. It is performed in two steps and requires a laboratory environment with unconventional recording materials and special equipment. In a typical application, source documents are first recorded at low reductions of 1:9 to 1:12, using conventional cameras and 35 mm microfilm. Alternatively, 35 mm microimages can be produced from computer-generated information by a COM recorder. These microimages are then further reduced by 1:10 or more, using photochromic microimaging (PCMI) materials.

Being grainless, photochromic materials can produce consistently high quality microimages at reductions exceeding the present capabilities of conventional microphotographic systems. These ultra high reduction microimages require no development and are inspected immediately following exposure. In the event of error, a microimage can be optically erased and re-exposed. When the master ultrafiche or ultrastrip is completed, special duplicators, designed to achieve uniform contact at high speed, are used to produce printing intermediates from which the required number of distribution copies are made. The interrelationship of document characteristics, image contrast, exposure time, and other quality-control parameters is more complex than in conventional microphotography and must be carefully monitored. Because printed characters measuring 2 mm to 3 mm high in full-size may be reduced to less than ten microns on ultrafiche or ultrastrips, a clean room environment is necessary to control dust during production. As an additional precaution, distribution copies are usually laminated to prevent scratches that might obscure or obliterate characters, lines, or even entire pages.

Ultrafiche are primarily intended for micropublishing applications where the high cost of producing a photochromic master will be recovered through the sale of a distribution copies. The break-even point for edition size varies with the application. In commercial applications, ultrafiche have been used for automotive parts catalogs and similar voluminous publications. When many copies are required, the cost per page compares favorably with conventional microforms and paper publications. During the late 1960s and early 1970s, ultrafiche were used in a number of ambitious micropublishing projects involving out-of-print books and other library materials. While most of those projects have been abandoned, ultrafiche remains an important microform for legal publications.

Ultrafiche require a reader or reader-printer equipped with a high magnification lens, a powerful light source, and a short depth of focus. Ultrastrips are typically packaged in cartridges for use in specially designed retrieval units. One type of reader accepts externally-stored cartridges containing fifty ultrastrips each; a more automated model features an internal drum that holds 512 ultrastrips with a total microimage capacity approaching 1.3 million letter-size pages. Access to individual images is controlled by a computer-maintained index.

Opaque Microforms

As their name suggests, opaque microforms—sometimes called micro-opaques—feature paper rather than film substrates. Developed as micropublishing media for library applications, they are no longer being produced, although many libraries continue to maintain large microcard, Microlex, and Microprint collections that were purchased in the 1960s and 1970s. Introduced in the 1950s, microcards are 3 by 5 inch cards that contain up to forty photographically produced microimages. Microlex was a trade name for an opaque, card-type microform produced by Microlex Corporation. Primarily used for legal publications, they measure 6.5 by 8.5 inches and can contain up to 200 photographically produced microimages per side. Both formats were discontinued in the 1970s.

Microprint cards, the most successful micro-opaque format and the last to be commercially produced, measure 6 by 9 inches. Developed by Readex Microprint Corporation, they contain 100 microimages arranged in ten rows and ten columns. Typical reductions range from 1:12 to 1:24. Space at the top of each card is reserved for eye-legible bibliographic information. Like ultrafiche, Microprint cards required special production methodologies and equipment. Microimages of source documents recorded on 35 mm microfilm were

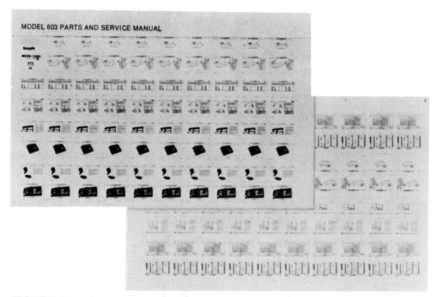

FIGURE 14.   An opaque microform.

stripped and mounted on special plates. The microimages were actually printed by offset lithography onto 100 percent rag-content paper. Because photographic chemicals were not used during printing, Microprint cards can be stored under the same environmental conditions as books. Microprint was utilized as a publishing medium for very large collections of specialized research materials. Microprint production was discontinued in the mid-1980s, and some Microprint products have been reformatted as microfiche publications.

3 Source Document Microfilming

As PREVIOUSLY DISCUSSED, microforms can be produced from source documents or from computer-generated data. Source document microphotography requires the use of special cameras to film office records, books, reports, technical manuals, engineering drawings, maps, and other documents at greatly reduced size. It is the older of the two microform production methodologies. As noted in Chapter One, 16 mm microfilm cameras for banking and other business applications were introduced in the late 1920s. Although the earliest library microfilming projects employed conventional 35 mm cameras configured with reduction lenses, microfilming equipment designed specifically for library materials became available in the 1930s.

With the introduction of cartridge systems, microfiche, microfilm jackets, and aperture cards in the 1950s and 1960s, source document microfilming activity increased, and applications broadened. Microfiche cameras, engineering-drawing cameras, microfilm processors, duplicators, jacket viewer/inserters, aperture card mounters, and a variety of supporting production devices and accessories were developed to simplify source document microfilm implementations. By the late 1960s, several hundred manufacturers offered source document microfilming equipment ranging from highly automated cameras and duplicators to manually-operated cartridge loaders and inspection devices. During the 1970s and 1980s, cameras and other source document microfilming devices increasingly incorporated microprocessor-based controllers and other computer-like electronic components, thereby enhancing both reliability and versatility. Benefitting from six decades of steady and significant product refinements, modern source document microfilming equipment can successfully address a broad range of application requirements.

As an overview of production procedures, figure 15 depicts the flow of work and interrelationship of equipment components in a typical source document microfilming implementation. The following explanations apply:

1. Preparation requirements—the series of work steps that make source documents "camera ready"—depend on several factors, including the characteristics of documents to be microfilmed and the type of camera to be used. As a minimum, correspondence, project files, insurance claims files, and similar office records must be removed from file folders, unfolded if necessary, and stacked neatly in the correct sequence for filming.

Most microfilm cameras require removal of staples and paper clips from source documents, and the removal of such fasteners usually improves filming productivity and the appearance of the resulting microimages, even where not required. Torn pages should be mended or photocopied prior to filming. Rolled engineering drawings, maps, and other large documents must be flattened. Books, reports, and other bound materials are most easily filmed if unbound, although some cameras can be equipped with specially-designed, spring-loaded book cradles. Additional preparation work steps, such as document numbering or the insertion of special flash targets between pages, are often associated with specific retrieval methodologies that will be described in Chapter Six.

2. Properly prepared, source documents are microfilmed by special cameras. While the characteristics and capabilities of source document cameras vary considerably, all are initially loaded with unexposed microfilm in 16 mm, 35 mm, or 105 mm widths. As discussed below, most microfilms intended for camera work are of the silver gelatin type.

3. Documents are recorded on film as miniaturized, latent images that require development before they are visible. Such development, which consists of a series of mechanical and chemical treatments, is performed by a microfilm processor. In most source document implementations, the processor is a separate device. It may be operated in-house or by a microfilm service bureau or photographic laboratory to which exposed film is sent. Alternatively, the microfilm camera and processor may be integrated in a single device called a camera/processor or processor/camera. Such devices expose and develop microimages in a continuous sequence of work steps.

4. Once developed, microimages must be inspected for sharpness, contrast, legibility, stability, and other characteristics. A variety of special devices and supplies—including microscopes, densitometers, light boxes, and archival testing kits—are required for this purpose. If microfilm processing and technical inspection are performed by a

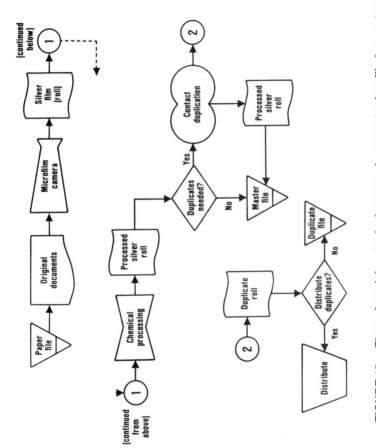

FIGURE 15. Flow of work in a typical source document microfilming system.

service bureau or photographic laboratory, in-house equipment requirements are simplified, but externally-processed film must still be inspected for legibility, image alignment, and other characteristics that affect its utility.

5. Microform duplication—the production of one or more microform copies from the camera original microfilm or, in some cases, from a previously created microform copy—is an optional, but recommended, work step in most source document applications. Such microform duplicates typically serve as working copies, permitting secure storage of the camera original microform. Like processing, duplication may be performed in-house or by a microfilm service bureau. Like source document cameras, duplicators are loaded with unexposed microfilm that records latent images requiring development to be made visible. Such development may be performed by the duplicator itself or by an external processor. Like their camera original counterparts, duplicate microforms must be inspected following processing.

6. As noted above, camera original microforms are typically stored in a secure location following processing, inspection, and duplication. In active records management applications, 16 mm microfilm working copies are often inserted into cartridges. Working copies of 16 mm or 35 mm reels may be cut up for insertion to microfilm jackets, card jackets, or aperture cards. Some microfiche cameras produce reels of 105 mm film which must subsequently be cut into individual microfiche.

The remainder of this chapter elaborates on each of these work steps. It provides more detailed descriptions of equipment and supplies utilized in source document microfilming and emphasizes features and functions that can influence the utility of specific types of devices in particular micrographic systems. The next chapter will provide a similar treatment of computer-output microfilming.

Recording Technologies

Despite much discussion of unconventional photographic technologies, silver gelatin microfilms remain the most important and widely used photographic media in source document applications. Diazo and vesicular microfilms, described later in this chapter, are widely used for microform duplication, but they are unsuitable for use in cameras. Silver gelatin microfilms are high performance, fine-grain photographic films named for their light-sensitive emulsion of silver halide crystals suspended in a gelatin layer. When exposed to light reflected from a source document, the silver halide crystals are converted to silver nuclei in areas of the film that correspond to light (usually, the background or noninformation) areas of the document. Containing text or other information, the dark areas of the source document absorb light. Little if any change occurs in the silver halide crystals that correspond to those areas.

Following exposure, silver gelatin images are complete but latent (invisible). Development reduces the altered silver gelatin crystals to visible black silver grains. The silver gelatin process is often described as negative-working or sign-reversing because the normal development of microimages produces a first generation microform with polarity characteristics that are opposite those of the original source document. As used in this context, the term polarity denotes the relationship between dark and light areas in a source document or a microform image made from that document. A microimage of positive polarity has dark information areas on a light background; a microimage of negative polarity has light information areas on a dark background.

The term *generation* denotes the remoteness of a particular microform from an original source document. A microfilm or microfiche produced by a source document camera is considered a first generation microform. A copy made from it is considered a second generation microform, a copy of that copy is considered a third generation microform, and so on. First generation microforms are sometimes erroneously equated with negative polarity, while second generation duplicate microforms are assumed to be of positive polarity. As will be discussed later in this chapter, however, there is no invariable relationship between generation and polarity. Second, third, or suc-ceeding microform generations may be negative or positive in appearance, depending on the duplicating process employed. Likewise, a special development technique called reversal processing can be used to create positive polarity, first generation microimages. The process uses positive-appearing source documents, such as x-rays and other photographs, which depend on the maintenance of tonal values to be meaningful.

The silver gelatin emulsion is coated on a film stock that is sup-plied in 16 mm, 35 mm, and 105 mm widths. Film length varies with the thickness of the base material. The industry standard measure of film thickness is a mil (.025 mm). Cellulose triacetate, the oldest microfilm base material, measures four to five mils in thickness, although the thickness of some 105 mm microfilms exceeds seven mils. Some vendors offer polyester-based microfilms in the same thicknesses. For source document applications, unexposed four- and five-mil silver gelatin microfilms are commonly supplied in 100-foot (30.5 m) lengths on spools of the type described in the ANSI/AIIM MS29 standard, *Cores and Spools for Recording Equipment—Dimensions.* Following exposure, the film may be wound onto reels, inserted into cartridges, or cut up for insertion into jackets or aperture cards.

Polyester-based microfilms are also available in a thickness of 2.5 mils. As a result, a greater amount of film can fit on a reel or cartridge. Unexposed, 16 mm polyester microfilms are typically supplied on standard-size spools in 215-foot (65.5m) lengths. While most older source document cameras were designed exclusively for 100-foot films, many newer models can accept 215-foot spools. The thinner microfilms are less expensive than their 100-foot counterparts. Their greater image capacities can significantly reduce the number of reels or cartridges in large backfile conversions and other high-volume applications. As noted in Chapter Two, a 100-foot reel of 16 mm microfilm can contain approximately 2,500 to 3,000 letter-size pages reduced 1:24. Depending on camera characteristics, a 215-foot reel of polyester microfilm can contain 5,400 or more letter-size pages reduced 1:24. Thus, a one-million-page file of paper documents that might occupy 400 reels or cartridges of 100-foot microfilm would require about 185 reels or cartridges in the 215-foot length.

As an additional advantage, longer microfilms can significantly improve productivity as they reduce the number of required camera loadings. The potential disadvantage of higher capacity reels, however, is that rolls of 215-foot film take twice as long to fill as their 100 foot counterpart. In low volume applications, a given roll may not be removed from the camera for days or even weeks after the first document was filmed. Microfilm can, of course, be cut following completion of a partial roll, but that defeats the purpose of using a higher capacity film. When faster turnaround time is desired in low-volume installations, the 100-foot format is preferred.

Both triacetate and polyester are nonflammable, safety-base film materials. When manufactured to current American national standards and processed in a manner described later in this chapter, both types of base materials are compatible with archival storage. Base material aside, light that passes through the silver gelatin emulsion can be reflected from the film base, causing ghost images—an undesirable effect known as halation. To prevent this, most microfilms feature an anti-halation undercoat (AHU) between the emulsion and base material. The undercoat is dissolved during processing. Compatible with most microfilm cameras, AHU microfilms yield high image quality, but they must be loaded and unloaded in subdued light. As an alternative method of halation prevention, some older microfilm cameras use dyeback films that feature a light-absorbing dye coated on the back of the base material. As an advantage, such films can be handled in ordinary room light.

In addition to their approach to halation prevention, silver gelatin microfilms differ in photographic speed, resolving power, color sensitivity and suitability for use in different cameras and with different types of source documents. Most microfilms designed for use in source document cameras are panchromatic and have high contrast properties to optimize the recording of textual documents and line drawings. Lower contrast microfilms are available for recording photographs. Generally, camera manufacturers specify the type of the silver gelatin microfilm they recommend for best results with their equipment. Micrographic systems analysts should be aware, however, of differences in film characteristics that may ultimately influence the selection of cameras and processing equipment.

While silver gelatin microfilms are well understood and offer very high image quality and exceptional stability, they require wet chemical development—a limitation that, at best, is inconvenient and, at worst, requires more attention to technical detail than can reasonably be expected of clerically-trained office personnel who work in most source document microfilming installations. Certainly, wet chemical development is a work step without counterpart in the electronic computing devices that currently dominate information management applications. An additional constraint discussed in Chapter Two is that silver gelatin microfilms lose their photographic sensitivity following exposure and development. Even though blank areas may remain, new images cannot be added to previously created microforms.

Where these limitations are significant, available source document production equipment can successfully address them. Some silver gelatin microfilm processors, for example, employ prepackaged fluids that can minimize the inconvenience of wet chemical development, and camera/processors virtually eliminate the microfilm user's perception of processing as a separate work step. Similarly, microfilm jackets or card jackets offer updateability, albeit with additional work steps.

As an alternative to silver gelatin microfilming, however, some source document cameras utilize unconventional photographic technologies. The updatable microfiche systems described in the preceding chapter are examples of such products. With its transparent electrophotographic film, the A.B. Dick updatable system employs a variant form of xerographic technology. The Bell and Howell Microx system uses a combination of electrophotography and thermal development to record microimages, while Memcom's MicrOvonic recording technology depends on energy-induced changes in a metallic film coating. The PCMI films used in ultrafiche production are another example of nonsilver microphotographic technology. As an alternative to wet chemical development, several vendors have offered source document cameras that use thermally-processed silver halide films, but such dry silver technology is more widely encountered in the COM installations to be described in Chapter Four.

Whether silver gelatin or alternative technologies are utilized, the foregoing discussion applies to black-and-white microfilms. Silver gelatin color microforms have been used successfully to miniaturize advertising files, catalogs, product labels, art works, maps, business graphics, navigational charts, interior design samples, anatomical documents, and other materials where color conveys essential information. Color microforms can be produced from 35 mm slides and three-dimensional objects as well as documents.

Although color microfilms do not offer the image sharpness of their black-and-white counterparts, quality should prove more than acceptable for applications that involve graphic rather than textual materials. Since color dyes are potentially unstable, the storage of color negatives at temperatures of 2C (35F) is recommended. Because the color microfilm base supports multiple emulsions, duplication of color microforms requires careful control of production facilities to avoid significant loss of color rendition, image sharpness, and contrast. Since the microform reader also affects color rendition, it should have high illumination and a gray screen. While color reader-printers are not available, photographic enlargers can produce color prints. As a final constraint, color microforms are much more expensive than black-and-white microforms.

Microfilm Cameras

Source document microfilm cameras are precision reprographic devices with specially designed optical systems. Based on their output formats, they can be divided into three broad groups: (1) those that produce roll microforms; (2) those that produce microfiche; and (3) those that produce other types of microforms. This section reviews the most important operating characteristics and capabilities of each product group, emphasizing features that influence the selection of microfilm cameras for particular source document applications.

Within the roll output group, microfilm cameras can be subdivided into rotary and planetary models. Rotary or flow-type cameras are designed for applications where work throughput is the primary consideration. Since their introduction in the late 1920s, they have been widely used to film business records of all types and sizes. Special models are available for unbursted computer printouts, electrocardiograms, oil well logs, and other continuous-form documents generated by medical or scientific instrumentation. Available rotary cameras produce 16 mm roll microfilm, in 100- or 215-foot lengths, depending on the model.

The rotary camera takes its name from its document feeding mechanism. Source documents, inserted into a narrow opening, are transported past a lens and a light source where they are recorded on microfilm. Input is limited to single sheets of paper with all staples, clips, and other fasteners removed. All torn pages must be mended, and special handling may be required for lightweight paper stock. Rotary cameras can usually film documents of any reasonable length. Acceptable document widths vary from model to model, although the typical maximum is fourteen inches.

The simplest rotary cameras, designed for low volume applications, support a single reduction—typically, 1:24 for letter-size pages. Documents must be manually inserted into the camera. They are recorded in the *simplex* format with one row of frames down the length of the film and one page recorded in each film frame. More complex models, designed for medium to high volume installations, feature

FIGURE 16. Rotary cameras.

Courtesy Bell & Howell.

Courtesy Eastman Kodak.

Courtesy Eastman Kodak.

Courtesy Fuji.

Courtesy 3M.

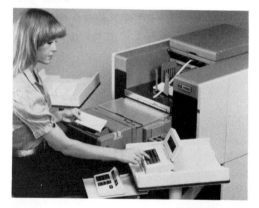

Courtesy Fuji.

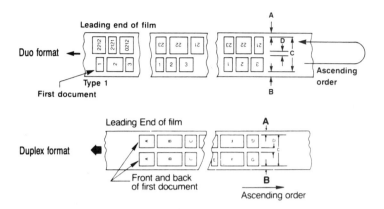

FIGURE 17. Multiplex image arrangements: the duo and duplex formats.

automatic feeders that can speed input for index cards, bank checks, and other small documents. Letter-size pages, however, must usually be fed by hand for best results. As an alternative to the simplex format, the most sophisticated microfilm cameras support *multiplex* recording with two or more rows of images per film frame.

Some rotary cameras, for example, can simultaneously record the front and back of two-sided documents. In this *duplex* filming format—which is widely used for bank checks and other negotiable instruments that contain an endorsement on the reverse side—each side of the document occupies one-half of a film frame. Typical reductions range from 1:32 to 1:50. In the *duo* filming format, which is also supported by equipment designed for medium to high volume applications, one-half of the film width (8 mm) is masked and the remainder exposed. When the full length of film has passed through the camera, it is removed and reloaded. The previously exposed portion is masked and the previously masked portion exposed. Sometimes called the 8 mm film principle, the duo format can be used at reductions of 1:32 to 1:50 to increase the microimage capacity of a single reel, although such high reductions—as discussed in Chapter One—may prove unacceptable for some source documents. Some rotary cameras support a combined duo-duplex format that records images of both the front and rear sides of source documents simultaneously on half of the width of the film, while the other film half is masked.

When compared to the planetary microfilmers described later, a rotary camera's document transport mechanism offers the advantage of greater filming speed, with consequently shorter job turnaround times and reduced labor costs. Without automatic document feeding, rates of 800 to 1,000 letter-size pages per hour, sustained by a single operator throughout a work day, are realistic. In some applications, however, the rotary camera's speed advantage may be negated by the degraded image quality that results from machine vibration and the necessity of photographing a moving document. Rotary camera image quality, while quite suitable for business records in good condition, may prove inadequate for books, journal articles, contracts, or other documents that contain footnotes or other printed text set in small type sizes. While the duplex format described above permits rapid, simultaneous microfilming of two-sided originals, significant amounts of show-through can occur. The rotary camera's inability to accept bound volumes or fragile documents is a further limitation in library applications.

Originally developed for library applications in the 1930s, planetary or flat-bed cameras are used to microfilm business documents, engineering drawings, maps, bound volumes, manuscripts, and other source documents in applications where high image quality is a paramount consideration. The typical planetary microfilmer is a relatively simple device that combines a camera unit, a flat exposure surface, a light source, and various operator controls in a tabletop or freestanding unit. The camera unit contains a lens system and film supply with a film advance mechanism. In some cases, a given camera unit can be easily removed and replaced with another, thus allowing the planetary microfilmer to be shared by several departments, each with its own camera.

Specific recording techniques vary with equipment design. The overhead-type planetary microfilmer is the oldest and still most common configuration. Source documents are individually positioned face-up on a flat copyboard for microfilming by an overhead planetary camera located on a vertical column. In an alternative approach, an

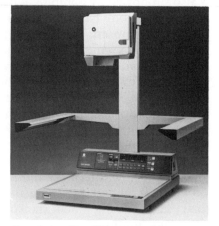

Courtesy Alos Micrographics.

Courtesy Minolta.

FIGURE 18.   16 mm planetary cameras for office documents.

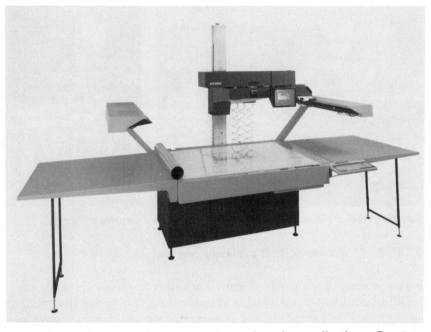

FIGURE 19. **35 mm planetary camera for engineering applications.** *Courtesy Alos Micrographics.*

inverted-type planetary microfilmer positions the camera unit and light source below or behind a glass exposure surface that resembles the platen of a photocopier. Source documents are positioned face-down on the glass surface for microfilming.

Whether the overhead or inverted design is used, input capabilities and output formats vary from model to model. Available tabletop planetary cameras, intended for office applications, can accept documents measuring up to 12 by 18 inches, although some models may be limited to 11 by 14 inch or smaller pages. Input restrictions aside, most tabletop planetary cameras produce 16 mm roll microfilm and typically operate at reductions ranging from 1:18 to 1:32 The most versatile models support multiple reductions. Larger, floor-standing models can accept documents measuring up to 24 by 36 inches. Operating at infinitely variable reductions ranging from less than 1:1.5 to more than 1:32, they can produce 16 mm or 35 mm microfilm. The most complex planetary cameras are designed for engineering applications. Operating at a wide range of reductions, they can microfilm drawings and other documents measuring up to 36 by 48 inches (E-size). Such cameras typically record documents on 35 mm microfilm which may subsequently be cut up for insertion into aperture cards.

With the simplest type of planetary cameras, individual source documents must be manually positioned for microfilming. A potentially significant advantage of planetary cameras over rotary cameras

 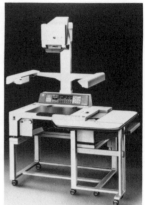

Courtesy Bell & Howell.   *Courtesy Minolta.*

FIGURE 20.   Automatic-feed planetary camera.

is that source documents remain stationary during exposure, thus, yielding excellent image quality suitable for a very broad spectrum of applications. As a disadvantage, however, planetary camera throughput rates are typically much lower than rates of their rotary camera counterparts. Without automatic document feeders, microfilming speed depends on operator skill. In applications involving properly prepared unbound documents, an experienced operator can sustain an average filming rate of 300 to 500 letter-size pages per hour. Fragile documents or bound volumes will reduce productivity considerably. As a further constraint with bound volumes, all planetary cameras impose limitations on document height or thickness. Typical limitations range from less than 1 inch to slightly more than 2 inches.

Addressing the throughput problem, automatic-feed planetary cameras provide high image quality at rotary camera speeds. Source documents, stacked in an automatic feeder, are individually transported to an exposure surface where they are stopped momentarily for filming. This design feature prevents the image degradation associated with conventional rotary cameras. Acceptable input sizes vary from model to model, but all pages must be unbound and free of staples or other fasteners. As with rotary cameras, typical throughput rates range from 800 to 1,000 pages per hour—including time for film loading, unloading, and related work routines—sustained throughout a work day.

Step-and-repeat cameras create microfiche by exposing source documents in a predetermined format of rows and columns on 105 mm microfilm. Depending on the model, the camera may accept 105 mm film in 50- or 100-foot rolls. The individual microfiche is cut to size following exposure and development. Alternatively, the camera may accept precut 105 by 148 mm sheets of unexposed film.

As discussed in Chapter Two, microfiche can be created in a variety of standard and nonstandard formats and reductions. Some step-and-repeat cameras feature a fixed reduction and can produce microfiche in one format only—typically, the 24/98 format that is most widely used in source document applications. While a choice of other lenses and microfiche formats may be available, the customer usually must specify the desired lens and format at the time the camera is purchased. More flexible, microprocessor-controlled step-and-repeat cameras, support multiple microfiche formats and interchangeable lenses. Such cameras are typically equipped with keyboards or similar controls that allow an operator to select the format appropriate to a specific application.

Formats and reductions aside, most step-and-repeat cameras resemble planetary microfilmers in design and operation. With manually-fed models, documents are individually positioned on a flat surface and remain stationary during filming. Following exposure, the document is removed, the camera automatically steps over to the next column position on film, another document is placed on the copyboard, and the process is repeated. As with their planetary camera counterparts, automatic-feed models enhance throughput by eliminating manual document positioning. As each row of images is completed, the step-and-repeat camera advances the film and begins exposure again in the first column. When an entire microfiche is exposed, the film is advanced to begin exposure of a new microfiche. Most step-and-repeat cameras can also record one or more lines of eye-legible information in the microfiche heading area. Newer models increasingly incorporate character generators for that purpose; others require the separate preparation of typewritten or printed title strips. Since they offer high image quality, step-and-repeat cameras, like planetary microfilmers, can produce legible microimages from a broad range of source documents.

While equipment for roll microforms and microfiche account for the majority of camera installations, several vendors offer devices that produce other types of microforms. Such devices are invariably planetary in operation, and most are designed as camera/processors. One of the best known examples, noted briefly in Chapter Two, records engineering drawings and other documents on 35 mm film chips pre-mounted in aperture cards. Exposed cards pass through a processing chamber and are delivered to the user in less than one minute. Designed for active records management applications involving growing files, a useful group of camera/processors produces fully developed pre-cut strips of 16 mm microfilm ready for insertion into jackets. Operating like photocopiers, these machines reduce the separate work steps of filming, processing, and film cutting by combining them into one operation.

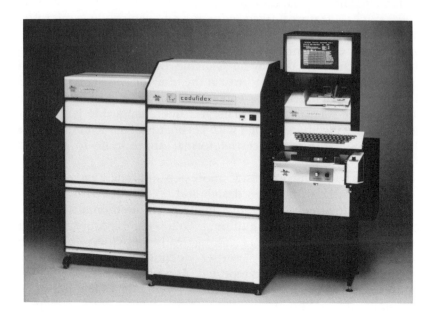

FIGURE 21. Step and repeat camera. *Courtesy Staude Micrographics.*

Camera selection is, of course, restricted to devices that can produce the types of microforms required by a given application. Within each product group, a successful source document microfilming system requires an effective match between application characteristics and camera capabilities. Among cameras that produce roll microforms, for example, rotary devices are preferred for the high speed creation of 16 mm microforms in applications where source documents are of uniformly good quality and work throughput is more important than resolution. They have been widely and successfully utilized in a variety of business applications. Planetary cameras are preferred for applications requiring very high quality 16 mm or 35 mm microimages. As discussed earlier, automatic-feed models overcome the throughput limitations associated with planetary microfilmers. For letter-size office records, their operating speeds favorably with rotary cameras, but the latter devices usually prove faster and more effective in applications involving bank checks, index cards, and other small documents.

Early microfilm cameras required many operator decisions that could only be made by specially trained technicians. Most newer models, however, are designed for operation in an office environment by nontechnical personnel with a minimum of training. Focus and film advance mechanisms are invariably automatic. Simplified control panels and pushbutton operation are the rule. Warning lights and audible alarms signal the end of film, improper loading, burned-out lamps, and other sources of potential operator error. In most cases, the camera will not operate until the malfunction is corrected. Simplified controls are especially important for step-and-repeat camera operators who must constantly be aware of the row and column position under exposure. To meet specific production requirements, the operator must be able to skip an image, advance a row, or move quickly to the first or last frame.

All microfilm cameras offer some type of exposure control to enable operators to compensate for variations in the color, texture, and other characteristics of source documents. With manual exposure control systems, optimal exposure settings are determined by performing a "step test" in which different types of documents are microfilmed at various exposures and the resulting images examined for clarity and utility. During actual filming, an operator must make necessary exposure adjustments on a case-by-case basis, using a rheostat mounted on a camera. To simplify this procedure, a number of microfilm cameras feature an automatic exposure control system as either a standard feature or an optional accessory. Such devices use a photocell to determine the reflectance value of each document and make corresponding adjustments in either lamp intensity or shutter speed. Exposure errors resulting from operator misjudgment are thereby eliminated. With high-speed rotary cameras and automatic-feed planetary and step-and-repeat models, automatic exposure is essential to maximum productivity and uniform image quality.

Microfilm loading and unloading are potentially time-consuming tasks. As previously discussed, the frequency of required film loading can be more than halved by selecting a camera that accepts 215-foot microfilm. To simplify loading by minimizing film handling, several cameras accept unexposed microfilm in specially designed cartridges. In some cases, such cartridges can be inserted directly into a processor following exposure. Some microfilmers, as previously noted, support interchangeable camera heads, each with its own lens system and film supply. This approach allows a single microfilmer to be shared by several departments within an organization.

FIGURE 22.   Cartridges of unexposed microfilm simplify camera loading.

Despite complaints that the ability to microfilm source documents of different sizes at varying reductions and in different formats has complicated the development of display and printing devices, interchangeable reductions remain a major camera selection criterion in many applications. Rotary cameras change reductions by interchanging filming units. Overhead-type planetary cameras usually change reductions by moving the camera head closer to or further away from the copyboard. Depending on the model, reductions may be preselected or infinitely variable between two extremes. Inverted-type planetary cameras typically use interchangeable lenses or film units to change reductions. As previously noted, some step-and-repeat cameras also support interchangeable lenses.

Other useful features that are selectively supported by microfilm cameras include the ability to expose two rolls of film simultaneously for applications that require both a working and a security copy of microfilmed documents; the ability to vary frame sizes and spacing to avoid waste in applications involving small documents; and the availability of spring-loaded book holders to keep bound volumes flat and correctly positioned during microfilming. Accessories that encode or otherwise index document images during microfilming will be discussed in Chapter Six.

Microfilm camera prices vary with equipment characteristics and capabilities. At the time this chapter was written, rotary camera prices ranged from about $10,000 for a low-to-medium-volume device capable of recording hand-fed documents in the simplex mode at a single reduction to more than $40,000 for a high-volume microfilmer configured with an automatic document feeder, multiple camera heads, duo and duplex filming capability, and special retrieval coding options. Planetary camera prices ranged from about $5,000 for a 16 mm desktop model to more than $50,000 for a 35 mm microfilmer designed for engineering drawings and other large documents. Step-and-repeat camera prices ranged from $15,000 for the simplest models to more than $100,000 for a multiformat microfiche production system equipped with multiple lenses, a high-speed automatic document transport, two-sided filming capability, and computer-generated titling. Regardless of price, careful attention should be given to the nature and extent of the camera's warranty, the vendor's provisions for operator training, and the availability and quality of maintenance service.

Microfilm Processing

A microfilm processor is a mechanical device that applies the physical and chemical treatments required to produce visible images from exposed microfilm. Conventional processing of silver gelatin microfilm begins with its immersion in an alkaline developing agent that reduces exposed silver grains to black metallic silver. Some processors briefly immerse the microfilm in an acid solution that stops the development process. For most processing, the developing agent is followed by a fixing solution that dissolves unexposed silver grains. These silver grains, if unremoved, would gradually darken on exposure to light. After a clean water wash that removes the dissolved grains, the processed microfilm is dried.

Microfilm processors perform these steps automatically and in succession. As discussed earlier in this chapter, normal development of silver gelatin microfilm is a polarity-reversing process that produces negative-appearing microimages from positive-appearing source documents. When negative-appearing source documents—such as x-rays or other photographic images—are involved, or when positive-appearing microforms are desired, some models support *reversal processing.* In full reversal processing, exposed silver grains are dissolved prior to fixing the image. The silver halide crystals remaining in areas corresponding to dark areas of the source document are then re-exposed, developed, and fixed. The result is a positive-appearing microimage of a positive-appearing source document or a negative-appearing microimage of a negative-appearing source document.

Some older microfilm processors use a simpler technique, called partial or halide reversal, in which the redevelopment or fixing steps are eliminated. Polarity characteristics aside, a microfilm processor must support complete edge-to-edge development at a uniform, repeatable density that is consistent from job to job. Processed microfilm must be properly dried and free from scratches, water spots, and other deformations.

Like microfilm cameras, processors vary in size, speed, and capabilities. Floor-standing equipment designed for high volume applications can develop up to 100 feet of microfilm per minute, accept film in widths ranging from 16 mm to 105 mm simultaneously, and support conventional or reversal processing. Such devices are widely used by microfilm service bureaus and micropublishers where they are often operated by photographic technicians. Processors can require elaborate site preparation, including external plumbing and waste disposal facilities. At the time this chapter was written, prices began at $10,000 and approached $50,000 for the most complex models.

For low to medium volume installations, simpler tabletop processors can develop 10 to 40 feet of microfilm per minute and can be operated by nontechnical personnel in an office environment. Depending on the model, such devices may accept 16 mm, 35 mm, and/or 105 mm microfilm. They feature a horizontal or serpentine film path and typically, operate at speeds ranging from 2 to 10 feet per minute. With some nominally slow models, effective throughput can be improved by processing several rolls simultaneously. Cartridge loading can simplify film handling, and some models utilize premixed chemicals in disposable containers. Several manufacturers even offer self-contained models that can operate without external plumbing. At

Courtesy Staude Micrographics.   **Courtesy Houston Fearless 76.**

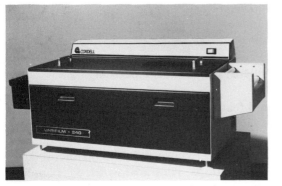

Courtesy Cordell.   **Courtesy Allen Products
Company.**

FIGURE 23. Microfilm processors in tabletop and high volume models.

the time this chapter was written, prices for tabletop processors ranged
from about $4,000 to $10,000, depending on operating speed and
features.

To comply with environmental regulations, some microfilm
processing installations include silver recovery units that reduce silver
concentration prior to the discharge of effluents into sewers or streams.
Silver removal also reduces the amount of fixing chemicals required
by processing operations, thereby lowering supply costs. As an additional advantage, recovered silver can be sold.

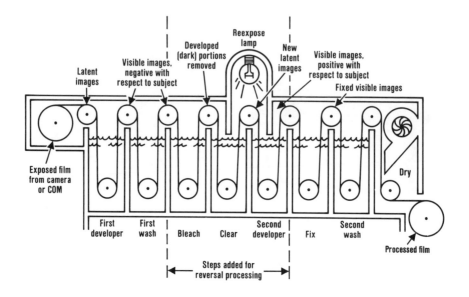

FIGURE 24. Steps in conventional and reversal processing.

Specific capabilities and features aside, conventional processors are standalone devices that require additional film handling and work steps. Camera/processors, as noted at the beginning of this chapter, are integrated units that automatically expose and develop microimages in a continuous sequence of operations. They are intended for applications where the user wants to avoid the inconvenience of external processing and/or where exposed microimages will be used immediately following development. In an engineering application, for example, newly completed drawings filmed by an aperture card camera/processor may be duplicated for immediate distribution to satellite files.

As the micrographic counterparts of photocopiers, camera/processors are available for most types of roll and flat microforms. Their obvious convenience is especially attractive to new micrographic users who want to avoid the technical procedures associated with conventional microfilm processing. As a potential disadvantage, however, camera throughput may be degraded by the comparative slowness of the film processor. Some camera/processors employ proprietary technologies that rely on unconventional photographic materials and/or modifications of the conventional silver gelatin film processing cycle. Special microfilm and processing chemicals may consequently be required, and such proprietary items are sometimes more expensive than their conventional counterparts.

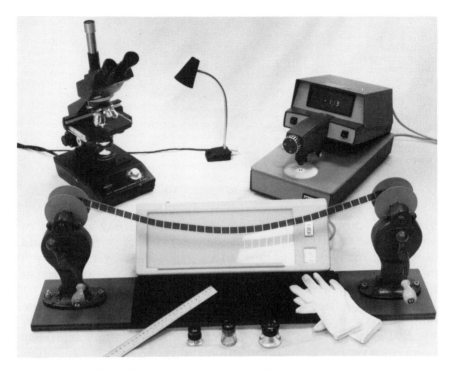

FIGURE 25. Microfilm inspection equipment.

Microfilm Inspection

Following processing, microimages must be inspected for image quality and stability. Recommended inspection procedures for source document microfilm production facilities are outlined in the ANSI/AIIM MS23 standard, *Practice for Operational Procedures/Inspection and Quality Control of First-Generation Silver-Gelatin Microfilm of Documents*. The ISO 3272/II standard, *Microfilming of Technical Drawings and Other Drawing Office Documents—Part II: Quality Criteria and Control* deals specifically with quality control procedures for engineering drawings. Required inspection equipment includes a densitometer, microscope, light box, a pair of rewinds, lint-free gloves, and editing and splicing equipment. Several manufacturers offer specially designed inspection stations that include light wells, rewind mounts, electrical outlets for test equipment, and drawers for supply storage.

The purpose of quality inspection is to ensure that the image quality of microimages is equal to or greater than an acceptable minimum level and to ensure duplicability of microimages through the required number of generations. Image quality inspections are typically based on resolution and density measurements. As applied to microfilm production, resolution is a measure of the ability of optical components and photographic materials to render fine detail visible. Expressed in terms of the number of lines or line pairs per millimeter

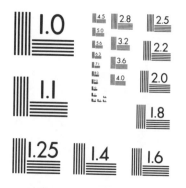

FIGURE 26.   Resolution test target.

that are discernible in a microimage, resolution is a function of photographic emulsions, camera lenses, camera vibration, and processing methods. It is most often determined by examining a microfilmed test target that contains numbered sets of lines of progressively decreasing size and spacing.

Resolution testing methods and test target specifications are outlined in the ANSI/ISO 3334 standard, *Microcopying ISO Test Chart No. 2—Description and Use in Photographic Documentary Reproduction*. The Association for Information and Image Management offers special resolution test targets for rotary and planetary cameras. They conform to requirements outlined in the ANSI/AIIM MS17 standard, *Test Chart for Rotary Microfilm Cameras*. The ANSI/AIIM MS24 standard, *Test Target for Use in Microrecording Engineering Graphics on 35 mm Microfilm*, describes a test target for use when microfilming large documents with planetary cameras.

Resolution test procedures are often criticized for their unavoidably subjective elements. Using a microscope to examine a microfilmed test target, a quality control technician must determine the smallest numbered line pattern where individual line pairs can be distinguished as separate. Resolvable line pairs per millimeter are then computed by multiplying that set number by the reduction. Thus, if the 5.0 line set is the smallest discernible in microimages reduced 1:24, the resolution is 120 lines or line pairs per millimeter. At 1:24, resolutions of 120 lines per millimeter or greater offer excellent microimage sharpness for viewing or duplication. Planetary cameras routinely support such high resolutions. Typical rotary cameras, by way of comparison, can resolve between 70 and 90 lines per millimeter. For office records in good condition, the resulting microimages will usually prove quite legible. Because some resolution is lost in duplication, the quality of multigenerational copies may prove unacceptable.

The legibility and duplicability of processed microfilm is strongly influenced by image contrast. As used in this context, contrast is a measure of the relationship between high and low density areas of a photographic image. Contrast is affected by camera exposure settings and processing operations. It is measured by a densitometer. Microimages with too little contrast may appear faded; where microimage density is too high, fine lines may be filled. In either case, the resulting microforms can prove difficult to duplicate or reproduce in reader-printers. Uniform densities are important for film that will be used in automatic duplicators and enlarger-printers. Background densities in the range 0.8 to 1.5 are generally acceptable for microimages made from source documents that are in good condition. Microimages produced from poor quality documents will often benefit from lower background densities. Because thin lines tend to fill at higher reductions, image densities may need to be reduced as reductions increase. Recommendation densities for specific situations are discussed in the ANSI/AIIM MS23 standard.

The stability of processed microforms is of great concern to records managers, archivists, librarians, and others who must retain microfilmed information for long periods of time. American national standards distinguish three levels of microform stability:

1. Archival microforms will retain their original information-bearing characteristics indefinitely; they are suitable for the preservation of records of permanent value.

2. Long-term microforms will retain their original information-bearing characteristics for at least 100 years.

3. Medium-term microforms will retain their original information-bearing characteristics for at least ten years.

Microform stability is affected by a number of factors, including the composition of photographic emulsions and microfilm base materials, the extent to which potentially harmful chemicals are removed during processing, and temperature and humidity conditions in the storage area. As noted in Chapter One, silver gelatin microforms offer archival potential. All silver gelatin microfilms sold in the United States are manufactured to specifications presented in the ANSI IT9.1 standard, *Imaging Media (Film)—Silver Gelatin Type—Specifications for Stability*.

To realize archival potential, however, exposed microfilm must be properly processed and stored. To prevent the deterioration of microimages, sufficient quantities of thiosulfate must be removed from film during processing. Thiosulfate is an agent used to remove unexposed silver halide crystals from microfilm during the fixing stage of development. Residual thiosulfate exceeding a prescribed amount will react with metallic silver, causing the image to fade and become discolored. Appropriate levels of residual thiosulfate and testing procedures are given in the ANSI PH4.8 standard, *Photography (Chemicals)—Residual Thiosulfate and Other Chemicals in Films, Plates, and Paper—Determination and Measurement*, and in ANSI IT9.1. The methylene blue test, the preferred test for residual thiosulfate,

TABLE 8   Recommended Microform Storage Conditions.*

Film Type	Base Material	Medium-term Humidity (%)	Medium-term Temperature (°C)	Archival Storage Humidity (%)	Archival Storage Temperature (°C)
Silver gelatin	acetate	15-60	25	15-40	21
Silver gelatin	polyester	30-60	25	30-40	21
Dry silver	polyester	15-60	25	15-50	21
Color	acetate	15-30	10	15-30	2
Color	polyester	25-30	10	25-30	2
Diazo	acetate	15-50	25	15-30	21
Diazo	polyester	15-50	25	15-30	21
Vesicular	polyester	15-60	25	15-50	21
Electrophotographic	polyester	15-60	25	15-50	21
Photoplastic	polyester	15-60	25	15-50	21

*From ANSI PH1.43-1985

measures the concentration of a blue dye formed during the analytical procedure. An alternative test, the silver densitometric method measures a density stain produced by residual thiosulfate but is not as precise as the methylene blue method at the low level of thiosulfate ion required for archival processing of silver-gelatin microfilm. Regardless of method, residual thiosulfate tests should be performed whenever film, chemicals, or the processor are changed.

To be considered archival, processed silver gelatin microfilm must be packaged and stored under conditions set forth in the ANSI PH 1.43 standard, *Photography (film)—Processed Safety Film—Storage.* That standard specifies storage in a tightly controlled environment where the temperature relative humidity are confined to specified ranges. As the accompanying table indicates, recommended temperature and humidity ranges vary with the type of microforms being stored. For archival storage of silver gelatin microforms, for example, the maximum temperature should not exceed 21 C (70 F). The relative humidity should range between 15 and forty percent for cellulose triacetate microfilms and between thirty and forty percent for polyester microfilms. A humid atmosphere encourages the development of a chemical reaction between metallic silver and residual thiosulfate and promotes the growth of fungus on silver gelatin microfilms. Rapid changes in temperature and humidity—any change greater than five degrees or percent in twenty-four hours— can produce condensation within microform containers and should be avoided. As might be expected, storage conditions for medium-term microforms are less stringent than their archival counterparts. The maximum temperature for extended storage can reach 25 C (77 F) and peak temperatures up to 32 C (90 F) can be tolerated for brief periods. The relative humidity should range between thirty and sixty percent. Additional protection can be obtained, of course, by storing medium-term films at lower temperatures and relative humidities.

The ANSI IT9.2 standard, *Processed Films, Plates, and Papers—Filing Enclosures and Storage Containers*, outlines physical and chemical requirements for microfilm storage containers and equipment. It recommends that microforms be stored in closed equipment or sealed containers. Microforms of different chemistry—silver gelatin and diazo microfiche, for example—should not be interfiled. The ANSI/AIIM MS45 standard, *Recommended Practice for Inspection of Stored Microfilm* specifies procedures for periodic inspection of stored microforms for mold, fungus, brittleness, discoloration, and other defects. There is some evidence that gold or selenium toning, applied during processing or as a post-processing treatment, provides additional protection against microscopic blemishes. However, the final conclusions are awaiting the completion of additional studies.

As a final point, archival microforms must not be subjected to the potential damage that is inherent in use. One or more nonarchival working copies should be made for use in display and printing equipment. Duplicating technologies suitable for that purpose are discussed in the next section.

Microform Duplication

Microform duplication is the production of single or multiple microform copies from a master microform. The master microform may be a camera original microform or a copy one or more generations removed from it. Microform duplicates may function as working copies, intended for distribution, or as printed intermediates, from which additional microform copies will be produced. When a large number of microform copies is required, the production of one or more intermediates is recommended to prevent deterioration of the master microform. Unlike original microphotography, which is an optical process, microform duplication relies on contact printing methodologies using silver gelatin, diazo, or vesicular film. The selection of an appropriate duplicating technology requires a detailed study of application requirements, including the desired polarity of the microform copies and the need for archival potential.

Silver gelatin duplicating films are termed *print films* to distinguish them from their camera counterparts, because they feature a light-sensitive emulsion of silver halide crystals suspended in a gelatin emulsion. Compared to diazo and vesicular processes, silver microform duplication can prove complicated, expensive, and time-consuming. Like camera films, silver gelatin print films must be exposed and processed in separate operations. They must be handled in darkness and require wet development. As a result, their use is typically limited to applications that require microform copies with archival potential. That is the case, for example, in updatable microfiche installations which use nonsilver, nonarchival camera films. As discussed in the next chapter, silver gelatin duplication can also produce archival copies of dry silver COM masters.

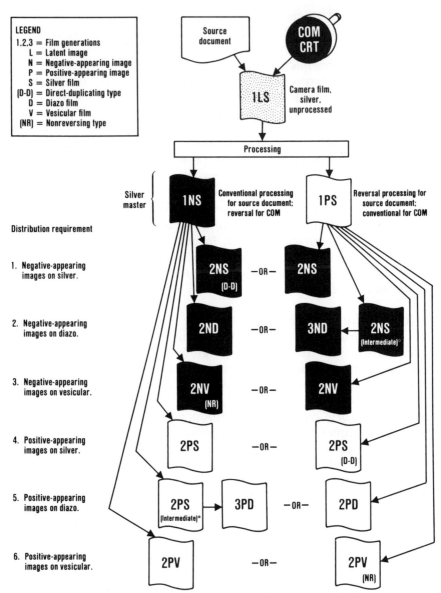

LEGEND
1,2,3 = Film generations
L = Latent image
N = Negative-appearing image
P = Positive-appearing image
S = Silver film
(D-D) = Direct-duplicating type
D = Diazo film
V = Vesicular film
(NR) = Nonreversing type

*In some system configurations, duplication intermediates may be required in any event for preservation or security purposes.

FIGURE 27. Relationship of processing and duplicating technologies to image polarity.

Silver gelatin print films offer a choice of polarity characteristics. Reversing silver gelatin print films changes the polarity of the master microform, making a positive-appearing duplicate from a negative-appearing master. Direct-duplicating silver gelatin print films maintain the polarity of the master microform, by producing a negative duplicate from a negative master.

Diazo microfilms feature an emulsion of diazonium salts. When exposed to ultraviolet light transmitted through a master microform, the salts are dispersed in areas of diazo copy film corresponding to light areas of the microimages being duplicated. Diazo film areas that correspond to dark areas of the master microform are protected from exposure and remain unchanged, forming a latent image that is developed with ammonia fumes. The ammonia couples with the remaining diazonium salts to produce deeply colored azo dyes. Some diazo duplicators feature anhydrous ammonia development systems which draw ammonia gas from a pressurized cylinder. Several other models employ aqueous ammonia development in which a mixture of ammonia and water is passed, via plastic or rubber tubes, into a development chamber where it is vaporized.

Maintaining the polarity of the microform being duplicated, the diazo process will make a negative-appearing copy of a negative-appearing master. Depending on the dye employed, diazo microimages will appear black, blue, or sepia. Black and blue diazo films are well suited to use in readers and reader-printers. Sepia diazo films are typically used to make intermediate copies.

Diazo technology offers several advantages over silver gelatin print films. The diazo process is simple and continuous, requiring minimal film handling or other operator intervention. Exposure and development components are integrated in diazo duplicating equipment intended for high-volume applications. Because diazo microfilms are grainless, resolution loss is minimized in successive generations of duplicates. Combining high resolution and high contrast, diazo films are well suited to the duplication of microimages produced at high reductions. Rather than residing in an emulsion that is coated on the microfilm's base material, diazo dyes are coupled with diazonium salts and resist abrasion during heavy use, an important consideration for working copies that will be referenced frequently. Because of their low photographic speed, unexposed diazo microfilms can be handled in daylight for short periods of time.

The diazo process is the duplicating technology of choice in applications where the polarity of the master microform must be maintained and archival potential is not required. When developed normally, camera original microforms made from positive-appearing source documents will be negative-appearing. By maintaining polarity, diazo microfilms produce negative-appearing working copies that are typically preferred in applications involving textual information or line drawings. Among their advantages, negative-appearing microforms hide scratches and can mask areas of uneven screen illumination. In addition, some reader-printers require negative-appearing microforms in order to produce positive-appearing paper prints.

The ANSI IT9.5 standard, *Photography (Film)—Ammonia-Processed Diazo Films—Specifications for Stability*, classifies diazo

TABLE 9   Microform Duplicating Technologies.

Film Type	Polarity	Stability	Typical Application
Silver gelatin (direct)	maintaining	archival	Archival storage copies from archival or nonarchival masters
Silver gelatin (reversing)	reversing	archival	Archival storage copies from archival or nonarchival masters
Diazo	maintaining	long-term	Working copies of source document microforms; duplication of reversal-processed COM masters
Vesicular	reversing	long-term	Working copies of conventionally-processed COM masters

microforms as long-term films that will remain stable for at least 100 years when stored under the archival conditions appropriate to silver gelatin films. It is important to note that this long-term designation applies only to storage copies. Working diazo duplicates, intended for use in display and printing equipment, are vulnerable to damage and/or deterioration from a variety of sources.

Vesicular duplicating films feature a light-sensitive emulsion suspended in a thermoplastic resin on a polyester base. The emulsion is hard and stable in an office environment, but exposure to ultraviolet light transmitted through a master microform creates pressure pockets that form a latent image. Rapid application of heat deforms the emulsion, developing the image. When heat is removed, the emulsion rehardens, fixing the image. Subsequent applications of heat must be avoided. The vesicular process is completely dry, requires no additional chemicals, and is convenient, fast, and odorless. Although vesicular films have a lower limiting resolution than their diazo counterparts, heightened contrast depending on the type of illumination can permit the duplication of microforms produced at reductions of up to 1:48. Vesicular microforms are not suitable for making contact prints as a printing master. They are readily identified by their distinctive beige, gray, or light blue color.

Although nonreversing vesicular microfilms are available, the vesicular process normally reverses the polarity of the microform being duplicated. As discussed in the next chapter, they are most widely used in COM applications where master microforms are often of positive polarity. Because vesicular microimages are formed by physical rather than chemical processes, they are particularly resistant to scratching. The ANSI PH1.67 standard, *Photography (Film)—Processed Vesicular Film— Specifications for Stability*, classifies vesicular microforms as long-term films, indicating that they will remain stable for at least 100 years when stored under the archival conditions appropriate to silver gelatin films. As with diazo microforms, this long-term designation applies only to storage copies.

FIGURE 28. Duplicators in low-volume and high-volume models. *Courtesy Micobra Corporation.*

A wide range of equipment is available for silver, diazo, and vesicular duplication of roll and flat microforms. Such devices can be divided into two broad groups: production-type duplicators and convenience-type duplicators. The distinction is based on the nature and volume of duplicating for which the devices are intended. Production-type equipment, as the name implies, is designed for centralized microfilming facilities, microfilm service bureaus, micropublishers, and other high-volume installations where duplication will be performed on a scheduled and more or less continuous basis. The typical production-type diazo or vesicular duplicator is a high speed, automatic unit that exposes and develops microform copies in one continuous operation with a minimum of operator intervention. A production-type microfiche duplicator, for example, can operate at speeds approaching 2,000 microfiche copies per hour. The most sophisticated units operate under microcomputer control and include in-line collators. Similar high-speed models are available for roll microfilm and aperture cards.

Production-type duplicators are primarily designed for applications where the number of required microform copies is known in advance and that entire quantity will be made at one time. Models are available for roll microforms, microfiche, and aperture cards. At the time this chapter was written, prices ranged from $10,000 for the simplest production-type units to more than $50,000 for the most sophisticated, microcomputer-controlled models intended for very high volume source document and COM installations. With prices ranging from $3,000 to $6,000, convenience-type duplicators are intended for low volume applications where one or several copies of a given microfiche, microfilm jacket, card jacket, or aperture card will be made on demand. They use diazo or vesicular technology. Unlike highly automated production-type models, convenience-type duplicators typically require manual operator intervention between the exposure and development stages of microform copying.

Most convenience-type devices have separate printer (exposure) and processor (development) sections. The two sections may be integrated in a single housing or embodied in separate units. In either case, the operator aligns a master microfiche or other flat microform with a sheet of diazo or vesicular copy film and inserts them into the printer. Following exposure to ultraviolet light, the master microform and copy film are separated. The copy film —which, at this point, contains latent microimages—is inserted into the processor for development. These work steps can be completed in thirty to sixty seconds, depending on the operator's skill.

While most duplicators generate copies in the same format as the master—roll to roll, microfiche to microfiche, or card to card, for example—some machines combine duplicating and reformatting capabilities. Typically operated by microfilm service bureaus, such devices can meet the special, usually occasional needs of particular applications. Examples include card-to-roll duplicators, which produce 35 mm roll microfilm copies from aperture cards, and microfiche-to-film duplicators, which create 16 mm roll microfilm copies from document images recorded on microfiche.

Like their camera counterparts, duplicate microforms must be inspected for resolution, density, and other characteristics. Inspection procedures are outlined in the ANSI/AIIM MS43 standard, *Recom-*

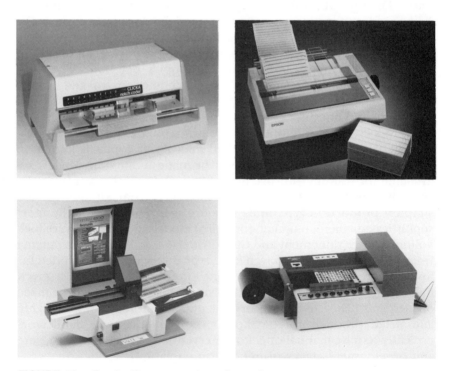

FIGURE 29. Production support equipment.

mended Practice for Operational Procedures/Inspection and Quality Control of Duplicate Microforms of Documents and From COM.

Production Support Equipment

Following processing and duplication, roll microfilm produced by rotary and planetary cameras may be converted to cartridges, microfilm jackets, card jackets, or aperture cards. While the ANSI standard cartridge is a simple collar-like enclosure for a reel of 16 mm microfilm, manual and motorized loaders are available for older-style cartridges. Special leaders and trailers must be spliced to the film and to the cartridge. Other equipment supports jacket loading and aperture card mounting.

A jacket viewer/inserter—variously called a viewer/filler or reader/filler—is a reader-like device that features a magnifying lens screen for the display and verification of images from a supply roll or film strips mounted on one side of the device. The jacket to be filled is inserted into a carrier assembly on the opposite side of the unit. Microfilm images are viewed on the screen. When the last image to be inserted into a given jacket channel is displayed, the operator pushes a button or lever to activate a knife, cutting the film and pushing it into the channel. The process is repeated until the jacket is filled. Similar devices are available for card jackets and aperture cards. To simplify labor requirements in high volume installations, automatic jacket viewer/inserters respond to variously sized opaque marks recorded beneath document images. The machine optically senses the marks, cuts the indicated film strips, and inserts them into jacket channels with little or no operator intervention. For very low volume applications, several companies offer simple, hand-held inserters.

Regardless of the type of equipment used, several standards provide valuable practical guidelines for the production of camera original microforms and duplicates from specific types of source documents. The ANSI/AIIM MS32 standard, *Microrecording of Engineering Source Documents on 35 mm Microfilm*, and the ISO 3272/I standard, *Microfilming of Technical Drawings and Other Drawing Office Documents—Part I: Operating Procedures*, describe reductions, image placements, and duplicating methodologies for engineering drawings. The ISO 3272/III standard, *Microcopying of Technical Drawings and Other Drawing Office Documents—Part III: Unitized 35 mm Microfilm Carriers*, outlines procedures for aperture card mounting. The ANSI/AIIM MS37 standard, *Recommended Practice for Microphotography of Cartographic Materials*, provides guidelines for black-and-white and color microfilming of maps, charts, and related graphic documents in various image formats. The ANSI/AIIM MS111 standard, *Recommended Practice for Microfilming Printed Newspapers on 35 mm Roll Microfilm*, provides format and quality control specifications for newspapers to be microfilmed by 35 mm planetary cameras. The ANSI/AIIM MS19 standard, *Recommended Practice for Identification of Microforms*, describes certification and bibliographic targets to be used when microfilming public records. Among guidelines that address special microfilming situations, the ANSI/AIIM MS18 standard, *Splices for Imaged Film—Dimensions and Operational Constraints*, discusses requirements for leaders, trailers, and other spliced microfilm segments, while the ANSI/AIIM MS42 standard, *Recommended Practice for the Expungement, Deletion, Correction or Amendment of Records on Microforms*, outlines procedures for the legally-mandated removal of microimages.

Microfilm Service Bureaus

A microfilm service bureau is a private business or other organization that provides micrographic services using a customer's own documents, data, or other source material. A given service bureau may offer any combination of microfilm production and support services, including source document microfilming, computer-output microfilming, microfilm processing, microfilm inspection, microform duplication, microfilm jacket or aperture card production, and microimage enlarging. Work may be performed at the service bureaus's facilities or at the customer's site.

To avoid the establishment of in-house production facilities, some organizations use service bureaus for all of their source document microfilming requirements, and many in-house facilities contract at least one phase of microform production to a service bureau. In source document microfilming, as noted in the introduction to this chapter, service bureaus can process and duplicate microforms produced by in-house cameras. Even organizations with extensive microform production facilities use service bureaus to supplement or enhance their own capabilities for high volume work that must be completed in a short time or for applications requiring special equipment or technical expertise that are unavailable in-house.

Service bureau capabilities and rates vary. The nature and acceptability of services to be rendered are matters for individual negotiation between the customer and service bureau. Important criteria for service bureau selection include a demonstrated understanding of the customer's application requirements, the ability to provide high quality service within the time allotted, and a record of satisfactory performance in similar applications. A tour of the service bureau's facilities prior to the award of any contract is essential for the customer to make a knowledgeable selection.

4 Computer-Output Microfilm

THE ACRONYM COM denotes the product (computer-output microfilm), the process (computer-output microfilming), and the device (computer-output microfilmer). Through the COM process machine-readable, computer-processible digital data is converted to human-readable textual or graphic information in microform without first becoming paper documents. Computer-output microfilmers, typically called COM recorders, were introduced in the late 1950s as high speed alternatives to mechanical plotters in scientific and technical applications. They were used for involving computer-generated graphics, including engineering drawings, maps, contour plots, and circuit diagrams. With the proliferation of computer-generated paper reports in the 1960s, alphanumeric, business-oriented COM recorders emerged as powerful records management tools. By the mid-1970s, COM recorders were commonly used as peripheral devices in centralized data processing facilities.

Today, several thousand corporations and government agencies operate one or more COM recorders, and many more organizations utilize microfilm or computer service bureaus to satisfy their COM production requirements. The continuing computerization of information management tasks has promoted the development of new COM applications. Among recent innovations, COM equipment has been introduced for office installations and for special applications, such as the recording of computer-generated engineering drawings on aperture cards.

As an overview of production procedures, figure 30 depicts the flow of work and interrelationship of system components in a typical COM implementation. The following explanations apply:

85

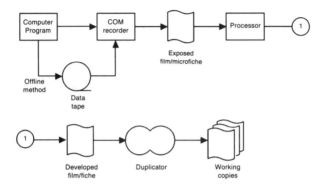

FIGURE 30.   Flow of work in computer-output microfilming.

1. From the data processing standpoint, COM recorders belong to the category of computer devices that are collectively termed *output peripherals*. As a group, such devices convert the machine-readable results of computer processing to the human-readable form required for reference or other use in specific applications. COM production begins with machine-readable data generated by an application program executed on a host computer. Produced by an output module within the application program, the data may be formatted as a tabular listing, columnar report, purchase order, engineering drawing, or other document suitable for printing on paper. While some computer applications are developed with microforms as the intended output medium, the typical COM implementation replaces paper output which is generated by an application program that predates the implementation of COM capabilities. Some modification of the program's output is consequently required. As discussed later in this chapter, such modification is accomplished by software that operates on the host computer or the COM recorder.

2. As computer peripheral devices, COM recorders are available in online and offline configurations. An online COM recorder is connected to a computer and receives data and commands directly from it. An offline recorder is a standalone device that accepts data and commands recorded on magnetic tape. The tape must be physically transported from the computer site to the offline recorder which may be located in the same facility, in a different department within an organization, or at a service bureau.

3. Like source document cameras, COM recorders are loaded with unexposed rolls of microfilm in 16 mm, 35 mm, or 105 mm widths. Specific film requirements vary from model to model. Some recorders use silver gelatin microfilm; others use dry silver film. In either case, the COM recorder converts the machine-readable data to human-readable page images that appear to have been first printed onto paper and subsequently microfilmed. If desired, static information can be

superimposed on the data to give the appearance of reports or other documents printed on specially designed business forms.

4. The COM recorder's output is roll microfilm or, more commonly, uncut rolls or precut sheets of microfiche. The microfilm contains latent images that must be developed to be made visible. As in source document installations, such development is performed by a microfilm processor that may be an external device or integrated with the COM recorder. The latter equipment configuration, which exposes and develops microimages in a continuous sequence of work steps, is termed a COM recorder/processor.

5. Following processing, COM-generated microforms are inspected, then duplicated to produce working copies. The duplicator is loaded with unexposed copy film. Most COM installations employ vesicular or diazo duplication. In some equipment configurations, the duplicator is attached to a COM recorder/processor. This attachment permits an automatic, continuous flow of work from the input of machine-readable data through production of human-readable distribution microfiche. Like their camera original counterparts, duplicate COM microforms must be inspected following processing.

6. The original COM film or microfiche is typically stored in a secure location following processing, inspection, and duplication. Depending on the recording technology used, the COM original film may be duplicated to create an archival storage copy. Working copies are distributed to designated users.

The remainder of this chapter elaborates on each of these work steps. It provides more detailed descriptions of equipment, software, and supplies used in computer-output microfilming and emphasizes features and capabilities that influence the design and implementation of COM systems.

COM Recorders

A COM recorder is a variant form of computer printer. It converts machine-readable, digital data to human-readable alphanumeric or graphic information on microfilm or microfiche without creating an intervening paper copy. It consequently functions as both a computer peripheral device and a high speed microfilmer. As noted earlier, online or offline operation is possible. Like other peripheral devices, an online COM recorder accepts input directly from an attached computer.

Historically, most online COM recorders have been designed for IBM mainframe installations in centralized data processing facilities where they function as plug-compatible replacements for paper printers. In such situations, the online COM recorder can be connected to an IBM mainframe through a selector or multiplexer channel. Recently, several COM equipment manufacturers have introduced recorders that can operate online in a broader range of computing environments, including non-IBM mainframe installations and office-

FIGURE 31.   COM recorders.

oriented minicomputer and microcomputer configurations. Online COM recorders designed for microcomputer installations are typically equipped with RS-232 serial or Centronics-type parallel interfaces. The host computer recognizes them as a conventional ASCII printer. They can be attached to a single microcomputer or operate as a print server, providing microform output capabilities to multiple workstations, in a local area network configuration.

Online COM recorders eliminate magnetic tape handling and, as a result, are more fully automated than their offline counterparts. From the data processing standpoint, this feature can prove particularly attractive in applications where COM will be used as the output medium for programmers' reports or other voluminous printouts that support software development activities. Online COM recorders are similarly well suited to the rapid production of small jobs, particularly when the recorder is configured with an inline processor as described later in this chapter.

Offline COM recorders include an integral or attached tape drive. Magnetic tapes, containing data to be recorded on film or microfiche, may be formatted on a host computer using one of several software techniques described later in this chapter. As an increasingly popular alternative, however, the offline COM recorder may incorporate a programmable minicomputer or microcomputer that accepts and reformats tapes containing data prepared for conventional paper printers. Some offline COM recorders are equipped with two or more tape drives. The additional drives can be used to mount and run jobs while the primary drive is rewinding, thereby improving work throughput. Alternatively, a single tape drive may be shared by two or more offline recorders.

As a potentially attractive capability, offline COM recorders can accept data prepared by multiple computers, including mainframe, minicomputer, and microcomputer configurations for which equivalent online models may not be available. Offline recorders can operate during periods of computer downtime, and they can rerun a given job without additional computer involvement. As a further advantage in certain situations, the offline COM recorder need not be installed in the computer room or managed by the data processing activity. Offline recorders can, for example, be operated by a micrographic services department, and they are widely used by microfilm service bureaus. As a potential disadvantage, the cost of the required magnetic tape drive makes the offline recorder more expensive than its online counterpart.

Most COM recorders are available in online and offline models. Following installation, an online device can be reconfigured for offline operation by adding a tape drive; alternatively, an offline model can be equipped with an online interface. For maximum flexibility, some vendors offer switchable recorders that are capable of either online or offline operation. Typically, such devices operate online to an IBM mainframe and accept appropriately formatted tapes prepared by other computers. Because they must include both an online interface and a tape drive, switchable recorders are more expensive than conventional online or offline models. As another interesting equipment configuration, some COM recorders can operate in tandem with paper printers to serve applications that require the concurrent or alternate production of paper and microform output from a single data source.

COM recorder prices vary with the characteristics and capabilities of particular equipment configurations. Some manufacturers have published list prices; others will only quote prices in response to customer requests for proposals. Typically limited to microfiche production, the least expensive online recorder/processors can be purchased for less than $70,000, although prices for some fiche-only devices can approach $100,000. As previously noted, offline configurations are invariably more expensive than their online counterparts. General-purpose COM recorders designed for high-volume production of microfiche and 16 mm roll microfilm are typically priced between $100,000 and $150,000. Prices for COM recorders with graphics capabilities typically exceed $200,000. COM recorder/processors designed specifically for aperture card production can be purchased for less than $60,000. Regardless of configuration, the price of a COM recorder should not be confused with the cost of a complete COM installation which also includes a processor, duplicator, inspection devices, and other production equipment.

Recording Technology

Whether operating online or offline, a COM recorder's logical circuitry accepts machine-readable, digital input generated by a computer program. The input stream contains data to be recorded on film or microfiche, accompanied by control signals and formatting instructions. Two recording technologies, CRT photography and laser beam recording, are widely used. Two older technologies, electron beam recording and light-emitting diode recording, were employed by several COM recorders introduced in the late 1960s and early 1970s. While not widely encountered, electron beam recording is used in special-purpose COM devices designed for graphic applications. Light-emitting diode recording has not been used since the 1960s. It is consequently omitted from this discussion.

CRT photography is the oldest and historically most prevalent COM recording technology. Data from magnetic tape or, in the case of online COM recorders, from an attached computer is displayed as a page of information on the screen of a specially designed cathode-ray tube located inside a COM recorder. The displayed page is photographed by a high speed microfilm camera, the film is advanced, the display erased, a new page displayed, and the process repeated. Typical recording speeds range from two to four pages per second (10,000 to 20,000 lines per minute), although some models operate at speeds as low as 7,500 lines per minute or as high as 30,000 lines per minute. Within this broad range, the actual speed attained in a given application will depend on such factors as the input rate, data format, microform produced, and page format.

Character generation techniques vary from one CRT-type recorder to another. Some models use electron beam strokes to draw characters on the CRT screen. Others define individual characters from a matrix of illuminated dots. While both methods can produce acceptable results, stroke-generated characters are typically more fully formed and legible than their dot matrix counterparts. With dot matrix displays, character legibility varies with matrix sizes which may range from 5 by 7 to 9 by 12 dots. As an alternative character generation method, one group of COM recorders directs a stream of electrons through a specially-designed character template located in the neck of cathode-ray tube. The electron beam illuminates the phosphorescent surface of the CRT, producing highly legible, clearly formed characters.

Regardless of the character generation method, most CRT-type recorders utilize an orthochromatic, black-and-white, polyester-based silver-gelatin microfilm that is specifically designed for CRT photography. Several COM equipment manufacturers have offered recorders with full color capability, but installations have been limited to a small number of highly specialized graphics applications. With conventional blue or green phosphor cathode-ray tubes, the amount of light at the film plane is relatively low, and the COM recording medium is accordingly restricted to highly sensitive silver gelatin photographic materials. While they are optimized for CRT photography, such COM films require wet chemical processing. Introduced in the late 1970s, CRT-type COM recorders with bright orange phosphors can expose dry silver microfilms. As briefly described in Chapter Three, dry silver microfilm is a light-sensitive recording medium that is developed by heat without wet chemicals. Thermal development offers a particularly attractive alternative to silver gelatin technology in computer room installations. This type of development appeals to data processing personnel who may be uncomfortable with wet chemical processing. In most cases, the dry silver processor operates inline to the COM recorder.

Dry silver microfilm is also used in laser beam recording. Unlike ordinary light, which consists of a mixture of wavelengths or colors, laser light is concentrated and more powerful. It can consequently be used to expose unconventional photographic media. Laser beam COM recorders deflect lasers with great precision to expose points in a dot matrix pattern on microfilm or microfiche, thereby writing individual characters. Mirrors are used to move the laser from line to line across each page. Conceptually similar to laser-based paper printers, laser beam

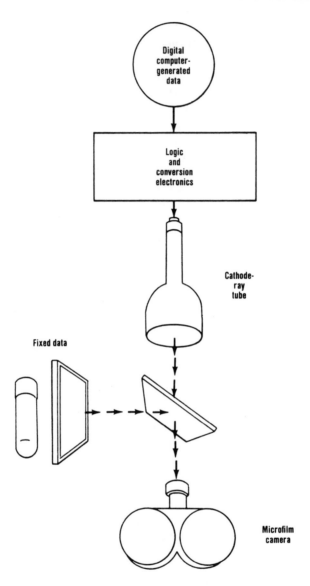

FIGURE 32.   COM recording using CRT photography.

COM recorders have proven especially popular in computer room installations. Typical recording speeds range from two to three pages per second (10,000 to 15,000 lines per minute).

    Electron beam recording is actually a variant of CRT photography. However, rather than using an electron beam to generate characters on the phosphorescent faceplate of a cathode ray tube, the electron beam writes human-readable information directly onto the film itself. Electron beam technology—which is, in effect, stroke-oriented CRT

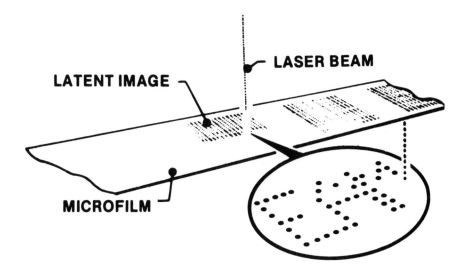

FIGURE 33. COM recording using laser beam technology. *Courtesy 3M.*

recording with the CRT faceplate removed—offers high resolution and is compatible with both silver gelatin and dry silver microfilms. It was the first COM recording technology to use dry silver media, but it has been supplanted by laser beam recording in business COM applications.

Forms Recording

Most COM recorders emulate document printing by printing business forms on specially designed paper. The COM recorder can merge computer-generated data with a static format to give the appearance of printing onto specially designed business forms. Such forms recording capability is typically required in applications where COM-generated microfilm or microfiche will store copies of computer-generated invoices, purchase orders, payment vouchers, and other financial documents.

Forms recording is usually accomplished with a *form slide*, a transparent piece of glass or film bearing the image of a business form.

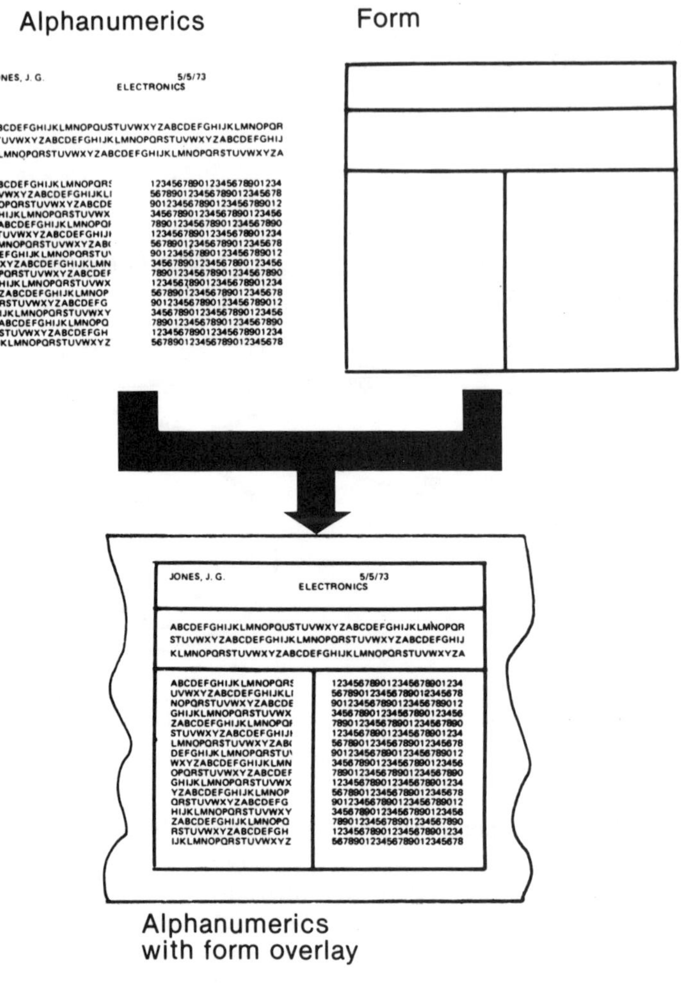

FIGURE 34.   A COM form slide.

Blank spaces are provided where variable information that is derived from the input data stream can be inserted on the printed copy. The form image is superimposed on the data during recording. Form slide artwork must be designed for optimum reproducibility at high reductions. Standard form slides—consisting of lines, shading, and frame borders—are used to establish frame limits and facilitate reading of columnar data. Customized form slides, based on an organization's existing business forms, can be created for particular applications. With both standard and customized slides, line placement accuracy is crucial to proper registration of the form image and data. Some COM recorders provide special loading mechanisms that allow multiple form slides to be interchanged within a single job.

As a supplement or alternative to form slides, several COM recorders feature computer programs that allow users to draw required forms using a variety of lines and geometric shapes. Text and bit-mapped logos can be added to form definitions, and optical scanners can be used to incorporate existing artwork. Once created, the electronically-defined forms are stored on magnetic disks until needed. This software-based approach to forms recording eliminates potential delays associated with form slide production. It eliminates problems of form registration, and also permits the use of multiple forms within a given microfilm or microfiche. This approach is also appropriate for infrequently executed jobs where the cost of a customized form slide cannot be justified.

COM Software

As noted in the introduction to this chapter, COM systems are widely implemented in applications that were originally designed to produce paper reports. In such situations, a computer program includes output commands that generate data interleaved with the control codes and formatting instructions required by a specific paper printer. The control codes and formatting instructions tell the printer when to change lines, begin a new page, indent to a specified print position, or perform other operations. For COM production, printer-specific control codes and formatting instructions must be converted to the form required by a particular COM recorder. Microfiche title information, index specifications, and other COM-specific instructions must also be included.

These tasks are accomplished by formatting software that can be implemented in either of two ways: (1) by modifying application programs to incorporate special COM formatting subroutines or (2) by using a translator program, operating on the host computer or the COM recorder itself, to reformat print files. The two methods differ in programming requirements, ease of implementation, host computer involvement, and COM recorder capabilities.

Widely used through the mid-1970s, the subroutine approach to data preparation is flexible and efficient but requires programmer involvement. A subroutine is a program segment or module that is designed to accomplish a specific task. Programs that produce paper output typically include subroutines that generate print records. When linked to an application program, COM subroutines will intercept and restructure such print records, inserting control codes and formatting instructions appropriate to a specific COM recorder. The restructured print records are then transmitted to an online COM recorder or transferred to a magnetic tape which will be processed by an offline recorder. Such tapes are typically called COM tapes.

COM recorder manufacturers offer prewritten and pretested subroutine packages to their customers at no charge or nominal cost,

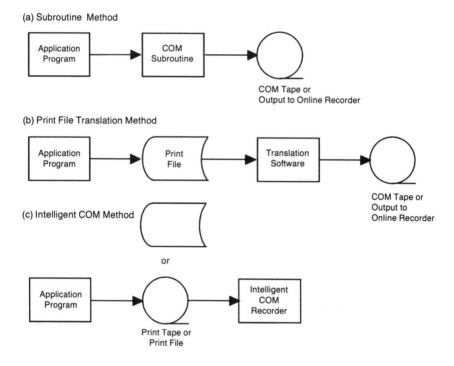

FIGURE 35.   COM software for data preparation.

but a programmer must adapt such subroutines to particular application requirements. Alternatively, users can create their own COM subroutines or obtain them from service bureaus or other third parties. Software sources aside, the subroutine method is a flexible and efficient approach to COM production that generates appropriately-formatted output with a single execution of a computer program. For programs that are executed frequently, it can save host computer time compared to other COM formatting methodologies, but such savings must be weighed against the cost of required programmer involvement. As an additional limitation, the host computer must support the programming language in which the COM subroutines are written. Most use assembler language for IBM mainframe installations and ANSI COBOL for other types computers.

In many data processing installations, output records generated by application programs are written into temporary files from which they are later printed. This technique, called *spooling*, has been used since the 1960s to minimize the speed differential between computers and printers. The file of records created in this way is variously called a spool file, print file, or a print-image file. Available from COM equipment manufacturers and other sources for a variety of computers, print file translation programs are prewritten software packages that reconstruct the contents of print files for COM recording. The reconstructed files can then be transmitted to an online recorder or transferred to a magnetic tape for use by an offline recorder. Programmer involvement and the modification of existing application programs are not required. Separate computer runs are necessary, however, to first produce then translate the print file. Additional computer time must consequently be available, and computer charges may increase significantly in some situations.

While COM subroutines and print file translation programs operating on host computers were widely used through the late 1970s, intelligent COM recorders that can perform print file translation without host computer involvement have since dominated the preparation of print data for COM recording. For most customers, intelligent COM recorders offer the fastest, simplest, and most effective method of formatting data for COM output. As its name suggests, an intelligent COM recorder features an integral minicomputer or microcomputer as a specialized front-end processor that controls the recorder's operations and reformats data intended for paper printers. The front-end processor is equipped with a library of software packages suitable for the translation of print files prepared by a wide variety of general-purpose computers. Intelligent COM recorders are available in both online and offline configurations. Online devices accept print records directly from a host computer. With offline models, print files are recorded on magnetic tape. Such devices have proven especially popular with COM services bureaus, allowing them to quickly and easily accommodate a wide variety of customer requirements.

Because print file translation is performed at the COM recorder, the host computer is freed for other work. In some cases, intelligent COM recorders can also translate print records prepared for other COM recorders. This capability can simplify conversions from one type of COM recorder to another or from one COM service bureau to another. In addition to reformatting print records and controlling COM operations, the intelligent recorder's integral computer can generate production reports, job statistics, and accounting information. It can also be used to simplify setup procedures and store parameters for repeatedly executed jobs. Intelligent COM recorders typically include programs that interactively solicit information about microfiche titling, indexing, page formats, and other production specifications. Once entered, such information is retained in magnetic disk files for retrieval when needed. Newer nonintelligent recorders also use microcomputers to create and store job-related information.

Whether intelligent or conventional in design, offline COM recorders read computer-processable data from appropriately formatted magnetic tapes. When planning a COM application, micrographic systems analysts must determine the tape sizes, recording densities, and coding formats required by a given offline recorder. Most COM recorders manufactured in the 1960s and 1970s—some of which remain in use—could accept seven or nine-track tapes recorded at densities of 200, 556, 800, or 1,600 bits per inch (bpi). Most newer COM recorders can accept tapes recorded at 800, 1,600, or 6,250 bits per inch. Several models can also accept data recorded on IBM 3480 tape cartridges. With respect to coding formats, most online and offline COM recorders can read data recorded in the Extended Binary Coded Decimal Interchange Code (EBCDIC), the internal system code utilized by IBM mainframes. Some offline models can also accept data tapes recorded in the American Standard Code for Information Interchange (ASCII). Some recorders may be optionally configured for compatibility with either coding scheme.

COM-Generated Microforms

Through the late 1970s, most business-oriented COM recorders could produce both 16 mm roll microfilm and 105 mm by 148 mm microfiche. Some models, intended primarily for engineering applications, could produce 35 mm roll microfilm. A few COM recorders could also produce 70 mm and 82.5 mm roll microfilm, the latter being used to create tabulating-size microfiche. When one output capability was offered as a standard feature, it was typically 16 mm microfilm. Microfiche capability was optional. Since the early 1980s, however, the opposite situation has prevailed. Microfiche is now the overwhelmingly dominant microform in business-oriented COM applications. In their standard configurations, many COM recorders produce microfiche only. Roll microfilm capability, if available at all, is increasingly an extra-cost option.

As defined in Chapter One, reduction is a measure of the number of times a given linear dimension of a document is reduced through microphotography. Because paper documents are not involved in COM recording, COM reductions are termed *effective* reductions. For purposes of this discussion, an effective reduction is a measure of the number of times a given linear dimension of an imaginary document would have to be reduced to equal the size of the corresponding linear dimension of a COM microimage. In most applications, the imaginary document is an 11 by 14 inch computer printout page, although some COM output formats are based on letter-size pages or engineering drawings.

In source document microphotography, as previously discussed, the variable quality of office records, business forms, newspapers, books, and other materials necessitates the use of medium-range reductions, seldom exceeding 1:24 for letter-size pages and 1:32 for computer printout-size documents. In COM recording, however, document quality is not an issue. Within the COM recorder, careful control of typefaces, type sizes, and image density permits the use of reductions that are much higher than those acceptable for source document microfilming. As previously discussed in Chapter Two, the ANSI/AIIM standard 48/270 microfiche format—the most widely used format for COM-generated microfiche—specifies an effective reduction of 1:48 and contains the equivalent of 270 computer printout-size pages arranged in 15 rows and 18 columns. The permissible reduction range is 1:47 to 1:50. The ANSI/AIIM standard 48/420 microfiche format specifies an effective reduction of 1:48 with the equivalent of 420 letter-size pages arranged in 15 rows and 28 columns. It is suitable for applications where COM will serve as the output medium for documents generated by computer-based word processing, electronic messaging, and publishing programs.

While it is no longer an ANSI/AIIM standard, the 42/208 format is still supported by some COM recorders and remains in use in many applications, although the 48/270 format is invariably preferred where available. As its name indicates, the 42/208 format provides an effective reduction of 1:42 with the equivalent of 208 computer printout-size pages arranged in 13 rows and 16 columns. The permissible reduction range is 1:41 to 1:44. The 42/325 format provides an effective reduction of 1:42 with the equivalent of 325 letter-size pages arranged in 13 rows and 25 columns. Although it was supported by a number of COM recorders in the 1970s, the ANSI/AIIM standard 24/63 microfiche format is now seldom encountered in COM applications. This standard format specifies an effective reduction of 1:24 and contains the equivalent of 63 letter-size pages arranged in seven rows and nine columns.

From the systems design standpoint, higher COM reductions are attractive because they increase microform capacity, thereby reducing duplication costs and minimizing microform handling where large numbers of microfiche are involved. Thus, a 500-page report will require three microfiche created in the 42/208 format but only two microfiche in the 48/270 format. The considerable length of many computer-generated reports has stimulated an interest in even higher COM reductions. Though not covered by ANSI/AIIM standards at the time this chapter was written, several COM recorders routinely support an effective reduction of 1:72 for the production of microfiche containing over 600 computer printout-size pages, and some recorders can produce microfiche at effective reductions exceeding 1:90. With continuing improvements in microfilm emulsions and COM recording technology, it is possible that very high and ultra high COM reductions will be more widely used in the future.

Where 16 mm microfilm capabilities are supported by a given COM recorder, a 100-foot reel or cartridge can contain the equivalent of 1,800 to 2,000 computer printout-size pages created in the cine mode at an effective reduction of 1:24. Where higher capacity is desired, an effective reduction of 1:42 can record two document images per frame in the comic mode. In that format, a 100-foot reel or cartridge can store about 4,000 computer printout-size pages. At an effective reduction of 1:48, a 100-foot reel or cartridge of 16 mm microfilm can store approximately 7,200 computer printout-size pages recorded in the cine mode with four images per frame. Because any given image can prove difficult to locate, these 1:42 and 1:48 roll microfilm formats are typically reserved for applications where high storage capacity is an important consideration and the microforms will be infrequently referenced.

Image Characteristics

Since the introduction of COM technology in the late 1950s, separate types of recorders have been developed for alphanumeric (business) and graphic (technical) applications. As their name implies, alphanumeric COM recorders can generate alphabetic characters, numeric digits, punctuation marks, and other symbols commonly encountered in textual documents. As such, they resemble the majority of computer printers. In addition to full alphanumeric capabilities, graphic COM recorders can generate the often complex geometric

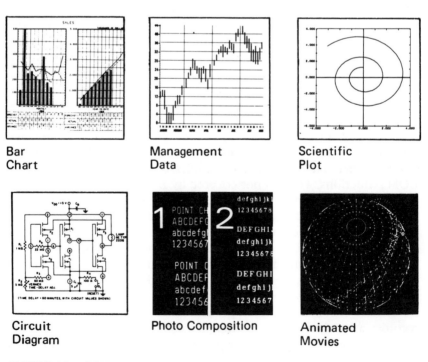

Bar
Chart

Management
Data

Scientific
Plot

Circuit
Diagram

Photo Composition

Animated
Movies

FIGURE 36. COM-generated graphics.

shapes associated with engineering drawings, charts, graphs, plots, network diagrams, circuit diagrams, and similar computer-generated images. They are the microform counterpart of computer plotters, and they further differ from most alphanumeric COM recorders in their ability to produce 35 mm roll microfilm as well as 16 mm microfilm and microfiche.

As outlined at the beginning of this chapter, graphic recorders were the earliest COM devices, but, since the 1960s, the micrographic industry has emphasized alphanumeric devices for business data processing. Graphic recorders remain a highly specialized product group manufactured by a small number of companies. As an indication of their future potential, however, the proliferation of computer-aided design and computer-aided manufacturing applications—so-called CAD/CAM systems—has resulted in a significant increase in the availability of machine-readable graphic data within engineering organizations. Rather than using plotters to print computer-generated engineering drawings onto paper for subsequent microfilming by planetary cameras, graphic COM devices permit the direct recording of computer-generated drawing images on 35 mm microfilm. A recently developed group of graphic COM recorders can even produce fully developed 35 mm microfilm images premounted in aperture cards. Graphic COM devices can also be used to record digitized document images stored on magnetic or optical media, thereby providing a stable long-term or backup storage medium for electronic document imaging systems. Such document storage configurations will be described more fully in Chapter Eight.

Alphanumeric COM recorders can generate a variety of textual documents. Like their paper printer counterparts, typographic capabilities of the earliest alphanumeric COM recorders were quite primitive. Through the mid-1970s, the typical recorder's printing repertoire was limited to sixty or seventy characters and did not even include the lower case alphabet as a standard feature. Responding to the increasingly sophisticated expectations of computer users, typographic capabilities have broadened considerably since the late 1970s. Most alphanumeric COM recorders can now generate at least 128 different characters, and some models support special expanded character sets supporting 190 to 256 different symbols. COM recorders that support Cyrillic, Katakana, and other non-Roman character sets have been available for more than a decade, and special character sets can be designed for specific installations.

Regardless of the specific characters being printed, most COM recorders feature a sans serif type font that is specifically designed for legible viewing and duplication. While there is no standard COM type font, several manufacturers utilize the OCR-B alphanumeric character set. The simplest alphanumeric COM recorders support a single type font, although several models offer italic and boldface capabilities. Some

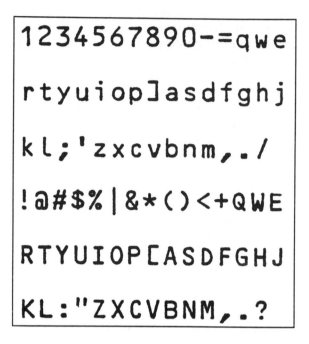

FIGURE 37. The OCR-B character set.

alphanumeric recorders can generate a given type font in several sizes and intensities. In some cases, sizes and intensities can be varied within a microimage—in order, for example, to emphasize section titles or headings within a report. Several recorders also support underlining. Graphic COM recorders typically offer a more varied typographic repertoire than alphanumeric devices. The most sophisticated models, which are suitable for micropublishing applications, support a wide selection of type fonts, styles, and sizes.

As noted in the preceding discussion of effective reductions, the most widely encountered COM page format emulates an 11 by 14 inch computer printout page containing sixty to 64 lines of text with up to 132 characters per line—the equivalent of six lines per vertical inch and ten characters per horizontal inch. Where greater information compaction is desired, some COM recorders can support other formats. Depending on the device, as many as 128 lines may be printed per page with 200 or more characters per line. Alternatively, line lengths can be reduced to 80 characters, producing the equivalent of letter-size document images—a page size used by the ANSI/AIIM 48/420 microfiche format.

COM-generated microfiche, as discussed in Chapter Two, are paginated vertically. Successive pages are recorded from top to bottom in individual columns. Images are typically recorded in the comic mode whereby the text runs parallel to the bottom edge of the microfiche. Some recorders offer rotation capabilities to generate cine mode and inverted cine mode images.

For 16 mm roll microfilm applications, some COM recorders feature a variable frame advance that can significantly increase information compaction by reducing the amount of space between frames. On both roll microfilm and microfiche, several COM recorders can enhance compaction by eliminating frames altogether. This technique, sometimes called *scrolling*, presents information on microfiche or cine mode 16 mm microfilm as a series of continuous lines.

Processing and Duplication

COM-generated microforms, as previously noted, contain latent images that require development. Once exposed, COM film can be removed from the recorder and taken to a separate processor for development. Alternatively, the COM recorder may be equipped with an *inline* processor that is directly connected to the recorder. Like the source document camera/processors described in the Chapter Three, these COM recorder/processors automatically expose and develop microforms in one continuous sequence. Operating as self-contained devices, several COM recorder/processors produce fully-developed, precut microfiche from silver gelatin microfilm. While they utilize liquid processing chemistry, it is conveniently packaged for simplified replenishment. Because external plumbing is not required, computer room or office installations are possible.

Because cathode-ray tubes display light characters on a dark background, normal development of COM original film will result in a first generation microform of positive polarity. The vesicular process can be used to produce the negative-appearing working copies that are generally preferred for use in readers and reader-printers. As discussed in Chapter Three, the vesicular process reverses the polarity of the microform being duplicated. Alternatively, reversal processing of the COM original microform can produce a negative-appearing master suitable for diazo duplication.

When dry silver film is used, the original COM microform is invariably of positive polarity. Vesicular duplication is commonly used to create negative-appearing distribution copies for use in readers and reader-printers. As a potential limitation, dry silver microforms do not have archival potential, although they will remain stable for many years when properly stored. Accelerated aging tests suggest a potential useful life of 100 years when stored under archival conditions appropriate to silver gelatin microforms. Because many COM-generated reports are updated by replacement at regular intervals, an archivally stable recording medium is not required. Where archival potential is essential, dry silver microforms can be duplicated onto silver gelatin microfilm stock.

COM installations are typically equipped with production duplicators of the type described in Chapter Three. Microfiche models can produce several thousand copy microfiche per hour from a single master. A given device may accept precut 105 mm by 148 mm microfiche masters, uncut 105 mm rolls, or both. To simplify job setup, the newest duplicators can interpret bar-coded instructions recorded in the microfiche title area. As noted earlier in this chapter, some duplicators can operate inline to a COM recorder/processor. The most sophisticated equipment configurations include an inline sorter that automatically collates microfiche sets for distribution. Such devices can respond to barcoded instructions or to commands entered at an operator console.

Quality control procedures for alphanumeric COM installations are outlined in the ANSI/AIIM MS1 standard, *Recommended Practice for Alphanumeric Computer-Output Microforms—Operational Practices for Inspection and Quality Control*. Quality control practices for graphics COM installations are delineated in the two ANSI/AIIM standards: MS38, *Microrecording of Engineering Graphics—Computer-Output Microfilm*, and MS39, *Recommended Practice for Operational Procedures, Quality Control and Inspection of Graphic Computer-Output Microforms*. The legibility of recorded information is the primary consideration in COM inspection and quality control procedures. Unlike their source document counterparts, COM resolution targets, which are contained in special form slides, do not measure character resolution. Instead, they are used to establish optimum focus. To evaluate character legibility, quality control technicians typically compare characters generated by the COM recorder with those contained on a reference form slide.

COM As A Computer Output Alternative

Since the late 1960s, COM recorders have been used as high-speed paperless replacements for line printers in applications requiring the timely production of voluminous printed reports from machine-readable data. While there are several types of available line printers, the most widely used models are impact-type output devices featuring a printing chain consisting of characters represented on embossed metal slugs linked in an endless loop. The chain rotates horizontally to bring characters into their appropriate print positions. A bank of hammers behind each print position is selectively activated to drive a sheet of paper into contact with an inked ribbon and the chain, thereby printing characters on the paper. Since several hammers may be activated simultaneously, the device appears to print entire lines at one time, hence its name. Despite recent advances in nonimpact printing technology, line printers remain widely used in mainframe and minicomputer installations.

As computer output peripherals, COM recorders offer significant throughput advantages when compared to line printers. The rated or maximum speeds of line printers have increased over the years to the current high of approximately 3,000 lines per minute. Actual speeds depend on several factors, including the size of the printable character set, and will typically prove significantly lower than rated speeds. The most widely used line printers operate at speeds ranging from 900 to 1,500 lines per minute. Multiple copies are generally produced on four- or five-play interleaved carbon form sets. For copies in excess of the form-set size, the print program must be re-executed. This combination of low actual output speed and multiple copy production via carbon paper can result in excessively long printing times for reports intended for distribution to many users. The production of twenty copies of a 200-page report, for example, can easily require one hour of printing plus additional time for decollating, bursting, binding, and distribution of output.

By way of contrast, typical COM recorder speeds, as previously noted, range from 10,000 to 20,000 lines per minute. The production of a COM master of a 200-page report on a single 1:48 microfiche requires less than five minutes. Allowing additional time for microfilm processing and diazo or vesicular duplication, twenty copies can be ready for distribution within half an hour. With its greater speed, a single COM recorder offers output capacity equivalent to perhaps ten line printers—without a tenfold increase in cost. By replacing line printers with COM recorders, computing centers and service bureaus translate increased recording speed into cost savings which can, in turn, be passed on to clients in the form of lower output charges.

Compared to line printers, COM offers potential for very substantial cost reduction in applications involving long, multicopy reports that are updated on a frequent schedule. In such applications, cost reductions of forty to fifty percent are attainable. In addition to economies of production, COM offers certain economies of use that can prove significant in office applications. As discussed in Chapter One, storage space requirements for computer-generated reports will be sharply reduced. Conversion to COM-generated microforms can speed the retrieval of information when compared to the awkward handling often associated with bulky paper reports. COM can also reduce mailing, handling, and other distribution costs. As a non-economic advantage, microform distribution copies are made directly from the COM master. If appropriate quality control procedures are instituted, these copies should be of uniform quality. The legibility of fourth and fifth line printer copies in carbon-interleaved form-sets, however, is often marginal.

As state-of-the-art competition for COM recorders, the fastest computer printers can generate paper output at speeds exceeding two pages per second. Termed page printers, these devices employ lasers and xerographic technology to create latent images of individual characters that are developed by the application of a toner and transferred to paper, in the manner of photocopiers. In addition to overcoming the speed limitations of line printers, they produce highly legible output on letter-size pages that are more conveniently handled than 11 by 14 inch print-outs. Because individual characters are generated from definitions stored in internal memory circuits, page printers can produce documents in a wide range of type fonts, styles, and sizes.

There are significant similarities between page printers and COM recorders. Both are nonimpact recording devices, and laser recording is common to both product groups. Both offer fast, convenient, and versatile alternatives to line printers. Convenience and typographic versatility aside, however, page printers and COM recorders differ in one important respect: page printers produce paper output, while COM recorders produce microforms. Page printers do nothing to address the fundamental problems of storage and dissemination associated with computer-generated paper reports. In fact, with their greater output speeds, they aggravate those problems. As discussed in Chapter One, the voluminous output of a single page printer can significantly increase storage space and file cabinet requirements in records management applications. By avoiding paper production entirely, COM recorders address these problems at their source. As an additional advantage, COM-generated microforms are easier and cheaper to distribute than an equivalent quantity of letter-size pages. COM recorders also retain a production advantage in applications involving very long reports that are distributed to many users on a frequent basis. Page printers must run such jobs repeatedly to produce the required number of copies. Although the repeated printings occur at very high speed, the COM production cycle is often shorter.

The preceding discussion emphasizes COM recorders' role as an alternative to paper printers in batch processing applications. As more and more computer applications are implemented as online systems, however, micrographic systems analysts have given considerable attention to COM's role in an online information processing environment. Three possibilities have been suggested: (1) COM as an alternative to online systems; (2) COM as a complement to online systems; and (3) COM as a supplement to online systems.

The view that COM represents an alternative to online systems in certain applications is based on a distinction between online systems in general and that subset of online systems which are designed to satisfy a requirement for real-time information. Although the terms *online* and *real-time* are often used interchangeably, online properly denotes a system configuration characterized by interconnected equipment, while real-time refers to a method of processing information. An online information retrieval system, for example, is one in which information stored on magnetic disk drives or other direct access devices is accessed via terminals. The terminals and the storage devices are physically connected to the computer on which the information is processed. The opposite of an online system is an offline equipment configuration, where hardware components are disconnected and data must be physically carried from one to another.

A real-time system, by way of contrast, is one in which information about a transaction or other event is processed by a computer at the time an event occurs. This is the case, for example, with airline reservation systems. The opposite of real-time processing is batch processing in which information is collected and processed in batches. Batch processing is suitable for information reflecting the occurrence of transactions or other events that can be collected and processed at regularly scheduled intervals some time after the events take place. Real-time information systems require online components, but some online systems provide access to information that is processed in batches. Alternatively, many batch-oriented systems rely on printed reports to convey information about previously processed transactions.

In information management applications, there is an obvious and direct relationship between the accuracy of information and its value. In transaction-oriented activities, the accuracy of information depends on its currency. Real-time systems, as defined above, provide access to up-to-the-minute information about the latest transactions. Where absolutely current information is required, there is no alternative to a real-time implementation. Many applications, however, can be satisfied with information that is current within the last business day. Batch processing is acceptable for such applications, but, given the relative slowness of line printers, in-house computing facilities and service bureaus are not always able to guarantee report production on a daily basis, especially when reports are long and many copies are required. The user may consequently be forced into an online system. Because they require direct access storage devices, telecommunication facilities, and terminals at individual inquiry sites, online implementations are typically more expensive than their batch processing counterparts.

With their impressive throughput capabilities, COM recorders and their associated production devices can enable computing centers and service bureaus to create long, multicopy reports on a frequent schedule, thus eliminating the need for an online implementation in applications where access to real-time information is not required. Where greater currency of information is required within a batch processing environment, COM recorders can produce reports at more frequent intervals than is possible with line printers. Batch-processed reports can be produced, for example, several times daily, thus providing users with information that is no more than a few hours old.

While COM can restore the viability of batch processing, real-time systems are sometimes required. Such systems, as previously noted, rely on online terminals to access information stored in disk files, but COM can play an important, complementary or supplementary role in real-time implementations. Consider, for example, a computer-based financial management system in which account-specific information for the two most recent fiscal years is maintained on magnetic disks. To conserve disk space, information for preceding years can be converted to document images, via COM, for microform storage.

In assessing COM's role as a supplement to online systems, it is important to note that computer hardware or software failure can result in partial or complete unavailability of data. COM-generated printouts can serve as a relatively inexpensive form of backup information in the event of an online system failure. Similarly, COM-generated microforms can play a useful role in applications where limitations and technical impediments prevent online access. Playing a supplementary role in an online information system, COM-generated reports can provide information to field offices or other sites where terminal access is unavailable.

5 Display and Printing Equipment

Mɪᴄᴏғᴏʀᴍ ᴅɪsᴘʟᴀʏ ᴀɴᴅ printing devices are indispensible components in most micrographic systems. The microforms used in a given application may be created by service bureaus or purchased from micropublishers, thereby eliminating the need for in-house cameras, COM recorders, processors, duplicators, and other production equipment discussed in preceding chapters. Nevertheless, on-site display and printing capabilities are essential if microfilmed information is to be referenced. Emphasizing compact storage of inactive records, early micrographic applications relied on photographic enlargers to make reference copies on those rare occasions when microfilmed documents needed to be consulted. As noted in Chapter One, however, the widespread availability of high-quality microform readers and reader-printers facilitated the transition from such archival microfilming to the active information management applications that have dominated micrographic systems since the 1960s. As the point where micrographic technology and users meet, microform display and printing devices play a pivotal role in successful micrographic system implementations.

Microform display and printing equipment can be divided into five broad groups: viewers, projectors, readers, reader-printers, and enlarger-printers. Marginally classifiable as display devices, viewers are handheld, usually monocular magnifiers that are intended for brief examination of flat microforms in situations where other display equipment cannot be effectively used. As an example, engineers, surveyors, and other technical personnel working at construction sites, well-drilling sites, or similar field locations where electricity is not conveniently available may use viewers to consult drawings or maps

FIGURE 38. An aperture card printer. *Courtesy 3M Company.*

recorded on aperture cards or microfiche. The typical microform viewer weighs less than half a pound and is small enough to fit in a pocket or purse, although a carrying case, strap, or belt loop holder is often provided. While designs vary slightly from model to model, the microform to be referenced is usually inserted into a slot and manually manipulated to position the desired sections for examination.

Microform projectors, as their name implies, magnify microimages for display on a wall or wall-mounted screen in applications requiring group examination and discussion of documents. They permit the use of microforms as presentation aids, thereby broadening the range of micrographic applications and providing an effective document display method in situations where photographic slides and transparencies typically prove impractical. In engineering and architectural project meetings, for example, microform projectors can display aperture card images as a convenient alternative to group examination of unwieldy blueprints, architectural renderings, site surveys, construction plans, and similar large documents. Microform projectors can also be used in business meetings to display COM-generated financial reports and similar documents.

A microform projector is essentially a microform reader without a screen. Broadly defined, a reader is a projection device that magnifies microimages for display on an integral screen. Available in models for roll and flat microforms, readers differ in projection methods, screen sizes, magnifications, and other features. As its name implies, a reader-printer combines the display characteristics of a microform reader with the ability to produce paper enlargements of displayed microimages. In effect, it is a reader with an integral copier. Some reader-printers produce copies on plain paper; others require specially-treated papers. Variations in magnifications, paper sizes, and other characteristics are

FIGURE 39.   Handheld viewers.

likewise encountered. Foregoing display capabilities, enlarger-printers
are specifically and exclusively designed to make paper prints from
magnified microimages. If they display microimages at all, it is to
facilitate document alignment prior to printing. If reader-printers are
the micrographic counterpart of convenience copiers, enlarger-printers
are analogous to high-speed duplicators.

While handheld viewers and microform projectors are intended
for special situations, readers, reader-printers, and enlarger-printers can
address a broad spectrum of information management applications.
Available in a wide range of attractive models from a variety of manufacturers, readers and reader-printers are the most widely encountered
types of microform display and printing devices. Enlarger-printers are
typically used in high-volume applications that conventional reader-
printers cannot effectively address. The following sections discuss the
most important characteristics and capabilities of microform readers,
reader-printers, and enlarger-printers, emphasizing features and
functions that can influence the performance of such equipment in
particular micrographic implementations.

Reader Design

When the typical microform reader of the late 1980s is compared
with devices manufactured in the early 1960s, significant improvements

are readily apparent in general engineering, image quality, ease of operation, application flexibility, appearance, and cost/performance characteristics. At a time when microform readers must compete with microcomputers, online terminals, telephone consoles, facsimile machines, and other business machines for limited amounts of work space, manufacturers are increasingly emphasizing compact designs. Base dimensions for desktop models have been reduced to about 8 by 11 inches. Overall dimensions vary with screen size, however, and may prove considerably larger than base measurements.

Where microforms must be used away from the office, portable readers are available in several configurations. Briefcase-style models, currently the most popular design, feature a microform projector built into an attache case. With the briefcase open, enlarged microimages are projected onto a screen built into the inside top cover of the case itself. Alternatively, with the top cover removed, enlarged images can be projected onto a wall or wall-mounted screen. Such devices are primarily intended for microfiche, microfilm jackets, card jackets, and aperture cards. In most instances, the briefcase contains additional space for the storage of microforms, files, books, or other materials.

While briefcase-style models are obviously designed for business use, lap-style portable readers were originally developed for study-type applications in libraries. About the size of a very large reference book, the typical lap-style portable reader features a rear projection screen and can be used on a desktop or while seated in a variety of casual postures. Most models are designed for flat microforms. In the early 1980s, several manufacturers introduced very compact portable readers which feature a collapsible design and a small rear projection screen that is capable of displaying part of a document. Sometimes described as handheld or palm-size readers, a typical model measures about 4 inches wide by 10 inches deep by 3 inches high and weighs less than three pounds.

Whether designed for portability or desktop installations, most newer microform readers are constructed of some combination of steel, aluminum, and high-impact plastic with glass parts. Plastic readers tend to be lighter, more readily transportable, and somewhat less expensive than metal models. Regardless of case materials, screens are typically unbreakable and shatterproof.

As discussed in Chapter Two, readers for 16 mm and 35 mm microfilm require manual reel mounting and film threading. Readers for 16 mm microfilm cartridges are typically self-threading, although a few low cost models require manual film handling. Threading mechanisms aside, the reader's transport mechanism, which advances the film to a desired image, may be manual or motorized. Operating at approximately 10 feet per second, motorized transports offer a traverse time of ten seconds per 100-foot reel or cartridge. Whether manual or motorized, the transport mechanism should not scratch or otherwise damage film.

FIGURE 40. Microfilm projectors.

Readers for flat microforms feature a carrier-type transport mechanism that holds the microform between two pieces of flat glass. The standard carrier accommodates one microform at a time. To minimize microform handling and facilitate the display of desired images, many microfiche readers can be equipped with a dual carrier which will accept two microfiche simultaneously. Regardless of carrier size, the transport operates on a slide and must move freely in both the horizontal and vertical directions. In most cases, the operator positions the carrier manually to display desired microimages. With microfiche readers, image location is facilitated by a simple grid and pointer mechanism that can be keyed to the most commonly encountered microfiche formats. Where automated image positioning is desired, several vendors offer motorized, microprocessor-controlled microfiche readers with calculator-like keypads for the entry of desired row and column coordinates. Some units require the manual insertion of microfiche; with others, microfiche are preloaded into special cartridges. As a potential limitation, some models will only work properly with microfiche produced in specific formats. If a given application, for example, requires a combination of source document microfiche produced in the 24/98 format and COM-generated microfiche produced in the 48/270 format, two separate readers will be required.

Readers intended for North American installations operate from a standard 120 volt, sixty cycle AC outlet. Most manufacturers also offer a 220/240 volt, fifty cycle configuration for use outside of North America. Recognizing the importance of energy costs in automated information processing systems, newer readers are specifically designed to minimize power consumption. For field operation, most portable readers can be optionally equipped with a rechargeable battery pack, and some models will also operate from a twelve volt, DC power source. Most newer readers are cooled by natural convection and are consequently silent in operation.

Because excessive heat can damage silver gelatin, dry silver, and vesicular microforms, the temperature at the reader's film gate should not exceed 158 F (70 C). Readers construction should conform to requirements outlined in the ANSI X.412 standard, *Safety of Office Appliances and Business Equipment*. For user protection, metal handle temperatures should not exceed 95 F (35 C). Unless labelled with a warning, the temperature of other reader areas should not exceed 152 F (60 C) for all other parts.

Optical Characteristics

From the optical standpoint, readers are straightforward devices. With equipment intended for transparent microforms, a condensing lens assembly collects light and transmits it through a microform onto a projection lens. Readers intended for use with Microprint and other opaque microforms described in Chapter One employ reflected rather than transmitted light. In either case, an integral lamp is the artificial light source. Depending on reader design, mirrors may be used to fold the optical path, thereby permitting compact equipment design. The ANSI/AIIM MS20 standard, *Microfilm Readers*, describes essential reader characters and establishes minimum performance expectations. That standard's contents are incorporated in the following discussion.

Currently available microform readers employ one of two projection methods: front and rear. Front projection readers display magnified microimages on an opaque—usually white or silver—screen that is positioned at or near desk level. Rear projection readers direct magnified microimages onto the back of a translucent, upright screen that the user views from the front. Depending on the model, the rear projection screen may be blue, green, or gray in color.

Comparative performance analyses have failed to demonstrate the superiority of either front or rear projection, and the micrographic industry has itself favored one or the other method at different points in time. The earliest microform readers were of the front projection type. Rear projection models dominated equipment design from the mid-1960s through the mid-1970s. A number of improved front projection models were introduced in the late 1970s, but rear projection readers remain the most widely encountered variety. Most manufacturers, however, include at least one front projection model in their product lines.

Rear projection readers offer a slight performance advantage in work environments where ambient light is uncontrolled. This is the case in the typical office installation where a variety of information processing tasks must be performed and room light cannot be optimized for microform display. With their translucent screen, rear projection readers absorb ambient light. With front projection readers, ambient light is reflected back at the user, although some models are equipped with a hood to minimize reflections. Because their screens are at desk level, however, front projection readers may prove more appealing than their rear projection counterparts for bifocal wearers. A reader with bifocals uses the bottom portion of corrective lenses for near vision, and a desk-level, front projection screen is in the natural visual path. With an upright, rear projection screen, however, a bifocal wearer must tilt his or her head slightly but uncomfortably backward to take advantage of the lens correction. To minimize problems, bifocal wearers are well advised to obtain reading glasses for prolonged use of microform readers and other image displays.

Regardless of display method, the image quality of a projection reader is evaluated in terms of resolution, contrast, and freedom from distortion. Resolution when applied to microform readers as it is to the source document cameras discussed in Chapter Three, denotes the ability of an optical system and screen to render fine detail visible. Reader resolution is determined by using a magnifying lens to examine an image of a microfilmed test target consisting of numbered patterns of closely spaced lines of decreasing size. The observer must determine the smallest pattern where contiguous lines can be distinguished as separate. The minimum acceptable reader resolution will vary with the type of material being displayed. Upper-case alphanumeric COM reports, for example, require a resolution of 2.5 lines per millimeter.

Typewritten office records require a minimum resolution of 3.2 lines per millimeter, while book pages set in eight-point type require a minimum resolution of 3.6 lines per millimeter. Readers selected for prolonged study of microfilmed newspapers must resolve more than four lines per millimeter. It should be noted, however, that even the highest resolution screens cannot enhance the quality of images produced from poor quality source documents or degraded by improper microfilming, processing, or duplicating procedures.

Screen contrast preserves the relationship between light and dark areas within a displayed microimage. All other characteristics being equal, readers with high contrast screens are preferred for applications involving black-and-white microimages of textual records or line drawings. Lower screen contrast is generally preferred for the display of half-tones in black-and-white or color. Contrast is affected by screen color where the darker shades offer the highest contrast. Most rear projection readers are equipped with blue screens for the high contrast display of silver gelatin and diazo microforms. Gray or green screens are often preferred for the display of vesicular microforms. Because they can display the full color spectrum, gray screens are recommended for applications that involve color microforms.

Distortions are optical defects which, for example, cause straight lines to appear curved at screen edges. Slight distortions are inevitable and typically insignificant in microform readers intended for business applications involving textual documents. Distortion-free screens are important for the display of maps, drawings, and other scaled originals.

Application Characteristics

Factors affecting the suitability of a microform reader for a given application include the types of microforms accepted, magnification, screen size and orientation, and the availability of special features. In terms of microforms accepted, readers can be divided into single-purpose and multipurpose devices. Single purpose readers, as the name implies, are designed specifically and exclusively for one type of microform—typically, a 16 mm microfilm cartridge, an aperture card, an ultrafiche, or an ultrastrip. They cannot physically accommodate other types of microforms.

Most readers, while primarily designed for one type of microform, are multipurpose devices in the sense that they can accept more than one form. Microfiche readers, for example, can accept microfilm jackets and card jackets. Some readers support interchangeable carriers that can accommodate two or more types of microforms. While such interchangeable carriers are an extra cost option, users can sometimes avoid the purchase of a second reader in installations where one type of microform is referenced frequently and another only occasionally. Popular combinations include microfiche with aperture cards, 16 mm microfilm reels with 16 mm cartridges, 16 mm microfilm reels with microfiche, and 35 mm microfilm reels with aperture cards.

Although a multipurpose reader may physically accept several different types of microforms, the reader's magnification may not be appropriate to any or all of them. The opposite of reduction, magnification is a measure of the relationship between a given linear dimension of an enlarged microimage and the corresponding linear dimension of the microimage itself. Magnification is expressed as 24x, 42x, 48x, and so on, where a given linear dimension of a microimage is enlarged 24, 42, or 48 times. Alternatively, magnification, like reduction, can be expressed as a ration—24:1, 42:1, or 48:1, for example. As with reductions, all expressions of magnification are nominal. The previously cited ANSI/AIIM MS20 standard permits variations of plus or minus five percent when comparing actual to nominal magnifications. Variations of plus or minus 1:1 at magnifications below 30:1 are typical. At 48:1, nominal and actual magnifications may vary by plus or minus 2.4:1.

The magnification selected for use with a given reader must be appropriate to the reduction at which the microforms were created to be displayed. Subject to slight variations in nominal expressions of reduction and magnification, a document reduced 1:24 will be displayed at or near original size when magnified 24:1. While such full-size display is often desirable for letter-size office documents, microimages of good quality can be legibly and usefully displayed at seventy to ninety percent of the original document's size. As discussed below, such under-magnification permits the use of readers with relatively small screens. Thus, microimages produced from legal-size pages reduced 1:29 may be magnified by 23:1 or 24:1 for display on a letter-size screen. Partial-size magnifications are widely used in COM applications where microimages of computer-printout size pages reduced 1:48 can be magnified 36:1 for display on screens measuring 11 by 8.5 inches.

When microimages contain typefaces or detailed graphics, higher magnifications—a 32:1 enlargement of a document reduced 1:24, for example—can facilitate reading or the close inspection of illustrations. Such overmagnifications are sometimes used in library materials to enhance the readability of microfilmed newspaper pages. They can also be used with microfilmed business forms, contracts, technical manuals, and other documents that contain text segments printed in very small type sizes.

In keeping with design trends established in the 1970s, newly manufactured microform readers invariably support multiple magnifications. Drop-in lenses are the most common method of implementing such multiple magnifications. As their name implies, drop-in lenses are easily interchanged by removal and substitution. While the specific lenses offered will vary from one reader product line to another, some combination of the following nominal magnifications is commonly encountered: 18:1 for the three-quarter size display of 24:1 source document and COM-generated microforms; 24:1 for the full-size display of letter-size source documents and the three-quarter size display of legal-size pages reduced 1:29; 32:1 for full-size display of computer printout-size source documents as well as the three-quarter size display of 42:1 COM-generated microforms; 36:1 for the three-quarter size display of 48:1 COM-generated microforms; and 42:1 or 48:1 for full-size COM display. Some readers also support 72:1 or 90:1 lenses for very high and ultra high reduction source document and COM-generated microfiche. Depending on the model, other magnifications may be offered as standard equipment or on special order.

In some office applications magnification changes are required. The same microfiche reader may be used to display microforms containing source document images reduced 1:24 reduction and COM-generated microforms produced at 1:48. Similarly, aperture card users may alternate between the partial-size display of complete drawings and a more highly magnified display of selected image areas. To minimize lens handling in applications where two magnifications will be interchanged frequently, some readers can be equipped with a dual lens mount a standard feature or a field-installed option. Alternatively, some models feature dual- or triple-lens turrets or tracks that can be rotated or slid into position in order to quickly change magnifications. Depending on the reader, such turret or track assemblies may have removable or captive lenses.

As another approach to magnification, a few readers are equipped with zoom lens systems that permit infinite magnification variations within a specified range. Although they are more expensive than readers with conventional lens systems, zoom lens models can prove especially useful where microfilmed engineering drawings, maps, or other graphic documents must be examined in both overview and detail.

TABLE 10   Common Reader Screen Sizes and Magnifications.

Height*	Width*	Applications	Magnifications
11	8.5	Full size display of letter-size source document images	24:1
8.5	11	Three-quarter size display of printout-size source document and COM images	18:1, 32:1, 36:1
11	11	Full size display of letter-size source documents; three-quarter size display of printout-size source document and COM images	18:1, 24:1, 32:1, 36:1
11	14	Full size display of source document and COM images	24:1, 42:1, 48:1
11	17	Two-page display of letter-size source documents; partial size display of engineering drawings	12:1, 24:1

*In inches

For effective reader operation, magnification must be coordinated with screen size. Screen sizes of available microform readers range from about 4 by 4 inches for the handheld portable models described above to larger than 24 by 36 inches for readers designed to display engineering drawings or other large documents at or near full-size. The majority of applications, however, are best served by some combination of the four most commonly encountered screen sizes: (1) 11 inches vertically by 8.5 inches horizontally, for the full-size display of letter-size source documents; (2) 8.5 inches vertically by 11 inches horizontally, for the three-quarter size display of COM-generated microforms; (3) 11 inches square, for the full-size display of letter-size source documents and the three-quarter size display of COM-generated microforms; and (4) 11 inches vertically by 14 inches horizontally, for the full-size display of both source document and COM-generated microimages. The accompanying table indicates magnifications commonly associated with each of these screen sizes.

As discussed in Chapter Two, document images may be recorded on 16 mm or 35 mm roll microforms in either the cine or comic orientation. Image rotation is a special reader feature that enables users to turn displayed microimages to compensate for such variations in filming positions. While full 360 degree rotation offers the greatest flexibility, ninety degrees is the minimum rotation requirement in reel microfilm and cartridge applications. Although microfiche standards prescribe comic mode filming, technical reports and similar office documents may contain tables, charts, and graphic materials which, while filmed vertically, must be read horizontally. Image rotation is a useful feature in such situations.

Image scanning permits the examination of microimages that are magnified at a size larger than a reader's screen dimensions. Image scanning is a standard capability with all flat microform readers and many roll microfilm models. It is particularly useful in roll microform applications where more than one document image is recorded per film frame. That is the case with 16 mm microfilm created in the duo or duplex formats that are discussed in Chapter Three.

As might be expected, the cost of a reader varies with the type of microforms it accepts, the size of its screen, the number and type of the magnifications it supports, and other features. At the time this chapter was written, a typical microfiche reader with an 8.5 by 11 inch screen could be purchased for $160 to $200, while prices for a microfiche reader with an 11 by 14 inch screen ranged from about $225 to $260. These prices include a single drop-in lens and a 4 by 6 inch microform carrier suitable for standard-size microfiche and the most popular microfilm jackets. Prices for additional lenses ranged from $50 to $100 each. As briefly noted in Chapter Two, roll microform readers are three to five times more expensive than microfiche models with comparable features. Prices for large-screen aperture card readers designed for engineering applications can exceed $1,000.

Human Factors

Human factors—variously called ergonomics or human engineering—is an interdisciplinary field. Ergonomics recognizes and emphasizes those elements that influence people's effectiveness in using equipment to accomplish its intended purpose. Microform systems analysts and equipment manufacturers have long recognized the significance of human factors in minimizing user resistance to microforms. User resistance, the reluctance or refusal of users to accept microforms as an alternative to paper documents, is fostered by perceived discrepancies between the way a given information task is performed with paper documents and the way the same task is performed with microforms. Properly designed microform readers minimize such perceived discrepancies.

Among the most important human factors considerations is a reader's focusing capability. Microform readers must be able to easily establish focus and maintain it consistently from frame to frame. The ANSI/AIIM MS20 standard, Microfilm Readers, recommends a minimum luminance of 35 candelas/meter^2 with a minimum luminance of 140 candelas/meter^2 at the center of the screen when measured at the eyepoint. The ambient illumination on the screen should be 10 lux or less during the time of measurement. Because their light source is above the display surface, front projection readers typically provide fairly uniform screen illumination. The screens of some older rear projection readers suffered from hot spots or deficiencies of diffusion that manifested in a halo effect. Such problems are largely corrected in newer models, most of which offer better screen luminance with diffused light. Some readers offer a feature that allows operators to adjust the lamp intensity. This is an attractive feature for applications involving positive-appearing images.

As previously noted, most newer readers are cooled by natural convection. Where present, fan noise can be a significant irritant in applications requiring prolonged microform use. Such noise should not exceed sixty decibels above the threshold of hearing.

The need for user instructions is common to all equipment-dependent information systems. While most microform readers are easy to operate, potential problems can be minimized by placing step-by-step instructions, with diagrams, near the reader. Several readers have operating instructions permanently inscribed on their front or side panels. In the absence of such instructions, a reader's operating controls should be clearly labelled and conveniently positioned near the lower front of the reader. Controls should be readily accessible and conveniently capable of being operated by both right- and left-handed persons. Reader operation should be predictable. When the film advance knob is turned clockwise, for example, the film should move forward.

Reader-Printer Design

Despite the considerable attention that has been given to so-called paperless information systems since the late 1970s, many micrographic applications require the ability to make paper enlargements for reference, distribution, or other purposes. In such situations, the availability of one or more reader-printers is essential to overcoming user resistance to microforms, just as video display terminals are often configured with printers in order to make occasional hard copies. As explained at the beginning of this chapter, reader-printers can both display enlarged microimages on a screen and make paper prints of those images on demand. Their most important characteristics and operating capabilities are outlined in the ANSI/AIIM MS36 standard, *Reader-Printers*. Recommendations made in that standard are incorporated in the following discussion.

In theory, the preceding discussion of reader characteristics applies to reader-printers as well. As display devices, most models feature rear projection screens and interchangeable lenses suitable for displaying microimages in a variety of sizes and magnifications. Screen measurements range from 9 inches high by 12 inches wide for models designed for the three-quarter size display of COM-generated microfiche to 18 inches high by 24 inches wide for devices intended for engineering applications. The majority of reader-printers, however, might be more accurately described as locator-printers, since they are rarely used for prolonged reading. Instead, their display capabilities permit the identification and alignment of microimages for printing.

Like their display-only counterparts, reader-printers are nominally designed for desktop operation in an ordinary office environment, although some large models are best installed on special workstations offered by their manufacturers. The smallest models measure about 2 feet wide by 2 feet deep. The largest devices approach 3 feet wide by 3 feet deep. Most reader-printers fall about midway between those two extremes. With weights beginning at around 75 pounds, reader-printers can hardly be considered portable, and some models cannot even be relocated easily. Construction typically combines steel and/or aluminum with plastic and glass parts.

In terms of equipment components, reader-printers include a display module with its associated screen, optical system, and microform carrier, plus a printing module that includes a copying mechanism, paper, and any required chemicals. In most cases, display and printing modules are integrated in a single chassis, although a few vendors do sell their reader-printers in display-only configurations with the printing module removed.

As business machines, reader-printers are easy to operate. The user loads the appropriate microform, locates the desired image, aligns it on the screen, adjusts the focus, and presses a print button. Roll film models typically include a motorized film transport with a manual ad-

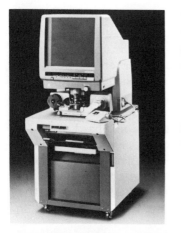
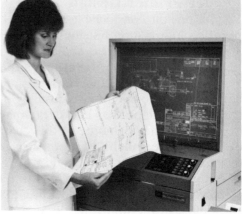

FIGURE 41.   Microform reader-printers.

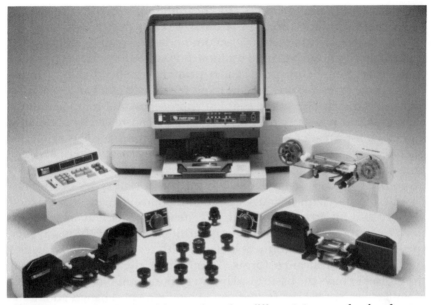

FIGURE 42. Interchangeable carriers for different types of microforms.
Courtesy Fuji.

vance for precise image positioning, although film transports may be
optionally available at a lower price. Carriers for flat microforms are
usually manual and open automatically when the carrier is pulled forward. Most reader-printers provide indicator lights to reflect readiness
for printing and to alert the operator to low paper levels or other conditions which require attention prior to use. Like photocopiers, most
newer models are microprocessor-controlled and will display diagnostic
messages indicating paper jams or other malfunctions.

While most reader-printers provide a manual exposure adjustment
which allows the operator to compensate for variations in film density,
some models feature electronic exposure controls that make such
adjustments automatically. Other controls include a print size selector
and, where appropriate to the print process, a polarity selector. With
some models, the operator must press the print button repeatedly to
obtain multiple copies of a displayed image; others provide a dial or
keypad for multicopy print selection. Like photocopiers, such devices
feature light-emitting diode displays which indicate the number of
copies selected and which count down as successive prints are made.
Depending on equipment design, prints may be delivered at the
top, bottom, or side of the machine. Bottom and side delivery are
somewhat more convenient for a seated operator and permit the
stacking of successive prints on a desktop or other work surface. Typical
printing speeds range between eight and ten seconds per letter-size
page. While subsequent copies of a given image may be produced at
a slightly faster rate, no reader-printers operate at the high speeds

associated with photocopiers. In the multicopy mode, the fastest devices can produce about 15 letter-size prints per minute.

In terms of microforms accommodated, reader-printers are available in single purpose and multipurpose varieties. Like their reader counterparts, single purpose reader-printers are specifically and exclusively designed for one type of microform, such as a particular style of microfilm cartridge. In the simplest approach to multipurpose equipment design, a reel or cartridge transport mechanism can be optionally purchased for a reader-printer. Such a transport mechanism is primarily intended for microfiche or other flat microforms. As an alternative approach, several manufacturers offer *universal* reader-printers that can be configured with interchangeable carriers for all types of roll and flat microforms. With such devices, roll film transports are not designed as mere add-on attachments but offer features—such as image rotation and motorized controls with infinitely variable film advance speeds—that are commonly associated with reader-printers designed specifically for roll microforms. To minimize the initial investment, the customer buys the basic display and printing unit plus those carriers that meet current needs. As application requirements change, additional carriers can be purchased. All carriers can be easily installed and removed without special tools. Interchangeable lenses allow these multipurpose reader-printers to be configured for a wide range of applications.

Depending on the model selected, a given reader-printer will make copies on roll paper or precut sheets. Because they can cut copies to various lengths, roll-fed models typically support a broader range of output sizes than sheet-fed models. Typically, the screen size determines the maximum print size. In some cases, the copy length can be infinitely adjusted to eliminate unwanted portions of a displayed document image, thereby minimizing paper consumption. Reader-printers that use precut sheets require a paper change to produce copies in different sizes, and they use up a whole sheet of paper regardless of the desired image size. To simplify operation, some sheet-fed models utilize interchangeable paper cassettes. Some roll-fed models likewise employ cassette loading to minimize paper handling and the resulting waste sometimes associated with conventional paper loading systems.

Printing Technology

While specific features vary from model to model, most reader-printer users want convenient equipment that can produce good quality copies at a reasonable cost. To meet these requirements, available models employ one of three printing technologies: the dry silver process, the electrofax process, and the xerographic process. Two previously available printing technologies, the electrochemical process and the stabilized silver process, are of historical interest only, and will not be discussed here.

Dry silver microfilm, as previously noted, is used by some source document cameras and COM recorders. Implemented as a reader-printer technology, the dry silver process employs a specially-treated print paper that is exposed to light but developed by heat without processing fluids or other chemicals. The process is clean and, as the name indicates, completely dry. Dry silver reader-printers operate with a single supply item: thermally-sensitive paper. Supply replenishment is limited to paper replacement, and machine cleaning is not required. Well suited to source document and COM-generated microforms with a broad range of photographic characteristics, the dry silver process produces good, usable prints with fairly high contrast to enhance the readability of textual documents and the clarity of line drawings. The process can also make fair to good enlargements of microfilmed photographs. Dry silver print paper is obviously coated and has a slight waxy feel that is noticeable but seldom objectionable. Dry silver copies can be annotated, although the ink used in some porous tip pens may not satisfactorily permeate the paper's coating.

While it is convenient and reliable, certain characteristics of the dry silver process limit its utility as a reader-printer technology. As discussed in Chapter Four, the dry silver process is invariably polarity-reversing. It always makes positive-appearing enlargements from negative-appearing microforms, and negative-appearing enlargements from positive-appearing microforms. Since reader-printer users want and expect positive-appearing prints, dry silver equipment is not suited to applications involving positive-appearing microforms. This is seldom a limitation in general business applications where controlled processing and duplication techniques can produce microforms of negative polarity. Many libraries, however, purchase micropublished editions of newspapers and periodical publications that contain photographs. Such micropublications are usually of positive polarity.

Dry silver print papers remain sensitive to light and heat following exposure and development. While they can be readily handled in ordinary working conditions, dry silver copies will fade if exposed to sunlight or strong artificial light for prolonged periods of time. They cannot, for example, be left on a desktop or credenza adjacent to uncurtained windows. In most micrographic implementations, however, microforms are the supposedly permanent copies, and reader-printer enlargements are working copies made for convenient reference and subsequent disposal. They may be filed for a brief time, and the stability of dry silver copies is suitable for that purpose. Dry silver prints stored in filing cabinets or notebooks should remain usable for months or years.

Because dry silver print papers contain silver, supply costs will fluctuate with the price of precious metals. Depending on the quantity of paper ordered, dry silver print supplies may cost 12 to 16 cents per letter-size copy. Since the other print processes described later in this section offer lower supply costs, the dry silver process is often selected for convenience rather than economy. Dry silver equipment costs are competitive with those of other reader-printer technologies. At the time this chapter was written, prices for dry silver microfiche reader-printers began at around $2,000 and ranged upward to $4,000. Prices for reel microfilm models began at around $5,000. Cartridge equipment prices ranged upward from $6,000.

The electrofax and xerographic print processes are both variants of the electrostatic technology that has dominated the photocopier industry since the 1950s. In the electrofax process, light transmitted through a microimage and lens forms a latent enlargement on a charged photoreceptive paper that is coated with zinc oxide in a resin binder. The latent image is developed by the application of an oppositely charged toner. With some electrofax reader-printers, the toner consists of fine carbon particles in liquid suspension. During the development phase, heat fuses the toner particles to the copy paper. Other electrofax models use a powdered toner that is fused to the copy paper with pressure. Dry toner eliminates any potential inconvenience resulting from the need to periodically replenish liquids, although liquid toner models frequently utilize prepackaged containers with all required processing chemistry.

Like dry silver technology, the electrofax process produces usable prints of good quality, especially when the images enlarged are of textual documents or line drawings. As a potential disadvantage, however, print contrast is sometimes lower than that of dry silver prints. Electrofax paper is very obviously coated, and some users may object to the odor of toner fluids in newly developed prints. Electrofax copies can be annotated with a variety of writing instruments. Electrofax images resist fading and are considered as permanent as the paper on which they rest. While most electrofax copy papers are of high-sulphite, high-acid content that cannot be considered archivally stable, they will perform effectively as working copies.

The polarity characteristics of electrofax prints varies with the type of reader-printer being used. Some models share a potential limitation of their dry silver counterparts in that they invariably reverse polarity. They produce positive-appearing prints from negative-appearing microforms and negative-appearing prints from positive-appearing microforms. The most versatile electrofax reader-printers, however, can produce positive-appearing prints from either positive-appearing or negative-appearing microforms. Often described as bimodal, such machines typically include a dial lever that is simply set to the polarity of the microform being copied. In some cases, bimodal requires a special print paper that may be more expensive than unimodal paper.

Since the electrofax process has been in use for more than three decades, it is well understood as a process. Electrofax reader-printers are reliable and easily maintained. Supply costs, for print paper and processing chemistry, typically range between six and 12 cents per letter-size copy, depending on the quantity of printing supplies purchased at one time. Equipment prices are comparable to those of dry silver models.

With xerographic reader-printers, light transmitted through a microimage and lens forms a latent enlargement on a charged photoreceptive surface. An oppositely charged toner is applied to this photoreceptor, to develop an image that is then transferred to plain paper and fused with heat. As with the electrofax process, the toner may be powdered or liquid. Because they closely resemble the copier-like output to which most office workers are accustomed, xerographic reader-printers can help minimize the resistance users experience toward microforms. Xerographic copies typically offer high contrast for excellent legibility. Depending on the model selected, xerographic reader-printers may reverse polarity or offer bimodal capabilities.

In addition to using ordinary, untreated paper, xerographic reader-printers can extend the range of micrographic applications by copying onto letterheads, special stationery, offset plates, and transparencies. Xerographic images are as permanent as the substrate on which they rest, and copies can be made on low-acid paper for long-term storage. Xerographic supplies are significantly less expensive than those required by dry silver and electrofax reader-printers, and cost saving is an important consideration in applications involving high-volume printing. Depending on quantities purchased, paper and toner costs will range between one and two cents per letter-size copy. Using technology employed in laser printers and low-priced photocopiers, some xerographic reader-printers also require periodic replacement of the photoreceptor, which is packaged with toner in a disposable cartridge. With such machines, supply costs range between four and six cents per letter-size copy. Equipment costs vary considerably. Prices for xerographic microfiche reader-printers that utilize replaceable photoreceptors begin at $3,000. Microfiche models with conventional photoreceptors are priced from $5,000. Prices for reel microfilm and cartridge models can exceed $15,000, depending on equipment design and the options selected.

Enlarger-Printers

As defined at the beginning of this chapter, an enlarger-printer is specifically designed to make enlarged paper prints from microimages. Reader-printers, are typically used to make one or several reference copies of selected microimages, while enlarger-printers are intended for high-volume applications requiring single or multiple copies of all or specified groups of document images recorded on a given microform. While reader-printers require an operator in constant attendance, most enlarger-printers will produce paper copies automatically once job parameters have been entered.

Enlarger-printers have been available for more than three decades. The earliest models printed enlarged images from 16 mm or 35 mm roll microfilm onto a continuous roll of plain paper which was subsequently cut into individual pages. Newer enlarger-printers can produce paper copies from various combinations of roll and flat microforms. Most models use xerographic printing technology and are microprocessor-controlled for versatility and reliability. Microfiche enlarger-printers, for example, will make one or more copies of all or selected images within a microfiche. A variety of enlarger-printers support the high-speed enlargement of engineering drawings recorded on aperture cards. The most versatile devices can accept a stack of cards and allow the operator to specify the desired print quantity for each. Copies can be produced in various sizes and magnifications. Output speeds can exceed 500 letter-size pages per hour. Sorters facilitate the handling of finished prints.

FIGURE 43. An aperture card enlarger-printer.

6 Retrieval Concepts and Systems

As DESCRIBED IN the preceding chapter, the micrographics industry offers a broad range of equipment for the display and printing of roll and flat microforms, but the identification and location of desired microimages is a precondition of such use. Consequently, the selection and implementation of appropriate retrieval methodologies are critical work steps in micrographic systems analysis. Over the past six decades, micrographic equipment manufacturers and systems analysts have developed a variety of concepts and methodologies to effectively support microimage retrieval at various levels of reference activity. The retrieval techniques employed in a particular situation will necessarily depend on application characteristics and reference requirements.

In applications that involve well organized, logically arranged records, micrographic implementations often miniaturize documents while retaining the original arrangement of paper files. As an example, retired personnel files, terminated patient files, or inactive student records that are arranged alphabetically may be simply removed from filing cabinets and filmed in alphabetical sequence on 16 mm microfilm reels or cartridges. Similarly, terminated case files that are arranged by case number may be microfilmed in that sequence. Technical reports, manuals, or other publications are routinely recorded on microfiche which are then arranged in alphabetic or numeric sequence by author, report number, or subject. Engineering drawings may be recorded on aperture cards which are then filed by project number or name. Alternatively, related drawings may be grouped in 35 mm microfilm jackets which are filed numerically or alphabetically.

A variety of manual and semiautomated retrieval techniques — including flash target indexing, odometer indexing, and sequential frame numbering—facilitate the location of desired document images in such situations. Easy to understand and apply, such techniques require little or no special equipment and are relatively inexpensive to implement. They are particularly well suited to inactive records management applications. In such cases space conservation is a paramount concern and little or no reference activity is anticipated. However, they can also perform effectively in active records management applications with straightforward retrieval requirements. Manual and semiautomated retrieval approaches have typically proven ineffective where documents are not, or cannot be, microfilmed in a readily usable sequence, however, or where individual images must be located and displayed very rapidly. Computer-assisted retrieval (CAR) methodologies can be employed in such situations. Widely and successfully implemented in a variety of active records management applications, CAR systems use computerized data bases to index and control the retrieval of document images recorded on microfilm, microfiche, or other microforms.

This chapter surveys the most important manual and automated microform retrieval concepts and systems. It emphasizes characteristics which promote or limit their utility in particular information management applications. The discussion begins with manual and semiautomated retrieval methodologies. Later sections discuss computer-assisted retrieval systems. The chapter concludes with a survey of microform storage cabinets and related equipment.

Flash Targets

The simplest microform retrieval techniques use flash targets in combination with blank frames to separate groups of microimages within a microform. The targets are specially prepared pages that contain eye-legible information, usually consisting of larger letters or numbers. In source document applications, flash targets may be handwritten or created by typesetting or desktop publishing systems. Most COM recorders can generate frames containing one or more eye-legible characters. Like folder tabs and dividers in conventional filing cabinets, flash targets direct the user to the area where a desired microimage is located but not necessarily to the microimage itself. While they can be effectively applied to microfiche and other flat microforms, flash targets are most commonly encountered in 16 mm and 35 mm roll microfilm implementations that contain files or other groups of related document images recorded in alphabetic or numeric sequence.

In the introduction to this chapter, an example was cited showing how 16 mm microfilm cartridges may be used to contain retired personnel files arranged alphabetically by employee name. In a simple source document microfilming implementation, flash targets are

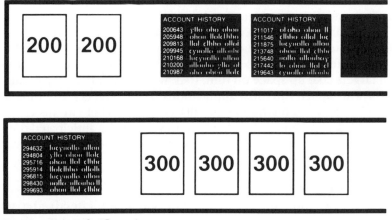

Numeric or Alpha by Sort Parameter

FIGURE 44.   Flash target indexing.

prepared for major alphabetic groupings like employee names arranged alphabetically or other file divisions and inserted into the stack of camera-ready source documents. Each target, which contains one or more eye-legible alphabetic characters, is filmed one or more times before the group of documents to which it pertains. The camera operator records several blank frames, on film to separate the last document in a given group from the flash target that precedes the next group. Adhesive labels are affixed to each cartridge to indicate the first and last personnel file recorded on a given roll.

To locate the file for a particular employee, a user first consults the labels to identify the appropriate cartridge. The cartridge is then inserted into an appropriate reader or reader-printer and the film is advanced rapidly. The appearance of a strip of blank frames indicates that a flash target follows. At that point, the film advance is slowed or halted and the flash target consulted to determine the alphabetic grouping of personnel files that follows the flash target. If the indicated alphabetic grouping matches the retrieval request, individual microimages are examined serially to locate the desired employee's file. If the alphabetic grouping does not match the retrieval parameter, the film is again advanced rapidly until the next target is encountered. This procedure is repeated until the desired file is located.

Flash targets are most effective in applications where documents are logically arranged and exact frame retrieval is not required. Individual targets are easy and inexpensive to prepare. Like the file folder guides and tabs that they emulate, their number and contents can be adjusted to support retrieval at any desired level of specificity. For applications that involve very inactive personnel records, for example, a single flash target may be prepared for each letter of the alphabet. Where more frequent reference is anticipated, however, multiletter targets can identify alphabetic subgroups.

Flash target retrieval is compatible with conventional readers, and reader-printers; no special equipment is required. Search procedures are straightforward, and user instruction is relatively simple. Although flash targets take up space on film, they will not significantly diminish microform capacity in most applications. Flash targets are compatible with other retrieval methodologies discussed elsewhere in this chapter. As a potential limitation, flash target retrieval must be anticipated during micrographic systems analysis. Flash targets cannot be conveniently inserted into previously created microforms.

Odometer Indexing

Odometer indexing is a simple but potentially effective retrieval technique that relates the locations of microimages to their distance from the start of a 16 mm or 35 mm roll microform. Like flash target retrieval, odometer indexing is intended for logically arranged document collections. In source document applications, roll microforms can be created on any rotary or planetary camera. An index is typically prepared by examining processed microimages on a reader or reader-printer equipped with an odometer. In an application involving retired personnel files, for example, a microfilm reel or cartridge is loaded and the film is advanced to the first frame. The operator records the name of the employee whose file appears on the screen, together with the odometer setting. The film is then advanced to the first page of the next employee's file and the odometer setting is noted. This procedure is repeated until odometer settings are recorded

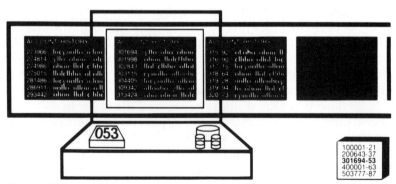

Measures Film Footage in Feet

FIGURE 45.   Odometer indexing.

for each file. The resulting list of employee names and the odometer setting may be written or typed on labels. Then the labels are affixed to microfilm reels or cartridges, recorded on sheets of paper, maintained in an index card file, or entered into a computerized data base.

As with flash target retrieval, the specificity of odometer indexing can be tailored to application requirements. Where infrequent reference is anticipated, for example, indexing may be limited to the first page in major alphabetic groups. If desired, odometer indexing can be combined with flash targets. In COM applications, software is available to derive odometer settings during data preparation. The resulting computer-generated odometer index can then be printed on paper or recorded as the first microimage on the reel or cartridge to which it pertains.

Regardless of index format and preparation method, retrieval procedures are straightforward. The index is first consulted to determine the roll number and odometer setting for the desired microimage. The user loads the appropriate reel or cartridge on a reader or reader-printer equipped with an odometer, advances the film to the first frame, resets the odometer to zero, and advances the film again until the indicated odometer setting is reached. Allowing for slight variations in the odometers of different readers and reader-printers, the user will then be at or very near the location of the desired microimage. Depending on application characteristics and the specificity of indexing, some images may have to be examined serially.

Odometer indexing is well suited to 16 mm and 35 mm reel and cartridge applications where documents are recorded on microfilm in alphabetic or numeric sequence. Odometer indexes are economical to prepare and easy to use. Special cameras are not required, and odometers are available as standard or optional equipment on the roll microform readers and reader-printers of most manufacturers. Odometer indexing requires no special film preparation and will not interfere with the simultaneous or subsequent application of other retrieval techniques. As a potentially significant advantage, it is one of the few retrieval techniques that can be applied to previously created microforms. Odometer indexing can consequently be used to improve retrieval of 16 mm or 35 mm microfilms created without flash targets or other retrieval aids.

Sequential Frame Numbering

In one of the most straightforward approaches to microform retrieval, sequentially-assigned numbers are recorded in each film frame, typically in one of the corners beneath the document image. While this technique can be used with microfiche, it is most often applied to 16 mm and 35 mm roll microforms. In source document applications, the numbered frames can be created by planetary cameras that incorporate digital counters in the photographic field. The counter may

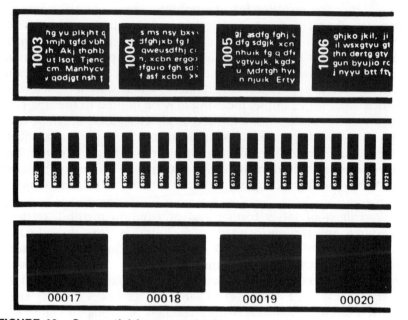

FIGURE 46.   Sequential frame numbering.

be mechanical or electronic; the latter typically employs a light-emitting diode display. In either case, the counter is automatically incremented following each exposure. Some rotary microfilmers can be equipped with an accessory that imprints a sequentially assigned number on each document prior to exposure. This numbering method takes advantage of the rotary camera's speed, but, because the document is defaced in the process, it may prove unacceptable in some applications. Most COM recorders support software that will position sequential numbers above or below each film frame. Such numbers may appear in either reduced or eye-legible size; the latter is similar to flash targets but occupies only a portion of a film frame.

Like the other manual and semiautomated retrieval techniques discussed in this chapter, sequential frame numbering is intended for logically arranged document collections. It is most easily applied to files that are in alphabetic or numeric sequence. As with odometer indexing, the user must prepare an index that relates document identifiers, such as names or case numbers, to frame numbers.

Specificity of indexing can be tailored to retrieval requirements. Indexing each microimage, while time consuming, permits exact frame retrieval. Where retrieval requirements are less stringent, indexing can be limited to selected frames. In an application involving retired personnel files microfilmed in alphabetic sequence by employee name, for example, an index may list the names of employees whose files are recorded on a given reel or cartridge, together with the numbers of the frames that contain the first page of each file. As with its counterpart, the odometer setting, a frame number index may be recorded on sheets of paper, written or typed on labels which are then affixed to microfilm reels or cartridges. The index may be maintained in an index card file, or even entered into a computerized data base. COM-generated indexes can be recorded as the first frame within a roll.

At retrieval time, a user first consults the index to determine the roll and frame number of a desired document image. The indicated microfilm reel or cartridge is then mounted on a reader or reader-printer and the film is advanced. The operator stops periodically to check the frame numbers until the desired frame is reached. If the index lists frame locations for the first page of a group of related documents, the microimages that follow it must be examined serially until a desired page is located.

Like flash target retrieval and odometer indexing, sequential frame numbering is a potentially effective and economical microform retrieval technique. Although some special production equipment is required, film preparation is uncomplicated, and conventional display and printing devices can be used. Retrieval procedures are straightforward, and user instruction is relatively simple. Frame numbers do not interfere with viewing; nor do they diminish microform capacity, or exclude the possibility of later conversion to other retrieval methods. Like flash target retrieval, however, sequential frame numbering must be anticipated during micrographic systems analysis, since frame numbers cannot be added to previously created microforms at a later time.

Blip Encoding

Blip encoding is a variant form of sequential frame numbering that is compatible with automated image retrieval. A blip is more descriptively termed an image count mark. It is an opaque rectangular mark that is usually positioned beneath each frame on 16 mm roll microforms. Blip locations, dimensions, and other characteristics are described in the ANSI/AIIM MS8 standard, *Image Mark (Blip) Used in Image Mark Retrieval Systems*. In source document applications, blips can be recorded by specially equipped rotary cameras. Most overhead-type planetary cameras can be easily modified for blip encoding by placing a dark covering over the copyboard and positioning a small piece of white paper in the lower portion of the photographic field. Alternatively, several planetary camera manufacturers offer special copyboards for blip encoding. In COM applications, a specially prepared form slide is used to record blips beneath each data frame.

Whether produced by source document cameras or COM recorders, blip-encoded microfilm is designed for use in special retrieval units. Such units are equipped with optical components and electronic circuitry capable of counting individual blips. The most commonly

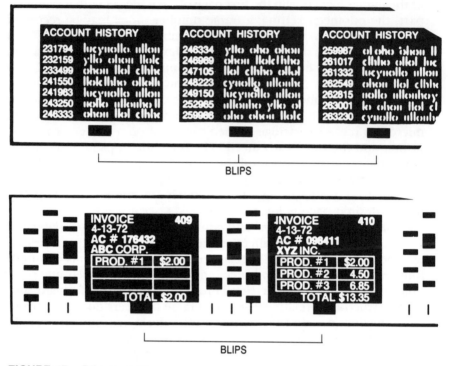

FIGURE 47. Blip encoding.

encountered blip-counting retrieval devices are reader-printers with calculator-style keypads for the entry of desired frame numbers. The retrieval unit advances the film, counts the blips, stops at the specified frame, and displays it for reading or printing. For visual confirmation of accurate retrieval, blip encoding may be combined with sequential frame numbering. Not to be confused with binary codes, blips simply mark frame locations. When properly counted, they indicate the position that a given microimage occupies from the start of a reel or cartridge. Blips do not contain index information that describes the contents of individual frames.

In the simplest source document and COM implementations, blips of uniform size and appearance are recorded beneath document images in the lower portion of individual film frames. As a potentially useful variation, some microfilm cameras can record blips in both the top and bottom portions of each film frame. Other models can record blips in two or three different sizes. Such capability for multilevel blip encoding are designed for applications where microfilmed documents will be retrieved by hierarchical relationships. In financial applications, for example, documents may grouped into blocks and batches for microfilming. At retrieval time, a desired document will be identified by the number of the block within which it was filmed, its batch

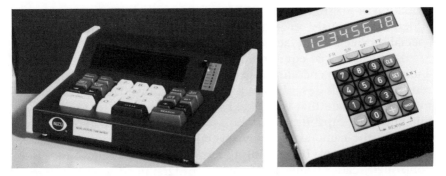

FIGURE 48. A blip counting attachment for reader-printer installations.

number within the specified block, and its item number within the specified batch. Similarly, in retail sales applications customer charge slips may be retrieved by store, sales register, and item numbers, while insurance claims are sometimes retrieved by group, claim, and attachment numbers. When multilevel blip encoding cameras are used, large-size blips will identify a block, store, or group; medium-size blips will identify intermediate groups; and the smallest blips will identify individual items.

Whether single level or multilevel blip encoding is employed, a separately prepared index indicates the roll and frame locations of individual microimages. As will be discussed later in this chapter, computer-assisted retrieval systems combine blip encoding with computer-maintained index data. However, conventional typed or handwritten indexes can also be used. In a straightforward application involving retired personnel files filmed in alphabetical sequence, an index would list the names of employees whose files are recorded on specific reels or cartridges, together with the number of the frame that contains the first page of each file. In a typical retrieval operation, the index will be consulted, the indicated reel or cartridge loaded into a blip-counting reader-printer, and the desired frame number entered. As noted above, the film is automatically advanced to the indicated frame. For a multilevel retrieval, the operator enters a combination of block, batch, and item numbers, and the frames will be counted accordingly.

Blip encoding is an effective, reliable method for high speed retrieval of exact frames. Retrieval procedures are straightforward, and user instructions are simple. Blips do not diminish microfilm storage capacity, interfere with viewing, or preclude the use of other retrieval techniques. As will be discussed later in this chapter, blip encoding is an important component in computer-assisted microfilm retrieval systems. Where the required cameras are available, micrographic systems analysts are well advised to routinely specify blip encoding for all 16 mm roll microforms. This encoding should be done in anticipation of possible future CAR implementations. While blips can be added to previously created roll microforms, the procedure requires special service bureau facilities and the process can prove expensive.

Because special equipment is required for both film preparation and retrieval, blip encoding is generally more expensive than the other retrieval methods described in preceding sections. Depending on the microfilm camera that is selected for use in a particular application, blip encoding capabilities may be a standard feature or an option that increases the cameras price by several hundred to several thousand dollars. The newest blip-counting retrieval units are microprocessor-controlled reader-printers that are preprogrammed to count several types of blips. Prices range from less than $10,000 to more than $15,000, depending on printing capabilities and options. As a less expensive alternative, several vendors offer accessories to convert conventional 16 mm readers and reader-printers to blip-counting retrieval units. The simplest of these devices consists of an electronic counter with a light-emitting diode display and a photocell designed for attachment to the screen of any reel or cartridge reader or reader-printer. After consulting an index to determine the roll and frame location of a given document image, the operator mounts the indicated reel or cartridge, advances the film at high speed, and watches the displayed frame numbers, stopping the film when the desired frame is reached. More fully automated and expensive attachments include calculator-style keypads, which operate under microprocessor control, and can count several types and sizes of blips. Prices for blip-counting attachments range from less than $1,000 to more than $5,000.

Microfiche Titling and Indexing

As with reels and cartridges, the retrieval of information from microfiche and other flat microforms requires that both the appropriate microform and the desired microimage within the microform be identified. In manual retrieval implementations, location of the appropriate microfiche, jacket, or aperture card is facilitated by eye-legible titling. As previously discussed in Chapter Two, microfiche standards reserve an area equivalent in size to one row of frames at the top of each microfiche for such titling. All COM recorders capable of producing microfiche can generate one or more lines of eye-legible characters in the title area. To meet special application requirements, some COM recorders can also position eye-legible titling along the bottom row of frames or in either end column. In source document applications, some step-and-repeat cameras include electronic character-generators that can create one or more lines of eye-legible titling information; others expose strips of paper containing handwritten or typed titles. Alternatively, an adhesive heading strip, which may be prepared on a typewriter, computer printer, typesetter, or other device, can then be affixed to the top row of a given microfiche. In

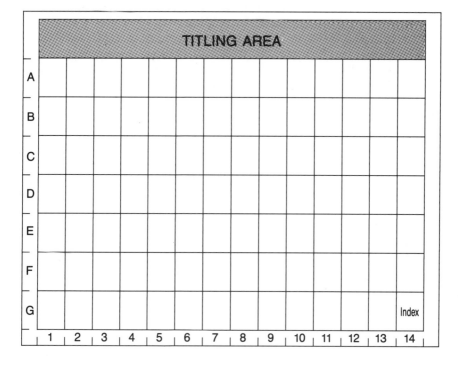

FIGURE 49. Microfiche titling and index frames.

some cases, polarity reversal is used to highlight all or selected portions of the title area. Color strips can be used to further distinguish
microfiche from one another.

Subject to application-specific variations, the content of eye-legible
microfiche titling typically includes a combination of a file or report
name, date, a microfiche sequence number (for multifiche sets), and
inclusive microfiche contents. The latter usually takes the form of a
from-to statement based on information contained in the first and last
frames. In COM applications, title information can be input directly
by the recorder operator or extracted by software from specified
portions of the input data. To facilitate reference, some COM-generated
microfiche provide additional eye-legible characters at the top of each
column or in other locations within a microfiche. As previously noted,
source document microfiche may also contain eye-legible flash targets
interspersed with document images.

As described in Chapter Two, microfilm jackets, like microfiche,
include a heading area that consists of matte-finished surface on which
eye-legible characters can be written, typed, computer-printed, or
otherwise inscribed. Heading sizes vary from jacket to jacket. The most

popular 4 by 6 inch jacket, for example, contains five channels for microfilm strips and features a heading area that measures 8 mm wide—sufficient for one line of typed information. Alternatively, the same jacket can be purchased in a four channel configuration with a 27 mm heading area. Jackets are available with larger heading areas, but as the heading size increases fewer channels are available for microfilm images.

While eye-legible titling identifies individual microfiche, internal indexes facilitate the location of desired frames. Microfiche indexing methodologies vary from implementation to implementation. Source document microfiche prepared from technical reports, monographs, and other publications may include an index prepared for the original work and keyed to page numbers in the paper document. Although information recorded on source document microfiche and certain alphabetically or numerically sequenced COM-generated reports may be retrievable without a specially prepared index, some source document applications and many COM-generated reports require a special index to associate data with its location in a particular microfiche frame. Such specially-prepared indexes use alphanumeric row and column designators to denote frame locations. In source document applications, a microfiche index may be prepared manually and filmed with the documents. In COM applications, software can extract specified index keys from each data frame and list them in the index with their associated microfiche row and column coordinates. A grid on the microfiche reader facilitates the location and display of microimages at designated row and column positions. Available for various standard and nonstandard microfiche formats, such grids are typically interchangeable.

Standard source document and COM microfiche formats specify an index as the last frame within a microfiche, positioned in the lower right-hand corner. If more than one index frame is required, they customarily occupy the last few corner frames. In COM applications, some recorders can place index frames at the top of each column within a microfiche. Such column indexes may be identical with, or more detailed versions of, the corner index. The column index technique sacrifices a few data frames to facilitate retrieval by making index information conveniently accessible.

In some COM applications, frequently updated data—such as descriptive entries in computer-generated parts catalogs or membership lists—is recorded on microfiche in random sequence. Supplementary data microfiche, containing new and revised entries, are generated periodically and added to the microfiche collection. Data microfiche are identified by eye-legible numbers recorded in the title area. Index frames are recorded on separate microfiche that are reissued at regular intervals to reflect changes or additions to the data microfiche. Index entries contain microfiche numbers and grid coordinates for the latest information recorded on the data microfiche. References to obsolete entries are deleted when indexes are updated, making them unretrievable.

The CAR Concept

The manual and semiautomated retrieval methodologies described in the preceding sections can successfully accommodate straightforward retrieval requirements in applications involving logically arranged document collections or computer-generated reports. In an application where one million pages of retired personnel files are recorded on 400 microfilm cartridges, for example, flash targets can identify and separate individual files, and the cartridges themselves can be labeled to reflect their inclusive contents. If desired, this simple approach can be enhanced by odometer indexing, sequential frame numbering, or—where a modest amount of automation is desired—conventional blip encoding.

As noted briefly in the introduction to this chapter, CAR systems are designed for applications where documents cannot be microfilmed in a readily usable sequence and/or where rapid retrieval by complex combinations of parameters is required. Broadly defined, the phrase computer-assisted retrieval (CAR) denotes an automated document storage and retrieval technology that uses computer hardware and software to index and locate documents or document images recorded on any media. CAR systems use data base management software to create, maintain, retrieve, and otherwise manipulate machine-readable records that contain index information accompanied by pointers to document locations. Most CAR systems support online data entry and retrieval via video display terminals. Computer-processible index records are stored on magnetic disks. At retrieval time, the index is searched to determine the existence and storage locations of documents pertinent to specific information needs. Alternatively, index records and document location information can be printed on paper or COM-generated microforms for offline reference, although the resulting retrieval capabilities will be limited.

While computer-assisted retrieval concepts can be applied to paper documents and to digitized document images recorded on magnetic disks, optical disks, or other computer-processible media, this discussion deals exclusively with CAR systems that utilize microforms for document storage. Viewed as a micrographic retrieval methodology, CAR is one of three technologies that comprise the so-called computer-micrographics interface; the other two are computer-output microfilm (COM), previously discussed in Chapter Four, and computer-input microfilm (CIM), which will be described briefly in Chapter Eight. Collectively, these technologies use a combination of computers and micrographics to address information processing requirements that cannot be satisfactorily addressed by either computers or micrographics alone. As its name suggests, CAR combines the substantial document management advantages of micrographic technology with the ability of computers to rapidly manipulate index data.

While the CAR concept gained considerable notoriety within the broader context of office automation in the late 1970s and early 1980s, automated microform retrieval systems were first proposed in the 1940s. During the 1950s and early 1960s, a number of experimental and custom-developed systems were implemented in government and corporate applications requiring the control and rapid retrieval of scientific and technical documentation. By the mid-1960s, several working systems were available for sale, and the acronym ADSTAR (for

FIGURE 50.   A turnkey CAR system. *Courtesy 3M.*

Automated Document Storage and Retrieval) was introduced to denote this emerging technology. At a time when computers were much more expensive and less powerful than they are today, early automated microform retrieval systems bypassed computers entirely. The best known and most widely used example, Eastman Kodak's MIRAcode system, recorded index data as photo-optical binary codes on microfilm, adjacent to the document images to which they pertained. A simpler product, the ORACLE system, recorded a limited amount of index data in a barcoded format beneath each film frame.

The first true CAR systems were implemented in the early 1960s as "one of a kind" installations using prototype microform retrievers and other customized components. Off-the-shelf CAR products—including blip-counting reader-printers and automated microfiche retrieval units—became available in the early 1970s. During the same period, several complete CAR systems—consisting of integrated, self-contained configurations of computer hardware, computer software, and micrographics equipment—were introduced for sale on a turnkey basis. Prewritten CAR software, intended for operation on customer-owned computers, became commercially available in the mid-1970s. Since that time, CAR has firmly established itself as an information management technology, and dozens of vendors have introduced CAR equipment components, prewritten CAR software, and complete turnkey CAR systems suitable for a variety of document storage and retrieval applications.

CAR System Components

A microform-based computer-assisted retrieval system includes computer and micrographic subsystems, each with its own data base. The computer data base, as previously noted, contains machine-readable index information. The micrographic data base is composed of document images recorded on microfilm, microfiche, or other microforms. The characteristics and capabilities of CAR implementations are best described with reference to the following hypothetical but realistic example:

Assume that the customer service office of an electronics manufacturing company has implemented a CAR system to control a file of product warranty registration forms which must be retrieved quickly and reliably in response to customer inquiries, complaints, service requests, product recall actions, and other events. Customer service representatives must be able, for example, to retrieve a warranty registration form submitted by a specified individual on a particular date, all warranty registration forms for a specified product sold in a particular geographic region, or all warranty registration for forms for products sold by a particular store during a specified time period.

Using this hypothetical application as an example, the accompanying flowchart depicts the interrelationship of microfilming and

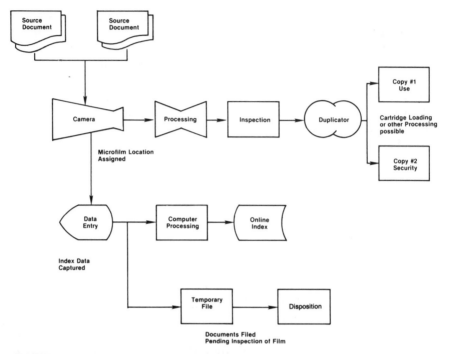

FIGURE 51.   Flow of work in CAR implementations.

data entry components and worksteps in a typical computer-assisted retrieval implementation. The following explanations apply:

1. As a preparatory work step common to all computer-assisted indexing and retrieval methodologies, a micrographic systems analyst or other application developer must determine indexing categories and establish procedures for the identification of index values appropriate to those categories. In this hypothetical example, each warranty registration form will be indexed by date, customer name, product name, the name of the store where the product was purchased, and the name of the geographic region where the store is located.

2. CAR systems can be implemented in several different ways, In one approach, documents are assigned identifying numbers on arrival at an indexing station. Where document images will be stored in 16 mm microfilm cartridges—the most common type of CAR implementation—identifying numbers are assigned to each page of multipage documents. Such numbers, which are assigned sequentially, indicate the microfilm roll and frame locations which individual pages will occupy. Thus, the number "0045-1325" identifies a page recorded on cartridge number 45 at frame number 1,325. In microfiche-based CAR implementations, document identifiers typically include a microfiche number, a row indicator, and a column designator. As an example, the number "0132-C7" identifies a page recorded on

microfiche number 132 at the intersection of row C and the seventh column.

As noted earlier in this chapter, specially equipped cameras can stamp identifying numbers on pages prior to microfilming and data entry. Alternatively, identifying numbers can be hand-stamped, written, or otherwise inscribed on pages. In some CAR installations, documents are filmed by cameras that number frames rather than pages. In CAR implementations involving engineering drawings, maps, or other documents recorded on aperture cards, frame locations are omitted from identifying information, since aperture cards—as described in Chapter Two—usually contain a single document image.

3. Following the assignment of identifying numbers in a format appropriate to the microform in use, the warranty registration forms are microfilmed. In most CAR applications, documents are filmed in the order in which they are received, thereby eliminating folder and label preparation, document sorting, interfiling, and other file maintenance routines typically associated with paper documents. Where 16 mm microfilm is used, images are typically blip-encoded. Exposed microfilm is processed and duplicated to produce working and storage copies in the manner discussed in Chapter Three.

4. In the approach to CAR implementation depicted in the accompanying flowchart, the warranty registration forms travel to a data entry terminal following filming. In such situations, the microfilm camera and data entry station may be located in different areas. Some CAR installations, however, use a special document-entry station that includes a microfilm camera linked to a data entry terminal. In other cases, documents are indexed from microimages following film processing, the images being displayed on a reader or reader-printer that may or may not be connected to a data entry terminal. Regardless of the approach employed, assigned index values are typed at the data entry terminal's keyboard in a manner prescribed by the CAR indexing software in use. The documents' identifying numbers, which represent their microform addresses, are entered as well. Most programs support specially formatted screens to facilitate data entry.

5. Using the entered data, computer software updates a data base of index records and supporting files that reflect the characteristics of documents stored in particular microfilm locations. In the hypothetical example discussed here, data base records will contain fields for each of the five retrieval parameters outlined: date, customer name, product name, the name of the store where the product was purchased, and the name of the geographic region where the store is located. Entered data is stored on magnetic disks for online retrieval. Security copies, intended for offline storage, may be recorded on magnetic tape, diskettes, write-once optical disk cartridges, or other media. For rapid retrieval, most CAR software creates inverted index files that are essentially alphabetical lists of selected field values with

pointers to the data base records that contain them. Thus, the following data entered from a warranty registration form:

Date: 12/10/89
Customer: Flynn T
Product: VDT170
Store: Sterling Electronics
Region: Midwest

will generate entries in the date index under 12/19/89, in the customer name index under Flynn T, in the product index under VDT170, in the store index under Sterling Electronics, and in the region index under Midwest. These index entries will contain pointers to data base records that include fields indicating the microfilm locations of document images with which the index values are associated.

6. Following indexing, paper documents can be transferred to a temporary file, where they are maintained in the sequence in which they were filmed, pending microform processing, duplication, and inspection. Once those work steps are completed, the paper documents are no longer required. Depending on an organization's records management policies and procedures, they may be destroyed or moved to off-site storage facilities. Working copies of microforms containing images of index documents are stored in file cabinets, on shelves, or in other containers to be described later in this chapter. Camera-original microforms, and any additional security copies, may be stored offsite, following the recommendations of film storage standards.

As outlined above, a CAR system's computer components support the entry, maintenance, and processing of index records that are linked to document images stored by the micrographic subsystem. The computer subsystem includes a central processor, an alphanumeric video display unit with keyboard, and sufficient magnetic disk capacity for online storage of data base records, supporting files, and CAR software. Optional hardware components include a printer and telecommunication links to other computer systems.

Computer configurations will necessarily vary with application characteristics. CAR systems have been successfully implemented in mainframe, minicomputer, and microcomputer environments. Turnkey CAR systems—preconfigured combinations of computer and micrographic components designed specifically for automated document storage and retrieval and purchased as a single product —typically employ minicomputers or microcomputers as their central processors. In most cases, a turnkey system's central processor is dedicated to CAR operations and cannot support other information processing tasks. A customized CAR system, by way of contrast, may use a timeshared or dedicated computer of any type or size. In timesharing implementation, the central processor may be operated by an organization's own data processing department or by an external service bureau. It can, of course, be used for other information management tasks.

A CAR system's micrographic components include a production and retrieval devices. In CAR applications that use 16 mm microfilm reels or cartridges, the micrographics subsystem can include any rotary or planetary camera capable of blip encoding. As discussed in Chapter Three, some or all phases of microfilm production can be performed by a service bureau or photographic laboratory. While source document applications are most widely encountered, CAR systems can also be used to index and retrieve COM-generated microforms.

The micrographics subsystem must also include an appropriate microform retrieval unit. Blip-counting readers and reader-printers, as previously discussed, support the rapid, exact display of designated 16 mm microfilm frames. While they are less widely encountered, several vendors offer similar automated display and printing devices for microfiche. Such readers and reader-printers typically use special cartridges or carousels to house individual microfiche for retrieval and display. An operator enters instructions on a keypad and the designated frames are retrieved and displayed. In many cases, the microfiche are

FIGURE 52. An automated retrieval unit for microfiche enclosed in cartridges. *Courtesy Map, U.S.A.*

attached to notched clips or stored in specially marked carriers to facilitate identification and automated retrieval.

In some CAR installations, microfilm and microfiche readers and reader-printers operate as offline retrieval units that are unattached to other system components. After searching a computer-maintained data base of index records, the operator selects a designated microfilm cartridge or microfiche from a filing cabinet or other storage location and manually loads it into the retrieval device. As an alternative to such standalone operation, many readers and reader-printers can be optionally equipped with an electronic interface that permits online operation to a computer. As described in the ANSI/AIIM MS40 standard, *Microfilm Computer Assisted Retrieval (CAR) Interface Commands*, this CAR interface converts a microform retrieval unit into a special-purpose, receive-only terminal. It typically connects a microform reader or reader-printer to the RS-232 serial port of an online video display terminal or microcomputer. Following an index search, the CAR system's central processor transmits the numbers of pertinent frames through the interface to the retrieval unit, thus eliminating the need to enter frame numbers manually. The operator, however, must still manually select and load the appropriate microforms.

CAR Software

The phrase *CAR software* denotes the programs that a CAR system's computer executes to establish, maintain, search, or otherwise process data base records associated with document images recorded on microfilm, microfiche, or other microforms. From the software standpoint, CAR systems can be implemented in any of four ways that differ in implementation time, cost, and other characteristics:

1. As is the case with computer software for any information processing application, document indexing and retrieval programs can be custom-developed for a specific CAR implementation. Time-consuming and expensive, such customized programming is an implementation option of last resort to be used in those rare instances where unusual indexing or retrieval requirements cannot be accommodated by available prewritten software.

2. A prewritten, general-purpose data base management software package can be adapted for document indexing and microform retrieval. Many mainframe and minicomputer installations have acquired such software packages for use in management information systems, automated library systems, or other data processing applications. Given their broad information storage and retrieval capabilities, they can usually be modified for CAR implementations, although some customized programming may be required. Microcomputer-based data base management programs, which are routinely encountered in office installations, can likewise be adapted to CAR implementations.

3. Prewritten document indexing and retrieval programs designed specifically for CAR implementations can be purchased from various micrographic system vendors and service bureaus. Such programs are available for popular computer configurations, including IBM Series 370 mainframes; minicomputers manufactured by Digital Equipment Corporation, Hewlett-Packard, Data General, Prime Computer, and others; and IBM-compatible microcomputers. Compared to general-purpose data base management programs, which must be adapted to CAR requirements, CAR-specific programs are designed expressly for microform indexing and retrieval and are easily implemented. Unlike some general-purpose packages, they do not require programming skill to take full advantage of their information processing capabilities. Some programs also include device-driver modules that can control microform retrieval units equipped with the CAR interfaces discussed earlier. General-purpose data base management programs do not offer such capabilities.

4. Turnkey CAR systems, as previously noted, feature prewritten software that is bundled for sale with computer and micrographics hardware. Such turnkey configurations offer the fastest and, in some respects, the simplest approach to CAR film system procurement and installation. In addition to rapid implementation, turnkey systems offer the advantage of simplified procurement and single vendor responsibility during system installation and subsequent operation.

In customer-developed CAR systems that incorporate hardware and software from different sources, it can prove difficult to determine the source of, and maintenance responsibility for, system malfunctions. A given system failure may be attributable, for example, to micrographics equipment, computer equipment, computer software, or some combination of those components. A turnkey system vendor typically assumes maintenance responsibility for all malfunctions.

The CAR software may be custom-developed, adapted from general-purpose data base management programs, purchased prewritten, or bundled in a turnkey system. Nevertheless, the CAR software must be able to support the creation and editing of data base records pertaining to document images recorded on microforms, and the location and display of records conforming to specified retrieval parameters. The ability to search an online index for the addresses of potentially relevant microimages distinguishes CAR systems from conventional approaches to both document filing and micrographics retrieval. While retrieval procedures vary, search specifications typically include a field name, a relational expression, and a field value to be matched. The most flexible programs permit retrieval commands containing combinations of search terms. Some programs also support search term truncation and wildcard symbols.

In most cases, a CAR system's initial response to a retrieval command is a report of the number of document images that satisfies a search specification. The operator can then broaden or narrow the search. When an appropriate number of presumably relevant items is identified, full or partial data base records are displayed for operator examination. While some CAR programs simply display the microform address field from retrieved records, the most flexible software packages give the application developer considerable control over the content and arrangement of displayed records. These records may be displayed in a full-screen format or in a tabular listing. Retrieved data base records can usually be printed as well. Once the displayed records are examined and the microform locations of document images are determined, the indicated microforms can be removed from filing cabinets or other storage locations and mounted on a reader or reader-printer for viewing or printing.

Microform Storage Equipment

Whether manual or automated retrieval methodologies are used, most micrographic implementations require storage facilities for reels, cartridges, microfiche, aperture cards, or other microforms when not in use. For roll microforms, drawer-type cabinets resemble filing equipment for paper records and offer high storage capacities with relatively little floor space consumption. As an example, a six-drawer unit measuring 36 inches wide by 30 inches high by 18 inches deep can store over 750 16 mm reels or cartridges. As an alternative to drawer-type cabinets, several filing equipment manufacturers offer open storage racks for roll microforms. Modular storage units, each with cubbyhole-like compartments for sixty to 100 rolls, can be stacked on top of one another to attain required storage capacities. Small configurations can be maintained on desk tops. Larger stacks can be mounted on casters or turntables. As a potential advantage over conventional filing equipment, such compartment-type storage units eliminate the necessity of opening cabinet drawers, thereby facilitating the removal of microfilm cartridges and improving total retrieval time in CAR installations.

Flat microforms can also be filed in drawer-type cabinets. Typically, 75 to 100 microfiche, microfilm jackets, aperture cards, or other flat microforms can be stored per linear inch of drawer space. A typical cabinet measuring 15 inches wide by 52 inches high by 27 inches deep can hold up to 15,000 standard-size microfiche. A cabinet measuring 24 inches wide by 58 inches high by 28 inches deep can store almost 55,000 aperture cards. As with paper files, groups of microfiche or aperture cards can be separated by tabbed dividers.

Tray-type files are open or covered containers into which microfiche or other flat microforms are inserted in an upright position. The simplest models are inexpensive cardboard boxes with interior dimensions appropriate to microfiche or aperture card storage. The most popular units, however, are constructed of plastic or metal and are identical with general-purpose filing equipment for index or

FIGURE 53.   Microform filing cabinets.

tabulating cards. Regardless of construction, tray-type files offer the compaction and economy of drawer files and are well suited to desktop installation adjacent to microform display and printing equipment. Several companies offer specially designed micrographic workstations that provide space for a reader or reader-printer and one or more tray files. Tray files can also be stored on shelves or in drawers for removal as required.

Drawer- and tray-type files offer excellent storage capacity at reasonable cost, but the necessity of repeatedly opening individual drawers or flipping through trays can make rapid retrieval difficult in very active applications. As a further constraint, conventional drawer- and tray-type files limit the title visibility that is essential to convenient microfiche identification and refiling. Addressing this limitation, several

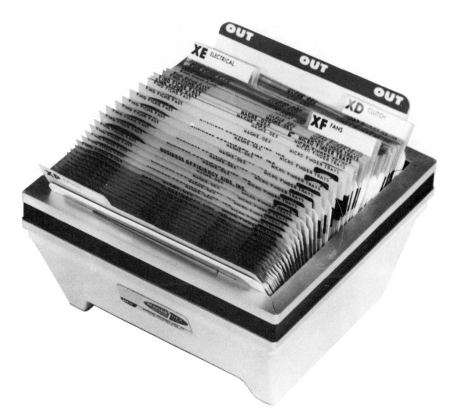

FIGURE 54. Desktop microfiche tray.

manufacturers have developed tray-type units with magnets or pop-up dividers that permit rapid scanning of microforms in all or selected portions of a tray. Alternatively, panel-type storage systems provide single- or double-sided panels with pockets for the insertion of microfiche or other flat microforms. The panels themselves are constructed of vinyl or paper reinforced by rigid plastic edge strips that facilitate attachment to various types of storage units, including ring binders, desk stands, carousels, wall-mounted brackets, and reader-mounted racks.

While manual filing equipment can perform effectively in many applications, several vendors offer random-access filing systems for the automated storage and retrieval of flat microforms. Introduced in the 1960s, such systems use notches or punches to identify particular microforms that are stored at random within a specially designed filing unit. In some cases, microforms are stored in special notched carriers; in others, the microforms themselves are notched or punched with identifying codes. Random-access filing systems will respond to a request for a particular numbered microform entered at a keyboard or through some other means by reading the notches to identify those items that satisfy the request. Such items identified are then ejected from the file for use in readers, reader-printers, or other devices. Following display or printing, the microforms can be returned to the file in any location. Refiling is simplified and, because microforms are stored at random, misfiling is eliminated.

FIGURE 55. Microfiche panel storage.

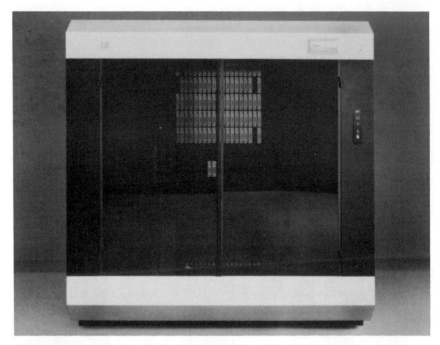

FIGURE 56.   An automated random-access microform file.

7 Micrographic Cost Analysis

THE PRECEDING CHAPTERS surveyed the various types of microforms and described methodologies and products that support their production, storage, retrieval, display, and printing. Firmly rooted in photography, micrographics is a well understood technology. As discussed in Chapter One, micrographic systems can speed retrieval, conserve storage space, simplify publication, improve distribution, and otherwise facilitate the management of active and inactive business records, engineering documentation, library materials, and other information. Based on six decades of application experience, micrographic systems design concepts are firmly established, and the micrographic industry currently offers equipment and supplies suitable for a broad range of source document and COM implementations.

With the notable exception of new data processing applications developed specifically for COM output, however, few information management systems are initially implemented with microforms in mind. Most source document and COM implementations are, instead, designed as alternatives to existing information processing methodologies based on paper records or, in some cases, machine-readable, computer-processible media. As discussed in preceding chapters, source document microfilm implementations often replace paper filing systems, while COM applications complement or replace paper printouts.

As a replacement technology, micrographics must offer affordable, demonstrably cost-effective solutions to information management problems. A cost-effective micrographic system is one that fully addresses the requirements of a given application at a cost lower than that of other information processing technologies or methodologies.

155

As an important facet of micrographic systems analysis, cost-effectiveness analysis is performed in two stages:

1. The cost of a proposed micrographic system is calculated, and an implementation budget and annualized cost estimate are prepared.

2. The costs are evaluated and a cost justification analysis is prepared.

Cost calculation and budget preparation require the identification and estimation of implementation and operating costs associated with a given micrographic application. Cost justification involves the preparation of realistic, reliable comparisons between a proposed micrographic system and alternative information management methodologies, typically emphasizing the methodology that the micrographic system is intended to replace. In the context of three hypothetical examples, the following sections illustrate principles and techniques used in micrographic cost analysis. Each example begins with a brief application description, followed by an estimate and explanation of the costs associated with a proposed micrographic implementation. The discussion concludes with a cost justification analysis that indicates potential cost savings offered by micrographic systems.

It is important to note that the cost estimates presented here reflect equipment prices, supply and service charges, wage rates, and other costs associated with micrographic implementations at the time this chapter was written. As an unavoidable limitation of any published cost analysis, prices and wages are subject to change, and cost calculations and justifications will necessarily be affected by such changes. As a further complication, some organizations—such as government agencies and educational institutions—may be able to purchase micrographic equipment, supplies, and services at substantial discounts when compared to prices presented here. In addition, some costs— such as wage rates—are subject to substantial local and regional variations. Rather than providing universally valid calculations and comparisons of specific micrographic costs, this chapter uses cost estimates as a means of presenting micrographic cost calculation and justification principles that are based on widely used systems analysis methodologies. The discussion should consequently retain its conceptual validity and utility despite changing prices.

Example 1: Microfilming Inactive Records

As discussed in Chapter One, micrographic systems can significantly reduce floor space costs and minimize filing equipment purchases associated with the storage of paper documents. As a more specific means of exploring the economic advantages of microfilming for long-term document storage, assume that the research and development division of a large manufacturing company is faced with the problem of maintaining one million pages of technical documentation pertaining to terminated laboratory projects completed between 1950 and 1980. Reflecting years of basic research and product development activity, these terminated project files represent valuable proprietary information which must be retained indefinitely, since records for older research projects contain test results, lab analyses, and other information pertinent to ongoing work. Reference activity, while occasional, occurs unpredictably. The terminated project files must consequently be conveniently available to researchers.

The typical project file contains several hundred pages of research reports, laboratory notebooks, technical memoranda, and similar documentation, all of which is letter-size or smaller. The files are closed in the sense that no new documents are added to individual folders. Individual files are stored in project number sequence in 85 four-drawer, vertical-style filing cabinets that occupy 510 square feet of contiguous floor space in the company's technical information center. The cabinets, which are in good condition, have a replacement value of $300 each. Floor space is valued at $20 per square foot. Available floor space is at a premium, as it is in many organizations, and the information center needs expansion room to accommodate its growing collections. If emptied, ten of the 85 cabinets would be used by the information center to accommodate new research files that will be created in the coming year. The company's purchasing department would distribute the remaining 75 cabinets to other organizational units as requisitions for comparable new cabinets are received. The company normally purchases more than that number of filing cabinets in any given year.

The division's administrative officer is exploring alternative records management methodologies and wants to know whether the conversion of these terminated project files to microfilm represents a sound business decision. To answer that question, a micrographics systems analyst must calculate the cost of a microfilm conversion and compare it to the cost of the existing paper filing system.

Table 11 presents an estimate of the cost of converting one million pages of terminated project files to 16 mm microfilm. For purposes of this discussion, it is assumed that the files will be microfilmed in project number sequence, exactly replicating their arrangement in filing cabinets. Records for individual projects will be separated by flash targets and blank frames. Conversion procedures will conform to the source document microfilming work steps previously flowcharted and discussed in Chapter Three. Camera original microforms will be maintained on 16 mm reels, and a duplicate set of working copies will be produced. In order to introduce a variety of cost factors and computation techniques, it is assumed that document preparation, filming, and work-finishing tasks will be performed in-house by the company's microfilming department with film processing and duplication being performed by a service bureau.

TABLE 11   Estimated Cost to Microfilm One Million Pages.

	Cost
A. Equipment	
1. Microfilm camera: 6-month portion of amortized purchase price	$1,500
2. Reader-printer	9,000
3. Equipment stand and chair	1,000
4. Cabinet	300
B. Supplies and Services	
1. Microfilm with processing prepaid: 190 rolls at $18 each	3,420
2. Diazo duplicates: 190 rolls at $16 each	3,040
3. Courier service: 26 weeks at $60 per week	1,560
C. Labor	
1. Document preparation: 1,000 hrs at $9.60/hr	9,600
2. Camera operation: 1,000 hrs at $9.60/hr	9,600
3. Microfilm inspection: 380 hrs at $9.60/hr	3,648
4. Supervision: 100 hrs at $16.70/hr	1,670
D. Other	
1. Camera maintenance contract	1,125
2. Reader-printer maintenance contract	675
3. Document destruction	500
4. Floor space: 200 square feet at $20/square foot for 6 months	2,000
Subtotal	**$48,638**
Contingency	2,432
Total Estimated Cost	**$51,070**

The estimates presented in Table 11 divide all costs into four broad groups: equipment, supplies and services, in-house labor, and miscellaneous. The following assumptions and explanations apply:

1. Documents will be recorded on 215 foot rolls of 16 mm microfilm by a rotary camera purchased for $15,000. The cost estimate presented in Table 11 represents a prorated portion of the camera's purchase price based on the percentage of the camera's total useful life consumed by this project. It is assumed that the company's microfilming department has a continuing need for the rotary camera and will use it for other assignments when this project is completed. At a work throughput rate of 1,000 pages per hour as discussed in Chapter Three, the filming of one million camera-ready pages will require 1,000 hours (six months), based on a single-shift operation. Assuming a useful camera life of five years (sixty months), this microfilming project will consume ten percent of that total. The $1,500 cost estimate consequently represents ten percent of the camera's $15,000 purchase price. For leased or rented equipment, the camera cost estimate would be limited to those payments made during the six months required to complete this microfilming project. Where an organization does not have a continuing need for a microfilm camera, the cost estimate would be based on the camera's purchase price minus its salvage value, for resale or trade-in, following completion of the file conversion. Alternatively, a camera could be rented for the duration of the microfilming project.

2. A 16 mm microfilm reader-printer, purchased for $9,000, will be used for simple inspection tasks during the microfilm conversion and for reference thereafter. An additional $1,000 is budgeted for an equipment stand and a chair for the reader-printer operator.

3. The terminated project files will occupy approximately 190 215 foot rolls of 16 mm microfilm. An additional 190 working copies will be produced, as discussed below. A drawer-type microfilm storage cabinet, with capacity for 400 rolls, will be purchased for $300.

4. Unexposed 16 mm microfilm, with processing prepaid, will be purchased from a service bureau for $18 per 215 foot roll. As noted above, this project will require approximately 190 rolls.

5. Exposed microfilm will be sent to a service bureau for processing. The service bureau will return the processed film on plastic reels, packaged in labeled boxes. A courier service will be used for pick up and delivery. The cost estimate presented in Table 11 assumes that exposed film will be picked up, and processed reels returned, three times a week at a charge of $20 per incident or $60 per week. The project's duration is 26 weeks.

6. The microfilm service bureau will also produce diazo working copies at a cost of $16 per 215 foot roll. Working copies will be delivered by the courier service.

7. The labor cost estimates presented in Table 11 assume that document preparation, filming, and quality control will be performed by entry level clerical employees being paid $14,400 per year plus 25 percent fringe benefits for an effective annual wage of $18,000 ($9.60 per hour based on 1,875 work-hours per year). As noted in the introduction to this chapter, labor costs are subject to considerable regional and local variation, and the wage rates used here may prove too high or too low for specific work environments. The assurance is that different skill levels are required by each of the microfilm production tasks, for example, camera operation and quality control are more difficult than document preparation. However, workers hired at the same wage level can be cross-trained and interchanged to minimize disruptions resulting from absenteeism, alleviate boredom, and improve morale, productivity, and accuracy.

8. Preparation will be limited to work steps required to make the terminated project files camera ready: documents will be removed from folders; staples, paper clips, and other fasteners removed; folded pages will be unfolded; and documents will be stacked for filming. Simple flash targets, containing eye-legible project numbers, will be inserted into the stack to separate individual project files. Following microfilming, documents will be placed in storage containers, pending destruction or other disposition to be discussed below. At a work throughput rate of 1,000 pages per hour, the preparation of one million pages of terminated project files will require 1,000 hours of labor. If source documents must be rearranged or if missing pages must be located, preparation time will be significantly increased.

9. At a work throughput rate of 1,000 pages per hour, camera operation will require 1,000 hours. That throughput estimate, as discussed in Chapter Three, assumes camera-ready documents that will be manually inserted into a rotary camera. The estimate includes time for camera loading, unloading, and related supporting tasks.

10. While the service bureau will perform technical inspections of processed microfilm, additional quality control procedures must be performed in-house. As a minimum, the camera-original microfilm reels and working copies received from the service bureau must be examined to confirm that the correct microforms were returned. Container labels must be checked for correct information, and selected frames examined for legibility. The labor cost estimates presented in Table 11 assume that a total of two hours will be required to inspect each camera-original roll and its associated working copy.

11. The cost estimate for supervisory labor assumes that ten percent of the microfilming department manager's time (approximately 100 hours over a six-month period) will be spent on this project. Among other tasks, the supervisor must establish work schedules for document preparation, camera operation, and inspection; monitor work throughput; prepare exposed microfilm for delivery to the service bureau; receive shipments of processed microfilm and working copies; and approve requests for payment by the service bureau. The cost estimate is based on an annual salary of $25,000 plus 25 percent fringe benefits for an effective annual wage of $31,250 or approximately $16.70 per hour.

12. The cost estimates for annual maintenance contracts for the microfilm camera and reader-printer are based on 15 percent of the equipment's purchase price. In both cases, charges are based on a six month period—the time required to complete the source document conversion. At the end of that time, the cost of the camera maintenance contract ($2,250 per year) will be charged to the next microfilming project for which it is used. The $675 charge represents the six-month cost of a reader-printer maintenance contract costing $1,350 per year. The contract's cost for the remainder of the year will be incorporated in an annual operating cost estimate to be presented below.

13. Source documents must be destroyed on termination of the conversion project to realize the fullest economic benefits of microfilming. The $500 cost estimate for document destruction assumes incineration of one million pages.

14. A floor space charge equivalent to $20 per square foot per year is imposed for a six-month period for 200 square feet of floor space occupied by document preparation, microfilming, and quality control operations.

15. The total estimated cost is increased by approximately five percent to create a contingency fund that will allow for film wastage, required refilming of selected documents, and other events that may

increase the costs delineated above. The resulting budget to convert one million pages of terminated project files to microfilm is approximately $51,070.

As this example indicates, source document microfilming projects typically involve substantial conversion costs which must be carefully evaluated and clearly justified in relation to anticipated benefits. The most common and persuasive type of justification demonstrates that the cost of a proposed micrographic system will be lower than that of any existing alternative system, including—in this case—the paper filing system it is designed to replace. As discussed in Chapter One, microfilming can significantly lower document storage costs. Based on the cost estimate presented in Table 11 and the application parameters outlined, the following discussion quantifies and analyzes the economic benefits associated with source document microfilming projects.

In every organization source document conversions and other proposed microfilming projects must compete with other activities for a necessarily limited amount of resources. In making decisions about the allocation of available funds to particular activities, financial officers and other administrators naturally prefer those projects that promise the most attractive return on investment. The prospects for such a return can be measured in several ways. One of the most common is break-even point analysis. Broadly defined, the break-even point is the period of time, in months or years, at which the accumulated savings associated with a particular activity equal the initial investment. In this example, the microfilming of terminated project files offers potential savings in two areas: (1) a reduction in the amount of floor space required for record storage; and (2) the ability to reuse the filing cabinets in which the paper records were originally stored, thereby avoiding the cost of purchasing an equivalent number of new cabinets. There may also be savings in retrieval time and associated document handling costs, but since this example involves relatively inactive records, the potential for such savings is limited.

TABLE 12   Break-even Point Calculation.

	Cost
Estimated cost of microfilm conversion (from Table 9)	**$51,070**
Less replacement value of 85 file cabinets at $300 each	**−25,500**
Net cost of conversion to be recovered through floor space savings	**$25,570**
Divide by annual value of net reduction in floor space: 460 square feet at $20/square foot	**$9,200**
Break-even point	**2.78 yrs**

Given floor space savings and the avoidance of filing equipment purchases as cost reduction parameters, the break-even point for a microfilm conversion project can be calculated by the formula:

$$B = \frac{C - (F \times P)}{S \times V}$$

where:

B =   the break-even point in years;
C =   the estimated cost of a microfilm conversion project;
F =   the number of filing cabinets that will be emptied and available for other uses following filming;
P =   the average replacement price of such cabinets, if purchased new;
S =   the amount of floor space, in square feet, that will be freed for other uses following filming; and
V =   the value of the floor space (annual cost per square foot).

Applying this formula, Table 12 presents a simple method of calculating the break-even point for a microfilm conversion costing $51,070, as previously calculated in Table 11. The calculation assumes that 85 file cabinets, with a replacement value of $300 each, will be emptied and available for other uses following filming. The estimated cost of conversion is first reduced by deducting the replacement value of the file cabinets. As noted in the preceding application description, some of the filing cabinets will be used by the technical information center to store current project files; the remainder will be distributed to other departments as new cabinets are requisitioned. In either case, the company experiences a cost avoidance, and a substantial portion of the microfilm conversion costs are immediately recovered. The break-even point—at which the accumulated savings equal the initial investment in conversion costs—is calculated by dividing the net cost of the conversion by the annual value of released floor space. As previously discussed, the 85 cabinets occupy 510 square feet of floor space valued at $20 per square foot. It is assumed that their micrographic replacement, consisting of a storage cabinet and a reader-printer workstation, will occupy fifty square feet, yielding a net floor space reduction of 460 square feet with an average value of $9,200. The resulting break-even point is approximately 2.78 years from completion of the microfilming project.

As this example indicates, break-even point calculation yields a numerical result that is only meaningful in a specific organizational context. While a short payback period is invariably preferable, every organization establishes acceptable break-even points for projects which it must fund. In most instances, microfilm conversion projects with break-even points shorter than three years are considered sound business investments. Some organizations consider a five-year break-even point acceptable. In unusual situations—when interest rates are very high, for example—a payback period of two years or even less may be required for project approval.

While the break-even point method of cost justification is widely used, critics correctly note that its exclusive emphasis on the payback period ignores savings that occur after the break-even point is reached. For that reason, break-even point analysis is typically supplemented by a multiyear cost comparison that indicates accumulated savings over some predetermined period of time. The break-even point calculation presented in Table 12 provides a simple, fast method of determining the probable cost-effectiveness of a given microfilming project.

TABLE 13   Annual Cost Calculation: Paper vs. Microfilm System.

Year	Paper System	Microfilm System
1	$35,700	$53,420
2	11,016	2,430
3	11,897	2,516
4	12,849	2,610
5	13,877	2,710
6	14,987	17,569
7	16,186	3,687
8	17,481	3,814
9	18,879	3,951
10	20,390	4,099

Providing a more formal and detailed cost justification analysis, Table 13 compares annual costs associated with the maintenance of one million pages of terminated project files in paper form and on microfilm. The cost of the paper system includes $25,500 for the purchase of 85 additional filing cabinets for use by the technical information center and other departments within the organization. As previously explained, that expense would be avoided if the files were microfilmed and the occupied cabinets released for other uses. The floor space required for document storage totals 510 square feet in the paper filing system and fifty square feet in the microfilm system. In both cases, floor space costs are assumed to increase by eight percent per year over the ten-year period. The microfilm system cost estimate includes $14,000 for the purchase of a replacement reader-printer in the sixth year. It also includes an annual allocation for reader-printer maintenance contracts based on fifteen percent of the equipment's purchase price. Reader-printer supply costs, assumed to be equivalent to photocopying supply costs in a paper filing system, are omitted from this analysis.

Indicating the cost savings ignored by break-even point analysis, Table 14 summarizes annual cumulative costs associated with paper

TABLE 14   Annual Cumulative Cost Comparison.

Year	Paper System	Microfilm System	Cumulative Savings
1	$ 35,700	$ 53,420	– $17,720
2	46,716	55,850	– 9,134
3	58,613	58,366	247
4	71,462	60,976	10,486
5	85,339	63,687	21,653
6	100,326	81,256	19,071
7	116,513	84,943	31,570
8	133,994	88,757	45,237
9	152,873	92,708	60,166
10	173,263	96,807	76,456

filing and microfilm systems. It is based on the annual cost calculations presented in Table 13. Note that savings begin in the third year when the values in the last column change from negative to positive, the break-even point having been reached near the end of that year. Estimated savings over the ten-year period total almost $75,000 or about $7,500 per year. This represents an annual return of almost 17 percent on the $44,430 investment required to complete the microfilm conversion.

While the preceding approach to cost justification goes beyond break-even point analysis in presenting an estimate of savings over a predetermined period of time, simple multiyear cost comparisons are sometimes criticized because they fail to consider the declining value of money expended in the later years of a system's operation. According to the present value method of accounting, the preceding cost comparisons need to be adjusted by multiplying each of the cost estimates by a discount factor to compensate for uneven cash expenditures experienced in the two systems. The present value method of cost analysis, sometimes called the discounted cash flow method, has the effect of penalizing those methodologies that require an initial expenditure of funds to convert information from one medium to another. Many organizations require present value calculations as a final step in cost justification analysis.

The present value method is easily applied. Multiyear cost comparisons are prepared in the manner described above, and a predetermined discount factor is multiplied by the estimated annual costs. In most organizations, financial planners and decision makers have selected a discount factor to be used for such analyses. Present value tables, similar to the one presented in Table 15, can be found in many accounting textbooks. For microcomputer users, present value functions are supported by many spreadsheet software packages. Once the appropriate discount factor is determined, each of the annual cost

TABLE 15   Excerpt from Present Value Table.

Year	Discount Factor										
	9%	10%	11%	12%	13%	14%	15%	16%	17%	18%	19%
1	1.0000	1.0000	1.0000	1.0000	1.0000	1.0000	1.0000	1.0000	1.0000	1.0000	1.0000
2	0.9174	0.9091	0.9009	0.8929	0.8850	0.8772	0.8696	0.8621	0.8547	0.8475	0.8403
3	0.8417	0.8264	0.8116	0.7972	0.7831	0.7695	0.7561	0.7432	0.7305	0.7182	0.7062
4	0.7722	0.7513	0.7312	0.7118	0.6931	0.6750	0.6575	0.6407	0.6244	0.6086	0.5934
5	0.7084	0.6830	0.6587	0.6355	0.6133	0.5921	0.5718	0.5523	0.5336	0.5158	0.4987
6	0.6499	0.6209	0.5935	0.5674	0.5428	0.5194	0.4972	0.4761	0.4561	0.4371	0.4190
7	0.5963	0.5645	0.5346	0.5066	0.4803	0.4556	0.4323	0.4104	0.3898	0.3704	0.3521
8	0.5470	0.5132	0.4817	0.4523	0.4251	0.3996	0.3759	0.3538	0.3332	0.3139	0.2959
9	0.5019	0.4665	0.4339	0.4039	0.3762	0.3506	0.3269	0.3030	0.2848	0.2660	0.2487
10	0.4604	0.4241	0.3909	0.3606	0.3329	0.3075	0.2843	0.2630	0.2434	0.2255	0.2090

estimates previously presented in Table 13 must be multiplied by the discounted value of a dollar for that year. The results, for the example under discussion here, are presented in Tables 16 and 17. In this case, the present value approach to cost analysis results in an extended break-even point and a somewhat smaller estimate of savings for the microfilm system over a ten-year period.

TABLE 16 Annual Cost Calculation: Paper vs. Microfilm System (Present Value Method).

Year	10% Discount Factor	Paper System	Microfilm System
1	1.0000	$35,700	$53,420
2	0.9091	10,015	2,209
3	0.8264	9,832	2,080
4	0.7513	9,654	1,961
5	0.6830	9,478	1,851
6	0.6209	9,306	10,909
7	0.5645	9,137	2,081
8	0.5132	8,971	1,957
9	0.4665	8,807	1,843
10	0.4241	8,647	1,738

TABLE 17 Annual Cumulative Cost Comparison (Present Value Method).

Year	Paper System	Microfilm System	Cumulative Savings
1	$ 35,700	$ 53,420	– $17,720
2	45,715	55,629	– 9,914
3	55,547	57,709	– 2,162
4	65,200	59,669	5,531
5	74,678	61,521	13,157
6	83,984	72,429	11,554
7	93,121	74,511	18,610
8	102,092	76,468	25,624
9	110,899	78,311	32,588
10	119,546	80,049	39,497

Example 2: Microfilming Active Records

The preceding example confirmed the potential for filing equip-ment and floor space savings when micrographic technology is applied to inactive records. As discussed in Chapter Six, computer-assisted retrieval (CAR) systems simplify file maintenance and expedite the retrieval of microimages in applications involving active records. In so doing, they can significantly reduce labor, space, and related costs associated with paper-based document storage and retrieval systems. To illustrate a CAR system's ability to reduce file maintenance costs in active records management applications, assume that the customer service department of a consumer products company maintains records pertaining to orders received from authorized distributors, wholesalers, department stores, and other customers. Customer service representatives use the records to answer telephone inquiries about the status of particular orders. The department's existing order information system is paper-based. Individual order files are arranged alphabetically by customer name. Records for individual customers are subdivided by order number. Each order file consists of some combination of the customer's purchase order, order cancellations and modifications, order confirmation forms, invoices, shipping papers, and correspondence. About sixty percent of the documents are received from customers; the remainder are produced internally in response to customer orders or inquiries. Thirty percent of order-related documents have multiple pages or attachments.

Approximately 80,000 orders are processed annually. Each order generates an average of 15 letter-size sheets of paper for a total annual file size of 1.2 million pages. Files for orders received in the most recent 18 months are stored in the customer service office where they occupy 165 four-drawer, vertical-style cabinets, each with a replacement value of $300. The cabinets occupy 1,260 square feet of floor space valued at $20 per square foot. Older files, packed in cubic foot containers, are stored off-site in a corporate records center for an additional five years. Each year, 1,300 cubic feet of customer order files are transferred to offsite storage. As a further complication, approximately sixty percent of the files are replicated in the company's shipping department where they are stored in sixty cabinets occupying 450 square feet of floor space. Those files are discarded six months following shipment of an order. Files in both locations are maintained by approximately 5.5 clerical persons who are responsible for folder preparation, labeling, filing, refiling, and the inventorying and packing of records for shipment to offsite storage.

Like other information management technologies, micrographic implementations involve a combination of start-up and ongoing costs. As the phrase suggests, start-up costs are incurred as a precondition of system implementation. Examples include the purchase prices of cameras, processors, duplicators, readers, reader-printers, storage cabinets, and other equipment to be used by in-house microfilm production facilities and reference workstations. Start-up costs are typically fixed in amount. While equipment prices may vary considerably from one device to another, depending on the capabilities and features of a particular model, the cost of a given camera, reader-printer, or other device will not vary with the amount of work it must perform. Whether a $15,000 microfilm camera will operate continuously on multiple shifts or sit idle for much of the workday, its price is unaffected.

Ongoing costs—those associated with the day-to-day operation of a given micrographic system—may be fixed or variable in nature. Examples of fixed ongoing costs include monthly payments for micrographics equipment that is leased or rented rather than purchased, and prices of maintenance contracts for customer-owned micrographics equipment. Variable costs depend on specific events for their occurrence and amount. Examples of variable ongoing costs encountered in micrographic implementations include the cost of unexposed microfilm and labor charges associated with microform production and use. Whether fixed or variable, ongoing costs are typically estimated on an annual basis.

When preparing a budget for a proposed micrographic implementation, estimated start-up and ongoing costs are often separately enumerated to differentiate capital investment requirements from costs that will be incurred over time. To simplify comparisons with other information management methodologies, however, start-up and ongoing costs associated with a proposed micrographic implementation may be combined in an annualized estimate of operating costs. The general formula for such annualized cost estimates is:

$$A = \frac{S}{U} + O$$

where:

A = the estimated annualized operating cost of a proposed system;

S = estimated start-up costs;

U = the projected useful life (in years) of system components for which start-up costs are incurred; and

O = estimated annual ongoing costs.

Essentially, this formula amortizes estimated start-up costs over a period of years equal to the anticipated useful life of system components and adds the result to the total of estimated annual ongoing costs. In some cases, start-up costs are amortized individually to allow for differences in the useful life of various components.

For the hypothetical example discussed here, cost effectiveness analysis involves a comparison of annual operating costs for the existing paper-based document filing system and a proposed CAR alternative. Applying the general formula presented above, Table 18 estimates the annual operating costs associated with the department's paper-based filing system. Filing labor costs assume that entry-level clerical workers will be paid $14,400 per year plus 25 percent fringe benefits for an effective annual wage of $18,000 ($9.60 per hour based on 1,875 work-hours per year). Supervision requires ten percent of the time of an of-

TABLE 18   Estimated Annual Cost of Paper Filing System.

	Cost
Filing cabinets: 225 at $300 each; 10 year amortization	$6,750
File folders and labels: 80,000 at 12 cents each	9,600
Clerical labor: 5.5 persons at $18,000 each, including fringe benefits	99,000
Supervision: 10 percent of supervisor's salary, including fringe benefits	3,125
Floor space: 1,700 square feet at $20 per square foot per year	34,000
Containers for off-site records storage 1,300 per year at 75 cents each	975
Off-site records storage: 6,500 cubic feet at $2 per cubic foot per year	13,000
Estimated Annual Cost	**$166,450**

fice manager being paid $25,000 plus 25 percent fringe benefits for an effective annual wage of $31,250 or approximately $16.70 per hour. As previously noted, labor costs vary considerably from location to location and organization to organization. The wage rates used here may consequently require upward or downward adjustment for specific work environments.

The replacement value of 180 filing cabinets is amortized over a ten-year useful life. Filing supply costs assume the purchase of conventional folders and self-adhesive labels at a substantial quantity discount. Each year, as previously noted, 1,300 feet of customer service files are transferred to an offsite record center where they are retained for five years. The annual cost estimate for offsite storage is based on charge of $2.00 per container per year. At any given time, 6,500 cubic feet of customer service files are stored offsite.

A CAR implementation for this hypothetical application will be based on components and work steps previously delineated in Chapter Six. As an alternative to conventional filing methodologies, CAR software will support the indexing and selective retrieval of document images recorded on blip-encoded microfilm packaged in 16 mm cartridges. Documents will be microfilmed on receipt by the customer service department and indexed by date, customer name, customer purchase order number, internal purchase order number, and a code representing the document type (purchase order, invoice, correspondence, etc.). Index data will be stored on magnetic disks for online access by retrieval workstations equipped with video display terminals and blip-counting reader-printers. Table 19 estimates annual operating costs for such a CAR implementation. The following assumptions and explanations apply:

1. The customer service department will purchase a minicomputer-based turnkey CAR system including computer hardware with sufficient disk storage space to accommodate four years of index data, indexing and retrieval software, one rotary camera, three data entry terminals, and two retrieval workstations equipped with

TABLE 19   Estimated Annual Cost of CAR System.

	Cost
A. Equipment	
1. Turnkey CAR system: $100,000; 4 year amortization	$25,000
2. Microfilm storage cabinets: $1,000; 10 year amortization	100
3. Office furniture	500
B. Supplies and Services	
1. Microfilm with processing prepaid: 225 rolls at $18 each	4,050
2. Diazo working copies: 2 sets, 450 rolls at $16 each	7,200
3. Cartridge loading: 450 rolls at $1.40 each	630
4. Delivery service at $100 per week	5,200
C. Labor	
1. Document preparation: 1,200 hrs at $9.60/hr	11,520
2. Camera operation: 1,200 hrs at $9.60/hr	11,520
3. Microfilm inspection: 500 hrs at $9.60/hr	4,800
4. Index data entry: 3,360 hrs at $12/hr	40,320
5. Supervision: 10 percent of supervisor's salary, including fringe benefits	3,125
D. Other	
1. Maintenance contract for turnkey CAR system	15,000
2. Floor space for film production and retrieval operations: 300 square feet at $20/square foot	6,000
3. Document destruction	600
4. Off-site storage for camera original microfilm: 30 cubic feet at $2 each	60
Estimated Annual Cost	**$135,625**

video display terminals and blip-counting reader-printers. The microfilm camera and data entry terminals will be installed in the customer service department. One of the retrieval workstations will be installed in customer service department; the other workstation, with a duplicate set of microfilm cartridges, will be installed in the company's shipping department where duplicate paper files are currently being maintained. To obtain an annual equivalent cost, the CAR system's purchase price of $100,000 is amortized over a four-year useful life.

2. Two storage cabinets, to be installed in the customer service office and the shipping department, will be purchased for $500 each and their cost amortized over a ten-year useful life. The equipment cost estimate includes an additional annual allocation of $500 for work area furniture.

3. The annual accumulation of customer service documents will occupy approximately 225 215 foot rolls of 16 mm microfilm. Documents will be prepared and filmed in-house. As discussed in the preceding example, unexposed 16 mm microfilm will be purchased, with processing prepaid, for $18 per 215-foot roll. Following exposure, the film will be sent to a service bureau for processing, technical inspection, and duplication. The service bureau will return the processed camera original film on plastic reels, packaged in marked boxes. A courier service will be used for pick-up and delivery. The cost estimate

presented in Table 18 assumes that exposed film will be picked up daily, taken to the service bureau for overnight processing, and returned by the delivery service the next day. Pickup and delivery costs will total $100 per week.

4. The microfilm service bureau will produce two sets of diazo working copies at a cost of $16 per 215 foot roll. One of the sets will be maintained in the customer service office; the other will be used by the shipping department where it will replace their duplicate paper file. The service bureau will package both sets of working copies in ANSI/AIIM standard microfilm cartridges.

5. The labor cost estimates presented in Table 19 assume that document preparation, filming, and in-house inspections will be performed by entry-level clerical employees being paid $14,400 per year plus 25 percent fringe benefits for an effective annual wage of $18,000 ($9.60 per hour based on 1,875 work-hours per year). As discussed in the preceding example, individual workers will be cross-trained and their tasks interchanged to minimize disruptions resulting from absenteeism, alleviate boredom, and improve morale, productivity, and accuracy.

6. Documents will be filmed and indexed in order of their arrival at the CAR system. Preparation will be limited to those work steps required to make source documents camera ready: staples, paper clips, and other fasteners removed; folded pages unfolded; and documents stacked for filming. Depending on the equipment and work steps used, documents may be indexed before, during, or after filming. Once filmed and indexed, customer service records will be placed in storage containers, pending destruction or other disposition to be discussed below. At a work throughput rate of 1,000 pages per hour, the preparation of 1.2 million pages of customer service files will require 1,200 hours of labor.

7. At a work throughput rate of 1,000 pages per hour, rotary camera operation will require 1,200 hours, including time for camera loading, unloading, and related supporting tasks.

8. The service bureau will perform technical inspections of processed microfilm. In-house quality control procedures will be limited to inspection of selected frames for legibility and examination of cartridge and box labels for correct information. The labor cost estimates presented in Table 19 assume that a total of two hours will be required to inspect each camera-original roll and its associated working copies.

9. As noted above, approximately thirty percent of the customer order documents created or received each year contain multiple pages or attachments. The annual total of indexable items is 840,000 items. At an average of forty characters of index data per item, the annual data entry workload is 33.6 million keystrokes. Assuming a throughput rate of 10,000 keystrokes per hour by operators working at video display terminals and typing information into specially formatted screens, the

required data entry time is 3,360 hours per year. The cost estimate further assumes that data entry personnel will be paid $18,000 per year plus 25 percent fringe benefits for an effective annual wage of $22,500 or approximately $12.00 per hour.

10. The cost estimate for supervisory labor assumes that ten percent of an office manager's time will be spent on this project. Among other tasks, the supervisor must establish work schedules for document preparation, camera operation, inspection, and data entry; monitor work throughput; prepare exposed microfilm for delivery to the service bureau; receive shipments of processed film and working copies; and approve requests for payment by the service bureau. The cost estimate is based on an annual salary of $25,000 plus 25 percent fringe benefits for an effective annual wage of $31,250 or approximately $16.70 per hour.

11. The estimated annual maintenance contract charge for CAR system hardware and software is based on fifteen percent of the system's purchase price.

12. To realize the fullest economic benefits of microfilming, the customer service documents must be destroyed following filming and indexing. The cost estimate for document destruction assumes incineration of 1.2 million pages per year.

13. A floor space charge equivalent to $20 per square foot per year is imposed for 300 square feet of floor space occupied by CAR system components and microfilm storage cabinets. The cost estimate includes a small additional charge for offsite storage of approximately thirty cubic feet of microfilm transferred from the customer service department. As with the paper documents from which they were created, these microforms will be retained for five years in the offsite location then destroyed.

In this hypothetical example, a CAR implementation reduces annual operating costs by $31,625—the equivalent of 1.8 clerical personnel—when compared to a paper-based filing system. While floor space reductions play an important role in these savings, this example illustrates a CAR system's ability to reduce file maintenance costs when compared to a paper-based information storage and retrieval system.

Example 3: COM vs. Paper Printers

As discussed in Chapter Three, computer-output microfilm offers a functionally attractive and potentially cost-effective alternative to paper printouts for reports, lists, and other computer-generated documents. Like their source document counterparts, COM-generated microforms minimize filing equipment purchases and reduce storage space requirements when compared to paper reports. A single 1:48 COM-generated microfiche, as previously discussed, can store 270 printout-size pages on a 105 by 148 mm piece of film that occupies less than one-sixth the area of a single 11 by 14 inch sheet of computer printout paper. A desktop tray file of COM-generated microfiche can contain the equivalent of many storage racks or filing cabinets filled with paper printouts. Compared to bulky paper printouts, COM generated microforms are more easily handled, referenced, and distributed. As a significant advantage in computing installations plagued by output bottlenecks, COM production equipment is faster than many paper printers, and, in certain situations, COM can significantly reduce output production costs.

Providing a more specific illustration of this potential, Table 20 compares paper and COM production costs for a 250-page, computer-generated budget report that is printed 15 times a month and distributed to twenty offices. The following assumptions and explanations apply:

1. The comparison assumes that paper reports will be produced on four-ply carbon interleaved forms by an impact printer capable of a sustained output rate of 1,000 lines per minute—the equivalent of 1,000 pages per hour, assuming that each 11 by 14 inch page contains sixty lines of text. A single printing will require 15 minutes, and the job must be executed five times to produce twenty distribution copies.

2. The printer is operated by an institutional or commercial computing center or service bureau at a charge of $50 per hour,

TABLE 20   COM vs. Paper Printer Costs.

	Cost
A. Paper Printer Costs	
1. Printing time: 1.25 hrs at $50 hr	$62.50
2. Paper: 1,250 pages at $35 per thousand	43.75
3. Binders: 20 at $1.25 each	25.00
4. Cost per update	$131.25
5. Monthly update frequency	× 15
6. Monthly printing cost	$1,968.75
B. COM Costs	
1. Print tape preparation	$15.00
2. Service bureau charges	
a. Master fiche: 3 cents per frame	8.10
b. Distribution copies: 20 at 25 cents each	5.00
c. Pickup and delivery	15.00
3. Cost per update	43.10
4. Monthly update frequency	× 15
5. Monthly COM production costs	$646.50
6. Reader amortization	122.25
7. Reader maintenance allowance	18.35
8. Monthly COM costs	$787.10
Monthly Savings with COM	**$1,181.65**
Annual Savings with COM	**$14,179.80**

including decollating and bursting of output. The entire printing job will require 1.25 hours.

3. Four-ply paper is priced at $35.00 per thousand sheets or 3.5 cents per page. The five print runs necessary to produce twenty distribution copies will require 1,250 pages.

4. Prior to distribution, the twenty paper copies are inserted into labeled pressboard binders at a cost of $1.25 each, including labor.

5. COM-generated microfiche will be produced in the 48/270 standard format by a microfilm service bureau from customer-supplied print-image tapes. The organization's computing center charges $15 to produce a print-image tape. The service bureau is equipped with an intelligent COM recorder that will reformat print records for microfilm output in a manner described in Chapter Four.

6. The service bureau charges three cents per frame to create the master COM microfiche. Partial microfiche are billed at the rate for 270 frames, hence the $8.10 charge in this example.

7. Vesicular working copies are priced at 25 cents per microfiche. This application will require twenty working copies. While the COM recording and duplicating costs used in this example are realistic, they are subject to regional and local variations. Some service bureaus, for example, may charge more for the preparation of COM master microfiche but less for working copies.

8. At $646.50, the estimated monthly tape production and service bureau charges for COM updates is lower than the cost of print paper alone, but COM-generated microfiche require display devices that have no counterpart in a system based on paper printouts. Twenty microfiche readers, each equipped with 11 by 11 inch screens and a 1:36 magnifying lens, are purchased for $200 each. The total cost of $4,000 is conservatively amortized over 36 months for a monthly equivalent charge of $122.25. The microfiche readers have a much longer useful life, but—in a volatile field like data processing—changing application requirements may render them inappropriate after three years. An additional $18.35 per month (approximately 15 percent of the readers' cost) is allocated for lamp replacement and other equipment maintenance.

In this example, COM's substantial production cost advantage—almost $1,200 per month—is a factor of report length, frequency of updating, and the number of required working copies. As a general rule, COM will offer substantial savings in production costs when compared to paper printouts in applications that involve long reports produced in multiple copies and updated frequently. While the specific length, distribution, and frequency requirements necessary to realize such savings will depend on local cost factors, COM will usually enjoy a economic advantage over line printers for reports that are longer than fifty pages, produced in more than five copies, and updated at least once per month. As the length of reports and distribution lists or update frequency increase, COM's cost advantage will increase as well. The savings cited here apply to production costs only. When compared to paper printouts, COM-generated reports also offer potential for significant reductions in filing equipment and supply purchases, storage space, and retrieval time at individual distribution points.

While the calculations presented in Table 20 compare the cost of COM and line printer output, COM production costs also compare favorably with page printer costs. In the example given here, a COM system produces 75,000 pages (twenty copies of a 250-page report produced 15 times) for an estimated monthly cost of $774.27 or slightly more than one cent per page, including display equipment amortization and maintenance costs. In page printer installations, supply (paper and toner) costs alone approach, or in some cases exceed, one cent per page.

8 Interfaces With Other Technologies

As DESCRIBED IN preceding chapters, micrographic systems can significantly reduce storage space requirements, speed retrieval, simplify file maintenance, facilitate document distribution, provide effective vital records protection, and generally reduce the cost of managing information in a variety of work environments. While micrographics was originally conceived as a self-contained, standalone image management technology, micrographic products and services can be incorporated in so-called "integrated" information systems. For purposes of this discussion, an integrated information system is one that combines two or more technologies to accomplish a given information processing task. Typically, such systems interface computer, image processing, and telecommunication components. By satisfying information management requirements that exceed the capabilities of a single technology, integrated information systems extend the range of automated information processing and promote their implementation.

Although they have been widely publicized since the mid-1980s, integrated information system concepts are at least a quarter of a century old, and micrographics-based configurations were among the earliest implementations. CAR systems that combine computer processing of index records with micrographic storage of document images, for example, date from the 1960s. Through the mid-1970s, however, computer-based data processing was widely promoted as the only state-of-the-art approach to automated information management. Dismissing micrographics, facsimile, and other technologies as transitional vestiges of the "pre-computer" period, many data processing specialists believed that those problems which were not readily and

177

immediately solvable by computerization alone would eventually yield to computer solutions, given the rapid development of electronic technology.

Since the late 1970s, however, information management professionals—including many computer specialists—have increasingly adopted a broader, more receptive view of other technologies. Much of the recent interest in integrated information systems stems from the data processing industry's failure to successfully address certain problems associated with computerization. As an example, the price/performance characteristics of online computer storage media and devices have improved continuously and dramatically over the past two decades, but the cost of converting information to machine-readable, computer-processable form remains high. Similarly, there has been little progress in the development of archivally stable computer storage media. Proponents of integrated information systems recognize that such limitations can be successfully addressed by a coordinated combination of complementary technologies, each designed to address a specific facet of the problem.

The so-called computer/micrographics interface— represented by the CAR systems described in Chapters Six—reflects this approach to information systems analysis. While online retrieval systems provide a convenient and powerful alternative to paper-based information management methodologies, computer-based systems rarely replicate the entire content of source documents. In most applications, the complete conversion of source document content to the machine-readable, character-coded form cannot be justified from the standpoint of either data-entry labor or online storage costs. As an additional constraint, certain applications require the preservation of a document's appearance as well as its content. Source documents, or photographic images of them, must sometimes be retained for legal reasons, even if their information content is entirely stored in computer-processable data bases.

CAR systems combine microform-based document storage with computer-based indexing. Thus, CAR systems provide a technically and economically viable approach to information management problems that computers alone cannot successfully address. CAR systems simplify data entry and online storage by limiting those activities to index data rather than entire documents. Microfilming a document takes less time and is far cheaper than entering the document contents by key, and the cost of microphotographic materials is lower than that of computer storage media. Preserving both the content and appearance of source documents, microforms—as previously discussed in Chapter One—are a legally acceptable substitute for paper records,

While interfaces between micrographics and data processing are well established, micrographic products and services can also be effectively combined with other information processing technologies and methodologies. This chapter examines actual and potential interfaces between micrographics and facsimile, electronic document imaging systems, optical character recognition, and word processing. It describes the most important characteristics of such integrated implementations and summarizes their most important advantages.

Microfacsimile

Facsimile, or fax, is an electronic messaging technology that transmits document images to remote locations via telephone lines or other communication facilities. From the hardware standpoint, a typical facsimile system includes a scanner and a receiver. The scanner converts a document to a pattern of digital or analog signals suitable for transmission over telephone lines, and the receiver decodes the signals and reconstructing the document image as a paper copy or facsimile, for which the technology is named. In most cases, transmission and reception capabilities are combined in a single unit called a facsimile transceiver. Such devices have been commercially available since the mid-1960s. While they have been routinely used in business applications since the mid-1970s, market acceptance increased dramatically in the 1980s, largely due to the development of standards for equipment compatibility and the introduction of attractively priced products capable of transmitting a letter-size page over telephone lines in less than one minute.

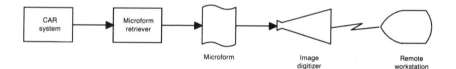

FIGURE 57.   Interrelationship of components in microfacsimile installation.

Conventional facsimile equipment is designed to transmit images of paper documents. Microfacsimile systems, as their name implies, can accept, transmit, and reproduce images from source document or COM-generated microforms. In a simple, "indirect" approach to microimage transmission, a reader-printer can produce paper enlargements for input to an ordinary facsimile transceiver. However, the microfacsimile method can prove time-consuming and labor-intensive in applications where large numbers of microimages are involved. As an additional constraint, some reader-printer copies may lack the sharpness and contrast required for satisfactory facsimile reproduction.

True microfacsimile systems—variously termed microimage transmission systems or videomicrographic systems—permit the direct
scanning of microimages. The microimages may be recorded on 16
mm or 35 mm roll microfilm, microfiche, aperture cards, or other
microforms produced by source document microphotography or COM
recorders. Regardless of the source, a microfacsimile system converts
microimages to digital form for transmission to remote display or
printing devices.

The accompanying diagram depicts the interrelationship of
computer, micrographic, and telecommunication components in a
typical microfacsimile installation. While specific components will
necessarily vary from one implementation to another, microfacsimile
configurations include an automated microform storage and retrieval
unit, an image scanner/transmitter, a receiving unit, and communications facilities. Rather than operating as a standalone technology,
microfacsimile capabilities are invariably implemented in the context
of a CAR system that identifies microimages which meet specified
search parameters. While conventional CAR systems rely on manual
extraction of microforms stored in filing cabinets or other containers,
microfacsimile systems feature automated microform retrievers.
Operating under computer control, an automated retriever will select
a microfilm cartridge, microfiche, or aperture card identified by an
index search; locate a microimage specified by CAR software; and
activate a scanner which converts the microimage to digital form for
transmission to a remote workstation.

A microfacsimile scanner combines the capabilities of a microdensitometer and an image digitizer. It divides a microimage into a
series of horizontal lines, each of which is subdivided into small
scannable areas called picture elements or pixels. The scanner measures
light from successively encountered pixels to determine whether it
exceeds some pre-established threshold value. If it does, the pixel is
considered white and is encoded as either a one or a zero bit; otherwise, it is judged to be black and is encoded as the opposite bit value.
The resulting digital signal may be routed to processing circuitry for
enhancement and/or compression prior to transmission. When
microforms contain images of photographs or other half-tone
documents, more elaborate multibit digitization schemes can be used
to represent gray-scale information, although such requirements have
rarely been encountered in microfacsimile implementations.

While conventional facsimile systems usually rely on the public
telephone network to transmit document images over long distances,
most microfacsimile implementations are designed for local area
network installations. In a typical configuration, a microform retriever
and scanner are located in a central file area, and digitized document
images are transmitted to decentralized workstations located within
the same building or office complex. Coaxial cable is generally utilized

FIGURE 58. Bit-mapped video monitor.

as a high speed communication link. Depending on the configuration, a microimage of a letter-size page may be transmitted in as little as two or three seconds. In most cases, digitized document images are initially transferred to a magnetic disk that serves as a temporary buffer to facilitate retransmission. In such situations, a workstation operator can browse through the buffer, thereby minimizing or eliminating rescanning for documents that must be redisplayed.

At the receiving location, digitized microimages are usually displayed on a high-resolution, bit-mapped video monitor. By selectively illuminating or darkening screen areas in a manner that conforms to the transmitted pattern of light and dark picture elements, such devices reconstruct scanned microimages, displaying them as a facsimile enlargements. Most microfacsimile retrieval stations are also equipped with laser printers for hardcopy output. Alternatively, digitized microimages may be transmitted directly to conventional facsimile receivers which will reproduce them as paper copies. The technical feasibility of microform output—in which the received document images are recorded on microfilm, microfiche, or aperture cards— has been demonstrated in several microfacsimile installations. A graphics-type COM recorder capable of reproducing digitized images serves as the output device in such implementations. As a potential constraint, however, delays associated with microfilm processing can defeat the purpose of high-speed microimage transmission.

While microfacsimile is often discussed as a new records management technology, experimental microimage transmission systems were implemented in the late 1950s, and operational installations date from the early 1960s. These early microfacsimile implementations typically employed one-of-a-kind devices developed for specific applications in large corporations and government agencies. While they demonstrated the technical feasibility of scanning and transmitting microimages, none of them led to commercially viable products.

Through the mid-1970s, the limited performance, unreliability, and relatively high cost of conventional facsimile equipment did little to stimulate interest in related document transmission technologies. While prototype microfacsimile products were routinely demonstrated at micrographics conferences and related trade shows, prospective customers were often confused about the technology's viability and availability. Product availability aside, the potential market for microfacsimile systems has historically been limited by the ease with which microforms can be duplicated for distribution to remote locations in anticipation of need. Microform collections can be inexpensively duplicated for decentralized storage at multiple locations. This option serves as an alternative to maintaining a centralized collection of microimages to be transmitted to remote workstations on demand. As a further impediment to microfacsimile's acceptance, the information industry obscured the importance of microfacsimile and other document-oriented technologies by emphasizing computer-based data storage and retrieval systems in the early-to-mid-1970s. During the late 1970s, however, some significant changes in information processing technology and information management practices led to renewed interest in microimage transmission. In particular, an intense interest in the productivity of office workers promoted an awareness of the importance of documents as information carriers, accompanied by a growing concern about the time wasted in document retrieval and dissemination. A number of information specialists, accustomed to centralized data processing operations, advocated similar centralization of document storage, retrieval, and distribution activities. At the same time, significant improvements in conventional facsimile products—especially the introduction of sub-minute digital transceivers—promoted user awareness and acceptance of document transmission technologies. New developments in communications technology—including the proliferation of terrestrial microwave, satellite, and coaxial cable facilities—created the infrastructure of wide-band linkages required for high-speed, high-resolution microimage transmission. Finally, the growing size of many microform files increased the cost of conventional duplication and distribution methodologies in some large-scale micrographic installations.

During the late 1970s and early 1980s, a number of ambitious microfacsimile systems were custom-developed by systems integrator and information management consulting firms for large-scale document storage and retrieval applications in corporations and government agencies. Several of those implementations have been widely publicized in information management publications. During the same period, several CAR system vendors began offering microimage transmission as an optional capability. Since the mid-1980s, several manufacturers have introduced document storage and retrieval systems that combine electronic document imaging and microfacsimile components, and such hybrid configurations are likely to dominate future microfacsimile implementations. Their characteristics and capabilities are described in the following section.

Micrographics and Electronic Document Imaging

Broadly defined, an electronic document imaging system is a computer-based hardware and software configuration that stores digitized document images and a supporting data base of character-coded index information for online, on-demand retrieval. As the accompanying flowchart indicates, electronic document imaging systems employ CAR-like document management methodologies. The following explanations apply:

1. As a preparatory work step common to all computer-based document indexing and retrieval systems, an information systems analyst or other application developer must determine index categories and establish procedures for identifying index values appropriate to those categories. Once index values are assigned, source documents must be prepared for input by removing staples, paper clips, and other fasteners.

2. Digitized document images are created in a manner described in the preceding section. The counterpart of a CAR system's microfilm camera, is the scanner which is also called an image digitizer or a document digitizer. Its function is to divide a document into a series scannable pixels. Using a solid-state array or other photosensitive component, the scanner measures the amount of light reflected by successively encountered pixels and transmits a corresponding electrical signal to image processing circuitry which converts it to digital codes. In the simplest and most widely used approach to document digitization, pixels that reflect light in excess of some specified amount are considered white and are encoded as either a one or a zero bit. Where the amount of reflected light is lower than the predetermined threshold amount, the scanned pixels are considered black and are represented by the opposite bit value. Depending on their relative lightness or darkness, gray pixels are encoded as either white or black. For effective digitization of photographs, some scanners—as noted above—employ multibit coding schemes to represent individual pixels. A four-bit coding scheme, for example, can represent 16 shades of gray, while an eight-bit coding scheme can represent 256 gray shades.

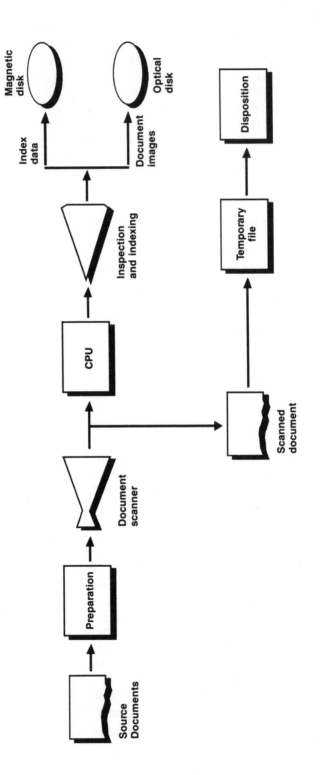

FIGURE 59.   Flow of work in electronic document imaging system.

FIGURE 60. Turnkey optical filing system.

3. Digitized document images are transmitted to a computer which displays them on a high-resolution monitor where an operator inspects the image and enters index data. Illegible or otherwise unacceptable documents can be rescanned. When satisfactory image quality is obtained, a document's assigned index values are key-entered in a manner prescribed by the system's data base management software.

4. As with microform-based CAR systems, the index records associated with specific document images are usually stored on magnetic disks.

5. Although digitized document images are typically processed by data compression algorithms, the resulting storage space requirements may still exceed the capacity of available magnetic media. As a result, digitized document images are typically recorded on high-capacity optical disks. The phrase ''optical filing systems'' is sometimes used to describe such document storage and retrieval configurations. However, they do not ''file'' documents in the traditional sense of

placing logically-related documents in close physical proximity to one another. Instead, like microform-based CAR systems, they rely on computer-based indexes that contain pointers to the optical disk locations of specific digitized document images. Optical disk drives use removable storage media encapsulated in protective plastic cartridges. Document image storage capacities range from less than 5,000 to more than 60,000 letter-size pages per double-sided cartridge.

Retrieval procedures resemble those employed by microform-based CAR systems: a computer-maintained data base of index records is searched to determine the existence and location of document images which meet specified parameters. Retrieved index records include the numbers of optical disk cartridges that contain their associated document images. In the simplest implementations, optical disk cartridges are stored offline in file cabinets, on shelves, or in other containers. When indicated by an index search, individual cartridges are manually removed from their storage locations and inserted into an optical disk drive. Retrieval software then locates and displays the appropriate document image. As with microform-based CAR systems, a given retrieval operation may require the examination of multiple document images located on several or many different cartridges, each of which must be mounted and removed from an optical disk drive. To simplify media handling, some electronic document imaging systems support jukebox retrieval units that will automatically extract specified cartridges from their storage locations and load them into an optical disk drive. Such jukebox retrieval units provide rapid online access to millions of document images.

Whether manual cartridge handling or jukebox retrieval is employed, the typical electronic document imaging system serves retrieval workstations located in a narrowly circumscribed geographic location. The simplest, microcomputer-based systems are limited to a single workstation. Larger microcomputer- and minicomputer-based configurations can support multiple workstations connected by a local area network. As an increasingly common option, some electronic document imaging systems permit long distance transmission of retrieved images over telephone lines to digital facsimile machines.

As a space-saving alternative to conventional paper files, both micrographics and electronic document imaging systems convert documents to miniaturized images for compact storage. As discussed above, both technologies are compatible with computer-assisted indexing and retrieval methodologies that support rapid, convenient document display and printing. Given these similarities, it is not surprising that microform-based CAR and electronic document imaging systems compete with one another in certain situations. However, the two technologies can complement one another just as well. By combining the special capabilities of micrographics and electronic document imaging, hybrid implementations can address a broad range of document storage and retrieval applications.

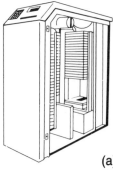

(a) Sixty-Four Disk Jukebox and
(b) Modular Jukebox Components

(a)

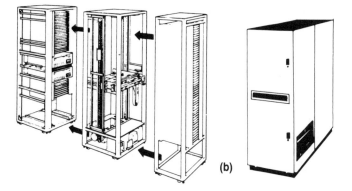

(b)

FIGURE 61. Optical disk jukeboxes.

Hybrid document storage and retrieval systems rely on the conceptual similarity of microform-based CAR and electronic document imaging technology, especially the use of a computer-maintained data base that contains pointers to the storage locations of document images associated with specific index terms. In a hybrid implementation, document images may be stored on either microforms or optical disks. A single data base of index records provides access to both types of media. An index search will indicate the microform and/or optical disk locations of document images pertinent to specific retrieval requirements. In the simplest hybrid configurations, an operator manually locates and loads those microforms and optical disk cartridges that contain pertinent document images. Retrieval workstations are equipped with bit-mapped video monitors for index searches and the display of digitized document images stored on optical disks, laser printers for hard copy reproduction of digitized document images, and reader-printers for the display and printing of microform images.

More complex equipment configurations incorporate optical disk jukeboxes and microform retrievers for completely automated media handling. In such installations, optical disk cartridges containing document images identified by an index search are automatically extracted from their jukebox storage locations and mounted in an optical disk drive for display and/or printing. Retrieval workstations, as described earlier, include bit-mapped video monitors and laser printers.

The availability of automated microform retrievers—including microfilm cartridge jukeboxes, microfiche retrievers, and aperture card selectors—was noted in the preceding discussion of microfacsimile systems. Operating under computer control, such devices will remove specified microforms from their storage locations, find microimages identified by an index search, and activate a scanning mechanism that digitizes those images for transmission to the same bit-mapped video monitors used for the display of document images stored on optical disks. Laser printers can produce paper copies for offline reference. Since digitized microimages and digitized document images recorded on optical disks are displayed and printed by the same devices, a given document's storage medium is both transparent and irrelevant to the user.

As with all equipment configurations that employ multiple technologies, systems that combine micrographics with electronic document imaging offer potentially more effective approaches to a broader range of information management tasks than can be success-fully accommodated by either technology alone. A hybrid system's op-tical disk components offer very high media capacity, the immediate availability of digitized images, convenient single-terminal access to both index data and document images, rapid online display and printing for active documents, and the ability to transmit digitized images to remote workstations or facsimile transceivers. The system's micrographics components offer low media cost, easy and inexpensive media duplication for vital records protection or distribution to multiple access points, firmly established legal acceptance of microfilm images, and excellent media stability with archival potential, if silver gelatin microforms are used.

Hybrid systems also offer an effective method of implementing electronic document imaging technology in applications where large numbers of documents are already recorded on microfilm, microfiche, aperture cards, or other microforms. While microimages can be digi-tized for conversion to optical disks, the required scanning procedures can prove time-consuming where very large microform collections are involved. A hybrid implementation can incorporate microimages without conversion. In addition to offering an effective approach to document storage and retrieval in its own right, a microform-based CAR system can also serve as an interim technology for those users who are considering the future implementation of an electronic document imaging system.

Computer-Input Microfilm

Mentioned briefly in Chapter Three as an example of the so-called computer/micrographics interface, computer-input microfilm (CIM) is a variant form of optical character recognition (OCR) technology. Operating as a computer peripheral device, a CIM unit scans microimages, recognizes the individual characters they contain, and converts those characters to machine-readable ASCII or other codes suitable for computer processing. Although both employ scanning methodologies, it is important to distinguish computer-input microfilm from the microimage digitization techniques employed by micro-facsimile and hybrid micrographic/optical disk systems. While digitization captures a microimage's appearance by converting microimages to a stream of bits that represent the tonal characteristics of successively encountered pixels, CIM devices—like conventional OCR counterparts—go beyond mere digitization in recognizing a microimage's textual content.

Unlike conventional OCR equipment, however, CIM devices scan microimages rather than paper documents. The advantages of microforms over paper in optical character recognition implementations have been recognized for many years. Being compact, microimages are easier to handle than paper records. Input documents need not be of uniform size or thickness, and the elimination of paper jamming permits higher document transport speeds. In addition, microimage scanning is accomplished by transmitted rather than the more powerful reflected light required by OCR systems that read opaque paper documents.

Computer-input microfilm is compatible with microforms created by either source document microfilming or COM. Some COM recorders, as discussed in Chapter Three, generate characters in the OCR-B type font for compatibility with computer-input microfilm technology. Conceptually, CIM is the opposite of COM, and that is the source of its substantial information processing potential. CIM technology allows microfilm to be used as a true computer storage medium. Compared to the magnetic and optical media currently employed by computer storage peripherals, microforms offer high storage capacity, relatively low media costs, convenient duplicability, and—when properly manufactured, processed, and stored—excellent stability. Widespread availability of CIM technology would permit the storage of information in a compact form that is both human-readable and computer-processible.

While it is easily described and its potential is readily appreciated, computer-input microfilm is one of the most enigmatic information management technologies. Although it has been frequently discussed in books, journal articles, and conference papers as a commercial available technology, few CIM systems have been implemented and relatively little is known about their operational characteristics. One of the earliest examples, the FOSDIC system, has operated since 1953 in various improved versions for the United States Census Bureau. This system actually employs mark-sense recognition rather than optical character recognition. It scans microfilmed copies of census forms for computer tabulation. During the 1970s, Information International Incorporated developed the Grafix system as a general purpose, multi-font OCR reader for source document and COM-generated microforms. The first Grafix system was built for the U.S. Navy. Published reports described it in several interesting applications, including computer processing of data recorded on COM-generated film and the scanning of microforms produced from bilingual documents that were used to create a legal data base. At the time this chapter was written, however, CIM equipment was not available on an off-the-shelf basis. CIM continues to be categorized as an emerging technology, although its present and future status is uncertain.

Microform Storage of Digital Data

Given their high resolution recording capabilities, potential stability, convenient duplicability, and relatively low cost, microforms are attractive candidates as storage media for the digitally-coded, computer-processible data that is currently being stored on magnetic and optical disks, tapes, and cards. Such data may consist of character-coded text, numeric values, or digitized images. As briefly noted in Chapter Six, several automated document storage and retrieval systems have recorded digitally-coded index information in photo-optical binary form on microfilm, adjacent to the document images to which they pertained. Index information was generated by keyboards attached to microfilm cameras or by special COM software. Such digitally-coded index information was designed to be processed by special-purpose microfilm retrieval devices rather than general-purpose computers. Since the late 1960s, however, various companies have demonstrated microfilm and microfiche products designed specifically for the recording and storage of computer-processible digital data. The development of write-once optical disks based on tellurium and other thin film technologies has stimulated interest in such microform-based data storage peripherals. While some interesting devices failed to develop beyond prototype implementations, several operational systems have been installed.

One such product can store up to five megabytes of digital data on a 105 mm by 148 mm microfiche. The binary-coded data is generated by dot matrix or graphics-type COM recorders. Proprietary error correction techniques compensate for media imperfections and contaminants. The resulting recording error rates are comparable to those encountered with write-once optical disks. The silver gelatin master microfiche provides an archivally stable storage medium. Working and backup copies can be made by diazo or vesicular technology. As an advantage over other computer storage media, high-speed duplicators permit the rapid production of distribution copies for multiple work-stations. An eye-legible title strip can identify the microfiche's content.

Digital data recorded on microfiche is read by a specially designed peripheral device that attaches to a microcomputer in the manner of an external disk drive. Device drivers are provided for various microcomputer configurations. At 208 kilobytes per square inch, the microfiche's areal recording density compares favorably with that of floppy disks but is lower than that of magnetic hard disks and optical disk cartridges. Microfiche loading requires approximately five seconds. With an average access time of half a second and a data transfer rate of one kilobyte per second, the system is slower than magnetic and optical disk drives, but faster operation is expected in future models.

COM and Word Processing

Since the 1970s, word processing systems have steadily replaced typewriters as the primary document preparation devices in corporations, government agencies, and other organizations. As their most important feature, such systems record typed keystrokes in machine-readable, character-coded form on magnetic media. Once recorded, the machine-readable text can be corrected, altered, moved, deleted, or otherwise revised without extensive retyping. When editing is completed, the text is dispatched to a printer which produces one or more paper copies. The machine-readable version can be retained in a text file for later reuse.

Word processing documents can, of course, be microfilmed by any of the cameras discussed in Chapter Three. As a faster, more automated alternative, however, COM recorders can produce microfilm or microfiche images from machine-readable text files, thereby avoiding document preparation, camera operation, and other work steps associated with source document microphotography. The word processing-to-COM approach also avoids quality impairments introduced by paper printers and permits the use of higher reductions than source document microphotography can routinely support.

While the most widely encountered COM formats are based on computer printout-size pages, the ANSI/AIIM 48/420 microfiche format is specifically designed for the letter-size pages produced by word processing programs and other text editing systems. As discussed in Chapter Two, the 48/420 format provides 420 microimages in 15 rows and 28 columns. The effective reduction is 48:1. At six lines per vertical inch and ten characters per horizontal inch, the typical page image contains fifty-four lines of text with sixty-five characters per line and one-inch margins on all sides. Some COM recorders also support the nonstandard 42/325 format which provides 325 letter-size microimages at an effective reduction of 42:1. For compatibility with source document applications, a few COM recorders can create microfiche in the 24/98 format.

The earliest word processing systems were special-purpose computer systems sold as an integrated configuration of hardware and software dedicated to text editing operations. During the 1970s, several companies demonstrated prototype interfaces between such dedicated word processors and COM recorders, but those prototypes were never developed into commercially available products. As an alternative to a direct word processing-to-COM connection, machine-readable text created by a dedicated word processing system can be transmitted to a mainframe, minicomputer, or microcomputer which will retransmit it to an online COM recorder or prepare a print-image tape for input to an offline COM recorder.

Since the early 1980s, the steady replacement of dedicated word processing systems by word processing software packages operating on general-purpose microcomputers, minicomputers, and mainframes has simplified the word processing-to-COM interface. Text files created by mainframe- and minicomputer-based word processing programs can be prepared for COM output like other data files. As discussed in Chapter Four, several vendors offer COM recorders that can operate online to microcomputers or as print servers in local area network installations. Word processing programs recognize them as conventional ASCII printers.

As a potential constraint discussed briefly in Chapter Four, the typographic capabilities of the typical COM recorder are more limited than those of the laser and dot matrix printers encountered in most word processing installations. While the upper and lower alphabet are now routinely supported, most COM recorders can only print characters in a single font and, in some cases, a single size. Where multiple fonts are supported, the recorder may not be able to combine them on the same page. Some, but not all, recorders support boldface printing and underlining. Italics, superscripts, subscripts, and other special features offered by paper printers are rarely supported.

Suggested
Additional
Readings

THE FOLLOWING BIBLIOGRAPHY contains citations to useful books, articles, and other publications dealing with micrographic technology and applications. Intended as a supplementary reading list and subdivided into broad topical categories, it contains references to more detailed treatments of specific subjects discussed in the preceding chapters. While it emphasizes books and articles published since the second edition of this book (1980), the bibliography includes a number of important older works that contain particularly clear or historically significant discussions of particular topics. Although many of the older works are out of print, they remain available through research and public libraries. Micrographic standards, an important group of publications intentionally omitted from this bibliography, are separately listed in Appendix Two.

Fundamentals

Brathal, Daniel A. and Langemo, Mark. Planning Conversions to Micrographic Systems. Prairie Village, KS: ARMA International, 1987.

Hawken, William R. Copying Methods Manual. Chicago: American Library Association, 1966.

Kish, Joseph L. Micrographics: A User's Manual. New York: Wiley, 1980.

Nelson, Carl E. Microfilm Technology. New York: McGraw-Hill, 1965.

Smith, Charles. Micrographics Handbook. Dedham, MA: Artech House, 1978.

Stevens, G.W.W. Microphotography: Photography and Photofabrication at Extreme Resolution. New York: John Wiley and Sons, 1968.

Verry, H.R. and Wright, G.H. Microcopying Methods. London: Focal Press, 1967.

Williams, B.J.S. Miniaturized Communications. London: Library Association, 1970.

History of Micrographics

Binkley, R.C. New tools for men of letters. Yale Review, vol. 24 (1935): 519-37.

Boni, Albert. Readex Microprint: How it began. Microdoc, vol. 11, no. 2 (1972): 5-10.

Born, Lester K. History of microfilm activity. Library Trends, vol. 8 (1960): 348-58.

Goldschmidt, Robert and Otlet, Paul M. Sur une Forme Nouvelle du Livre: Le Livre Microphotographique. Brussels: Institut International de Bibliographie, 1906.

Houghton, Sidney H. Preservation of records by microphotography in the United States. American Documentation, vol. 1 (1938): 156-61.

Leisinger, A.H., Jr. Selected aspects of microreproduction in the United States. Archivum, vol. 16 (1966): 127-50.

Luther, Frederic. Microfilm: A History, 1839-1900. Annapolis, MD: National Microfilm Association, 1959.

Luther, Frederic. Rene Dragon and the siege of Paris. American Documentation, vol. 1 (1957): 196-206.

Richards, Pamela S. Information science in wartime: Pioneer documentation activities in World War II. Journal of the American Society for Information Science, vol. 39 (1988): 301-307.

Rubin, Jack. A History of Micrographics: In the First Person. Silver Spring, MD: National Micrographics Association, 1980.

Seidell, Atherton. The photomicrographic reproduction of documents. Science, vol. 80 (August 24, 1934): 184-85.

Stevens, R.E. The microform revolution. Library Trends, vol. 19 (1971): 379-95.

Tate, Vernon D. From Binkley to Bush. American Archivist, vol. 10 (1947): 249-57.

Veaner, Allen. Micrographics: An eventful forty years — What next? In The American Library Association Yearbook. Chicago: American Library Association, 1976, pp. 45-56.

Types of Microforms

Baptie, Alex L. The 8 mm microfilm concept. Information and Records Management, vol. 5, no. 4 (1971): 57-60.

Beeman, Donald R. Micrographic standards for containers (cartridges and cassettes) for 16mm roll microfilm. Journal of Micrographics, vol. 9, no. 3 (1975): 51-54.

Bernstein, George B. Why $24 \times /48 \times$? Journal of Micrographics, vol. 5, no. 3 (1972): 295-300.

Carden, Ray C. A case for replacing the 35 mm aperture card with 105mm fiche. Journal of Micrographics, vol. 14, no. 10 (1981): 35-37.

Crew, Wynn D. The microaperture: a design to substitute for a book. Journal of Micrographics, vol. 4, no. 3 (1970): 3-11.

Davison, G.H. Microcards and microfiches: history and possibilities. Library Association Record, vol. 63 (1961): 69-78.

DeHaas, W. The microfiche. American Documentation, vol. 9 (1958): 99-106.

Disparti, Carl and Zagami, Robert W. New look to an old workhorse: the aperture card has come of age — again. Inform, vol. 2, no. 9 (1988): 28-30.

Hawken, William R. (1970). Microbook publications: a new approach for a new decade. Journal of Micrographics, vol. 3, no. 3 (1970): 188-93.

Otten, Klaus W. Ultrafiche technology. Journal of Micrographics, vol. 4, no. 4 (1971): 161-76.

Sall, Stuart N. and Disparti, Carl. Engineering microfilm systems: advantages, costs, and applications of the aperture card. Journal of Micrographics, vol. 14, no. 7 (1981): 35-40.

Symons, John. A new dimension for the 35 mm aperture card. Journal of Micrographics, vol. 15, no. 11 (1982): 20-25.

Van der Wolk, L.J. and Lannon, J.C. The microcopy on flat film as an aid in documentation. Revue de la Documentation, vol. 17 (1950): 134-41; vol. 18 (1951): 216-38.

Saffady, William. Microfilm jacket systems: a survey of available supplies and equipment. Micrographics Equipment Review, vol. 7 (1982): 9-40.

Verry, H.R. Micro-opaques. Aslib Proceedings, vol. 4 (1952): 153-62.

Wade, Henry J. The case for cartridge standardization. Journal of Micrographics, vol. 13, no. 6 (1979): 69-71.

Zagami, Robert W. The engineering aperture card. Journal of Information and Image Management, vol. 19, no. 8 (1986): 30-34.

Recording Technologies

Avedon, Don M. Standards: microfilm generation and polarity terminology. Journal of Micrographics, vol. 5, no. 3 (1972): 261-64.

Avedon, Don M. Archival quality and performance of microfilm. IMC Journal, vol. 1, no. 1 (1978): 12-14.

Bagg, Thomas C. Evaluation of Transparent Electro-Photographic Film and Camera System. Washington, DC: National Bureau of Standards, 1976.

Broadhurst, R.N. An Investigation of the Effects of Exposure to Light on Diazo Microfilm. Hatfield, England: National Reprographic Centre for documentation, 1976.

Dailey, Frank E., Jr. Films using organic photoconductors. In Proceedings of the Twenty-First Annual Conference and Exposition of the National Micrographics Association, ed. Ellen Meyer. Silver Spring, MD: National Micrographics Association, 1972, Section, 2, pp. 88-92.

Dailey, Frank E., Jr. and Bennett, E.W. Some considerations for a new photorecording technology. In Micrographics Science 1973: Winter Symposium, ed. Don Chenevert. Washington, DC: Society of Photographic Scientists and Engineers, 1973, pp. 194-203.

Dinaburg, M.S. Photosensitive Diazo Compounds and Their Uses. London: Focal Press, 1964.

Forbes, Edward J. and Bagg, Thomas C. Report of a Study of Requirements and Specifications for Serial and Monographic Microrecording for the National Library of Medicine. Washington, DC: National Bureau of Standards, 1966.

Habib, David P. and Plumadore, John D. A new microelectrophotographic system. Journal of Micrographics, vol. 7, no. 1 (1974): 249-54.

Kurtilla, Kenneth R. Dry silver film stability. Journal of Micrographics, vol. 10, no. 1 (1977): 113-17.

Lee, Leonard S. Updatable micrographics: panacea or placebo? Journal of Micrographics, vol. 10, no. 4 (1977): 335-41.

Lee, Leonard S. Everything you wanted to know about updatables but had no one to ask. Journal of Micrographics, vol. 12, no. 11 (1978): 187-97.

Lee, Leonard S. Are updatables archival? IMC Journal, vol. 2, no. 2 (1979): 7-11.

McGregor, H.H., Jr. Vesicular photography: an overview. Journal of Micrographics, vol. 9, no. 5 (1975): 13-20.

Meyers, Wilbur C. Laser micrographic recording on non-silver halide media. Journal of Micrographics, vol. 8, no. 4 (1975): 265-73.

Norcross, J.A. and Sampath, P.I. Non-silver photographic materials and lasers in the micrographics industry. In Micrographics Science 1973: Winter Symposium, ed. Don Chenevert. Washington, DC: Society of Photographic Scientists and Engineers, 1973, pp. 187-93.

Richman, W.W. Micrographic camera and duplicating films. In Proceedings of the Twenty-Seventh Annual Conference and Exposition of the National Micrographics Association, ed. Ellen Meyer. Silver Spring, MD: National Micrographics Association, 1978, pp. 48-54.

Saffady, William. Three updatable microfiche systems. Micrographics Equipment Review, vol. 5 (1980): 35-43.

Scott, Peter R. Basic microfilm technology. In Proceedings of the Twenty-Fourth Annual Conference and Exposition of the National Micrographics Association, ed. Ellen Meyer. Silver Spring, MD: National Micrographics Association, 1975, pp. 109-25.

Shepard, Joseph W. Dry silver film technology. In Proceedings of the Twenty-First Annual Conference and Exposition of the National Micrographics Association, ed. Ellen Meyer. Silver Spring, MD: National Micrographics Association, 1972, Section 2, pp. 88-92.

Stevens, G.W.W. Grainless emulsions and their technical applications. Journal of Micrographics, vol. 7, no. 4 (1973): 9-20.

Wolf, David R. The technologies and role of updatable micrographics. Journal of Micrographics, vol. 14, no. 8 (1981): 23-28.

Wolf, David R. Update on updatables: The technologies and role of updatable micrographic record systems. IMC Journal, vol. 23, no. 1 (1987): 44-49.

Source Document Microfilming

Avedon, Don M. Microfilm permanence and archival quality: Standards. Special Libraries, vol. 63 (1972): 586-88.

Avedon, Don M. Selecting a service bureau. Journal of Micrographics, vol. 10, no. 5 (1976): 3-8.

Balon, Brett J. Microfilm systems: Silver recovery is money recovery. Records Management Quarterly, vol. 21, no. 2 (1987): 31-32.

Bogue, David T. Choosing processors and duplicators. Journal of Micrographics, vol. 15, no. 4 (1982): 53-59.

Byer, Richard J. Densitometry: measuring for quality control. INFORM, vol. 2, no. 1 (1988): 7-9, 42.

Chase, Deborah. The microfilmer's guide to chemical regulations. INFORM, vol. 2, no. 10 (1988): 32-33, 46-47.

Cranwell, Gilbert S. Problems of establishing an international standard for micro-copying resolution testing. Journal of Micrographics, vol. 7, no. 4 (1974): 257-65.

Dorfmann, Harold. Quality criteria. Microfilm Techniques, vol. 5, no. 2 (1976): 9-10, 13, 28.

Dorfmann, Harold. Film inspection. Microfilm Techniques, vol. 8, no. 1 (1979): 24-25.

Gunn, Michael J. Document microphotography in colour. British Journal of Photography, vol. 10, no. 1 (1978): 121-25.

Gunn, Michael J. Colour microforms and their application to the visual arts. Microform Review, vol. 8 (1979): 187-92.

Gunn, Michael J. Manual of Document Microphotography. London: Butterworth, 1985.

Hobush, Paul A. Micrographics quality control: The human factor. INFORM, vol. 1, no. 12 (1987): 8.

Hollinger, James A. Production of good quality diazo duplicates from 35 mm silver gelatin film images. Journal of Micrographics, vol. 13, no. 1 (1980): 111-13.

James, Linda. Standing the Test of Time: Quality Assurance for State and Local Government Records Microfilming. St. Paul: Minnesota Historical Society, 1986.

Ling, Joseph T. Photo processing wastes: What needs to be done. Journal of Micrographics, vol. 8, no. 1 (1975): 109-13.

McCamy, C.S. and Pope, C.I. (1970): Redox blemishes: Their causes and prevention. Journal of Micrographics, vol. 3, no. 6 (1970): 165-70.

Miles, Charles S. SOM: A redefinition of a concept and a market. Journal of Micrographics, vol. 16, no. 1 (1983): 24-30.

Santisteban, John. Microfiche duplicators: Keeping up with technology. Journal of Information and Image Management, vol. 19, no. 3 (1986): 20-21, 32-33.

Smith, Kenneth M. Silver recovery. Journal of Micrographics, vol. 10, no. 1 (1977): 131-34.

Taubes, Ernest P. Color microfilming of large documents. Journal of Micrographics, vol. 12, no. 3 (1979): 285-88.

Thomas, Bill. Archival quality: The test for methylene blue. INFORM, vol. 1, no. 5 (1987): 6-7, 46-47.

Van Auken, John and Van Auken, Richard. Small office microfilm (SOM) products: A status report. Journal of Micrographics, vol. 5, no. 2 (1971): 5-11.

Watson, Andrew C. Micro-color images: Macro economies in color image management. Journal of Information and Image Management, vol. 19, no. 12 (1986): 30-34.

Wehsels, Gary. Quality control: Managing process materials. Journal of Information and Image Management, vol. 19, no. 12 (1986): 20-24.

Wise, Joseph. Four elements of microfilm quality control. Administrative Management, vol. 47, no. 10 (1986): 16-17.

Wise, Joseph. In-house or service bureau: Seven factors to consider. Administrative Management, vol. 47, no. 3 (1986): 20-21.

Witz, Wolfgang. Drafting technologies in engineering source document preparation. Journal of Micrographics, vol. 12, no. 6 (1979): 323-26.

Computer-Output Microfilm

Airhart, Truett. Computer output microfilm: A powerful systems tool. Journal of Micrographics, vol. 7, no. 5 (1974): 99-105.

Andors, Alice. Micrographics service in the information age. INFORM, vol. 1, no. 6 (1987): 26-29.

Avedon, Don M. Computer-Output Microfilm. Silver Spring, MD: National Microfilm Association, 1971.

Bolnick, Franklin I. On-line versus off-line COM systems. Journal of Micrographics, vol. 4, no. 3 (1971): 123-31.

Bordas, Richard R. The CAD-microfilm connection: linking for productivity. INFORM, vol. 2, no. 1 (1988): 28-29.

Boyd, Sherman H. Film requirements for computer output microfilm. In Proceedings of the Twenty-First Annual Conference and Exposition of the National Micrographics Association, ed. Ellen Meyer. Silver Spring, MD: National Micrographics Association, 1972, Section 3, pp. 35-49.

Boyd, Sherman H. Technology of computer output microfilm: Past, present, and future. TAPPI, vol. 56, no. 1 (1973): 107-10.

Colombetti, C. CAD and COM merging to manage engineering documents. INFORM, vol. 2, no. 7 (1988): 31-32, 39.

Exelbert, Rodd S. COM: Its relationship to management and the end user. Journal of Micrographics, vol. 10, no. 4 (1977): 245-53.

Furlong, J.D. Online/offline COM. Journal of Micrographics, vol. 14, no. 12 (1981): 38-39.

Gildenberg, Robert. Computer-Output-Microfilm Systems. Los Angeles: Melville Publishing Company, 1974.

Harrison, Tom L. CRT vs. COM: Real time vs. real time enough. Journal of Micrographics, vol. 7, no. 2 (1973): 37-44.

Hoberg, Richard P. Expanding roles for the micrographics service company. Journal of Information and Image Management, vol. 18, no. 4 (1985): 8-14.

Kerr, Thomas B. COM service bureaus: The emerging information managers. Journal of Information and Image Management, vol. 18, no. 4 (1985): 16-21.

Kober, S.A. What to look for in a COM service bureau. Journal of Micrographics, vol. 9, no. 2 (1976): 187-90.

Lewis, James. Productivity: The case for high reduction COM. Journal of Micrographics, vol. 14, no. 4 (1981): 44-46.

Malabarba, Frank J. Microfilm information systems (MIS): A data base alternative. Journal of Micrographics, vol. 9, no. 4 (1975): 3-11.

Malabarba, Frank J. and McCullough, William. On-line computer terminal versus COM systems. Proceedings of the Twenty-sixth Annual Conference and Exposition of the National Micrographics Association, ed. D.L. Harlow. Silver Spring, MD: National Micrographics Association, 1977, pp. 116-19.

McGinley, John. Linking CAD to microfilm. CAE, vol. 8, no. 6 (1989): 62, 65.

Morton, Rick. Graphic COM in factory automation. INFORM, vol. 1, no. 8 (1987): 26-29.

Ocon, Robert. When to go in-house with COM. Journal of Micrographics, vol. 15, no. 4 (1982): 30-32, 36.

Pauer, Tom R. Formslides: Information for the user. Journal of Micrographics, vol. 9, no. 5 (1976): 161-63.

Peoples, B.R. COM software: State of the art. In Proceedings of the Twenty-First Annual Conference and Exposition of the National Micrographics Association, ed. Ellen Meyer. Silver Spring, MD: National Micrographics Association, 1972, Section 2, pp. 84-90.

Reid, Marvin A. Bar code on microfiche. INFORM, vol. 1, no. 5 (1987): 20-23.

Saffady, William. Computer-Output Microfilm: Its Library Application. Chicago: American Library Association, 1978.

Saffady, William. COM recorders in the 1980s. Micrographics Equipment Review, vol. 8 (1983): 23-77.

Schrieber, Larry. Photocomposition on a COM recorder. Journal of Micrographics, vol. 8, no. 6 (1975): 251-54.

Schroeder, Chris (1988). CAD drives aperture card imaging systems. INFORM, vol. 2, no. 5 (1988): 9-10.

Smock, Sidney N. Microfiche poison index and management saves lives. Journal of Micrographics, vol. 8, no. 3 (1975): 127-30.

Stark, Thomas H. COM and CAD: film plotters will offer new convenience and speed. Journal of Micrographics, vol. 16, no. 3 (1983): 44-46.

Titus, Arthur C. On-line processing in a COM system. In Proceedings of the Twenty-First Annual Conference and Exposition of the National Micrographics Association, ed. Ellen Meyer. Silver Spring, MD: National Micrographics Association, 1972, Section 3, pp. 21-32.

Truax, David D. COM service bureaus: Selection guidelines. Journal of Micrographics, vol. 13, no. 5 (1980): 19-22.

Display and Printing

Baldwin, T.S. and Bailey, L.J. Readability of technical training materials presented on microfiche versus offset copy. Journal of Applied Psychology, vol. 55 (1971): 37-41.

Barr, Robert. Plain paper vs. dry silver technology: Which is right for your micrographics system? Journal of Information and Image Management, vol. 19, no. 5 (1986): 28-30.

Barrett, W.J. The evaluation of microfilm readers. Journal of Micrographics, vol. 6, no. 5 (1972): 51-63.

Boss, R.W. and Raikes, D. Developing Microform Reading Facilities. Westport, CT: Microform Review, 1981.

Christ, C.W., Jr. Microfiche: A study of user attitudes and reading habits. Journal of the American Society for Information Science, vol. 23 (1972): 30-35.

Greene, Robert J. Microform attitude and frequency of microform use. Journal of Micrographics, vol. 8, no. 2 (1975): 131-34.

Hawken, William R. Evaluating Microfiche Readers: A Handbook for Librarians. Washington, DC: Council on Library Resources, 1975.

Hultgren, G.V.; Knave, B.; and Werner, M. Eye discomfort when reading microfilm in different enlargers. Applied Ergonomics, vol. 5 (1975): 194-200.

Judisch, J.M. The effect of positive-negative microforms and front-rear projection on reading speed and comprehension. NMA Journal, vol. 2, no. 1 (1968): 58-61.

Kerber, Mindy S. and Hall, Hal W. A Microform Reader Maintenance Manual. Westport, CT: Meckler Publishing, 1983.

Landau, Robert M. Microfiche reader human factors. Journal of Micrographics, vol. 10, no. 3 (1977): 219-27.

Lee, David R. and Buck, James R. The effect of screen angle and luminance on microform reading. Human Factors, vol. 17 (1975): 461-69.

Lee, Leonard S. R.E.S.T.— Reader evaluation and selection techniques. Journal of Micrographics, vol. 12, no. 6 (1978): 13-17.

Lewis, Ralph W. User's reaction to microfiche: A preliminary study. College and Research Libraries, vol. 31 (1970): 260-68.

Spreitzer, Francis F. Selecting Microform Readers and Reader-Printers. Silver Spring, MD: Association for Information and Image Management, 1983.

Tanasescu, Leo. Microform reader system: A new approach in microform reader design. Journal of Micrographics, vol. 15, no. 1 (1982): 27-29.

Micropublishing

Ashby, Peter and Campbell, Robert. Microform Publishing. London: Butterworth, 1979.

Bailey, Herbert S., Jr. The limits of on-demand publishing. Scholarly Publishing, vol. 6 (1975): 291-98.

Ballou, Hubbard W. and Rather, John. Microfilm and microfacsimile publication. Library Trends, vol. 4 (1955): 182-94.

Gray, Edward. Subscriptions on microfiche: An irreversible trend. Journal of Micrographics, vol. 8, no. 2 (1975): 241-44.

Hernon, Peter. Microforms and Government Information. Westport, CT: Microform Review, 1981.

Josephs, Melvin J. Information dissemination with microforms. IEEE Transactions on Professional Communications, vol. 18 (1975): 164-67.

Meckler, Alan. Micropublishing: A History of Scholarly Micropublishing in America, 1938-80. Westport, CT: Greenwood Press, 1982.

Power, Eugene B. O-P books: A library breakthrough. American Documentation, vol. 4 (1958): 273-76.

Reno, Edward A., Jr. Some basic aspects of scholarly micropublishing. In Proceedings of the Twenty-Second Annual Conference and Exposition of the National Micrographics Association, ed. Ellen Meyer. Silver Spring, MD: National Micrographics Association, 1973, Section 2, pp. 282-93.

Sieger, Charles F. GPO micropublishing: An historical review and critical analysis. Library Acquisitions: Theory and Practice, vol. 2 (1978): 33-44.

Teague, S.J. Micropublishing in Great Britain. Microform Review, vol. 10 (1981): 7-12.

Veaner, Allen. The Evaluation of Micropublications: A Handbook for Librarians. Chicago: American Library Association, 1971.

Veaner, Allen, ed. Studies in Micropublishing. Westport, CT: Microform Review, 1977.

Records Management Applications

Brown, Connis O., Jr. The case against fore and aft certification. Journal of Micrographics, vol. 7, no. 2 (1974): 149-53.

Diamond, Susan Z. Records Management: A Practical Guide. New York: American Management Association, 1983.

Elkeles, G. The state of micrographics in the nuclear industry. IMC Journal, vol. 25, no. 3 (1989): 49-50.

Griffin, James. Microfilm medical records system: Cost effective bridge to the future. IMC Journal, vol. 25, no. 3 (1989): 57-59.

Hendley, Anthony M. The development of microfilm in engineering applications. IMC Journal, vol. 24, no. 2 (1988): 18-20.

Johnson, Mina and Kallaus, Norman. Records Management, 4th Edition. Cincinnati: South-Western Publishing, 1987.

Kaebnick, Greg. X-ray minification: Steady business, ready for growth. INFORM, vol. 1, no. 12 (1987): 6.

Kraushopf, Lutz. The legal status of microfilm in Europe. Microfiche Foundation Newsletter, no. 30 (1975): 7-11.

Lowell, Howard P. Preservation microfilming: An overview. Records Management Quarterly, vol. 19, no. 1 (1985): 22-29, 36.

Lundgren, Terry D. and Lundgren, Carol A. Records Management in the Computer Age. Boston: PWS-Kent Publishing Company, 1989.

Pelican, Greg. High-speed check processing. IMC Journal, vol. 25, no. 2 (1989): 30-32.

Reinhardt, Victor. Engineering documentation: A micrographic solution. INFORM, vol. 1, no. 12 (1987): 20-23.

Robek, Mary; Maedke, Wilmer; and Brown, Gerald F. Information and Records Management, 3rd Edition. Encino, CA: Glenco Publishing, 1987.

Rupp, Dale O. Active micrographics systems: Engineering link to the future. Journal of Information and Image Management, vol. 18, no. 12 (1985): 8-10, 16.

Saffady, William. Microfilm in Records Management. Silver Spring, MD: National Micrographics Association, 1982.

Skupsky, Donald S. The legal status of microfilm and other duplicate records. Records Management Quarterly, vol. 19, no. 1 (1985): 64-68.

Skupsky, Donald S. Legal liability of the records and information management professional. Records Management Quarterly, vol. 21, no. 2 (1987): 36-39.

Smith, Milburn. Information and Records Management: A Decision-Maker's Guide to Systems Planning and Implementation. New York: Quorum Books, 1986.

Stephens, David O. Making records retention decisions: Practical and theoretical considerations. Records Management Quarterly, vol. 22, no. 1 (1988): 3-7.

Thomas, Violet; Schubert, Dexter; and Lee, Jo Ann. Records Management: Systems and Administration. New York: Wiley, 1983.

Wallace, Patricia E. Records Management Applications. New York: Wiley, 1987.

White, Eugene T. The law and microfilm. In Proceedings of the Twenty-First Annual Conference and Exposition of the National Micrographics Association, ed. Ellen Meyer. Silver Spring, MD: National Micrographics Association, 1972, pp. 12-18.

Williams, Robert. Legality of Microfilm. Chicago: Cohasset Associates, 1979.

Wilson, Donald G. (1986). An alternative method for the long-term storage of microfilm. IMC Journal, vol. 22, no. 1 (1986): 15-17.

Library Applications

Baker, John P. Preservation programs of the New York Public Library. Microform Review, vol. 10 (1981): 25-28; vol. 11 (1982): 22-30.

Cruse, Larry, ed. Microcartography: Applications for Archives and Libraries. Santa Cruz, CA: Western Association of Map Libraries, 1981.

Fair, Judy H., ed. Microforms Management in Special Libraries: A Reader. Westport, CT: Microform Review, 1979.

Folcarelli, Ralph; Tannenbaum, Arthur; and Ferragamo, Ralph. The Microform Connection: A Basic Guide for Libraries. New York: R.R. Bowker, 1982.

Gabriel, Michael R. and Ladd, Dorothy. The Microform Revolution in Libraries. Greenwich, CT: JAI Press, 1980.

Gwinn, Nancy E., ed. Preservation Microfilming: A Guide for Librarians and Archivists. Chicago: American Library Association, 1987.

New, Peter. Reprography for Librarians. Hamden, CT: Linnet Books, 1975.

Rider, Fremont. The Scholar and the Future of the Research Library. New York: Hamden Press, 1944.

Saffady, William. Micrographics, 2nd Edition. Littleton, CO: Libraries Unlimited, 1985.

Teague, S.J. Microform Librarianship, 2nd Edition. Woburn, MA: Butterworth, 1982.

Veaner, Allen. Microfilm and the library: A retrospective. Drexel Library Quarterly, vol. 11 (1975): 3-16.

Retrieval Systems and Techniques

Baker, G.S. Information access methods for microfilm systems. Microdoc, vol. 13 (1974): 100-12.

Bush, Vannevar. As we may think. Atlantic Monthly, vol. 176, no. 7 (1945): 101-108.

Carden, Ray. Computer-assisted retrieval (CAR) as an information control tool. Journal of Micrographics, vol. 16, no. 3 (1983): 26-30.

Courtot, Marilyn. Microform Indexing and Retrieval Systems. Silver Spring, MD: National Micrographics Association, 1975.

Kalthoff, R.J. Automated document storage and retrieval: A perspective. Journal of Micrographics, vol. 8, no. 6 (1975): 61-72.

Kalthoff, R.J. and Lee, Leonard S. Productivity and Records Automation. Englewood Cliffs, NJ: Prentice-Hall, 1980.

Langemo, Mark. Selecting a successful CAR system. Journal of Information and Image Management, vol. 18, no. 10 (1985): 22-26.

Levine, Emil H. Effect of instantaneous retrieval on indexing criteria. Journal of the American Society for Information Science, vol. 25 (1974): 199-200.

Lidstad, Richard A. The impact of CAR. IMC Journal, vol. 22, no. 4 (1986): 16-19.

McConnell, P.M. Patentability searching using CCMSS. Journal of Micrographics, vol. 13, no. 1 (1979): 11-15.

Overhage, Carl F. and Reintjes, J.F. Project Intrex: A general review. Information Storage and Retrieval, vol. 10 (1974): 157-88.

Saffady, William. Personal computer software packages for computer-assisted microfilm retrieval. Micrographics and Optical Storage Equipment Review, vol. 11 (1986): 112-65.

Saffady, William. Document indexing in CAR and optical filing systems: Concepts and issues. Micrographics and Optical Storage Equipment Review, vol. 13 (1988): 97-124.

Saffady, William. Personal Computer Systems for Automated Document Storage and Retrieval. Silver Spring, MD: Association for Information and Image Management, 1989.

Sawasky, Larry. The CAR solution: Modernizing for automated document retrieval. Journal of Information and Image Management, vol. 19, no. 9 (1986): 30-33.

Smith, Robert J. Microfiche indexing systems. Proceedings of the Twenty-Fourth Annual Conference and Exposition of the National Micrographics Association, ed. Ellen Meyer. Silver Spring, MD: National Micrographics Association, 1975, pp. 244-53.

Tauber, Al. Fiche CAR: The preferred solution to microfiche-based office automation systems. Journal of Information and Image Management, vol. 19, no. 1 (1986): 18-20.

Teplitz, Arthur A. Computer-controlled retrieval: A primer. Journal of Micrographics, vol. 5, no. 3 (1971): 35-40.

Williams, B.J.S. Microforms in information retrieval and communication systems. Aslib Proceedings, vol. 19 (1967): 223-31.

Wise, Joseph. Evolution of a computer-assisted retrieval system. Journal of Information and Image Management, vol. 17, no. 11 (1984): 34-37.

Cost Analysis

Allord, W.E. Some economics: Microfilm and space. Records Management Quarterly, vol. 5, no. 2 (1971): 16-20.

Beyer, David C. Taking existing resources into account: Cost justification of engineering document management requires careful thinking. INFORM, vol. 3, no. 2 (1989): 29-31.

Britton, Joseph E. The cost justification of microfilm systems. Proceedings of the Twenty-Third Annual Conference and Exposition of the National Micrographics Association, ed. Ellen Meyer. Silver Spring, MD: National Micrographics Association, 1974, Section 2, pp. 229-33.

Lynden, Frederick C. Replacement of hard copy by microforms. Microform Review, vol. 4 (1975): 9-14.

Power, Eugene. Microfilm as a substitute for binding. American Documentation, vol. 2 (1951): 33-39.

Pritsker, Alan B. and Sadler, J.W. An evaluation of microfilm as a method of book storage. College and Research Libraries, vol. 18 (1957): 290-96.

Raffel, Jeffrey A. and Shishko, R. Systematic Analysis of University Libraries: An Application of Cost-Benefit Analysis to the MIT Libraries. Cambridge, MD: MIT Press, 1969.

Reed, Jutta R. Cost comparison of periodicals in hard copy and on microform. Microform Review, vol. 5: 185-92 (1976).

Schowen, Jeffrey C. Micrographic economics. INFORM, vol. 3, no. 5 (1989): 36-37, 47.

Thompson, D.D. Comparing costs: An examination of the real and hidden costs of different methods of storage. ASIS Bulletin, vol. 7 (1980): 14-15.

Interfaces With Other Technologies

Anderson, McRae; Varson, R.J.; and Wilkins, E.E. Micrographics and computer technology joined to process 1980 census data. Journal of Micrographics, vol. 13, no. 7 (1980): 37-40.

Avedon, Don M. Micrographics in the 1980s: A technological assessment. IMC Journal, vol. 3, no. 2 (1980): 19-22.

Bagg, Thomas C. Digitizing documents: Guidelines for image quality. INFORM, vol. 1, no. 11 (1987): 6-9.

Black, David. The new breed of mixed-media image management systems. IMC Journal, vol. 25, no. 1 (1989): 9-13.

Brown, Colin J. New generation videomicrographics set to impact information systems market. Journal of Information and Image Management, vol. 18, no. 11 (1985): 8-13.

Cinnamon, Barry. Optical Disk Document Storage and Retrieval Systems. Silver Spring, MD: Association for Information and Image Management, 1988.

Costigan, Daniel M. Microfacsimile: A status report. Journal of Micrographics, vol. 4, no. 3 (1971): 189-99.

Costigan, Daniel M. Electronic Delivery of Documents and Graphics. New York: Van Nostrand Reinhold, 1978.

Costigan, Daniel M. and Burger, Robert J. Videomicrographics: A positive new trend in online information retrieval. Journal of Micrographics, vol. 15, no. 4 (1982): 16-24.

Douglas, Paul E. The power of integration: Issues for engineering data management. INFORM, vol. 2, no. 2 (1988): 25-27.

Fain, David and Gruener, Garrett. Automated records management system. Journal of Micrographics, vol. 12, no. 5 (1979): 331-35.

Follet, Brian L. Word processing to COM: Software interfaces. Journal of Micrographics, vol. 13, no. 5 (1980): 15-18.

Frase, H.M. and Frager, S.A. Videomicrographics: Multi-media image management. INFORM, vol. 1, no. 4 (1987): 26-29.

French, Margaret. Future applications of the Navy's Microfiche Image Transmission System (MITS). Journal of Micrographics, vol. 14, no. 6 (1981): 25-31.

Frey, Henry C. An assessment of micrographics in advanced office information technologies. Journal of Micrographics, vol. 15, no. 2 (1982): 12-19.

Furlong, J.D. Micrographics and word processing. In Proceedings of the Twenty-Sixth Annual Conference and Exposition of the National Micrographics Association, ed. D.L. Harlow. Silver Spring, MD: National Micrographics Association, 1977, pp. 28-31.

Gallenberger, J. EIM: Electronic image micrographics?, INFORM, vol. 3, no. 4 (1989): 14-17.

Griffith, Arnold. From Gutenberg to Grafix I: New directions in OCR. Journal of Micrographics, vol. 9, no. 6, pp. 81-89.

Griffith, Arnold and Harris, Barry. Practical considerations of the COM/CIM marriage. In Proceedings of the Twenty-Sixth Annual Conference and Exposition of the National Micrographics Association, ed. D.L. Harlow. Silver Spring, MD: ational Micrographics Association, 1977, pp. 67-70.

Grigsby, Mason. Merging micrographics with MIS. Infosystems, vol. 33, no. 5 (1986): 94-97.

Harper, James. Microfilm reformatting: Linking past, present, and future. INFORM, vol. 1, no. 10 (1987): 14-16.

Harritatos, Fred and Mincieli, John. Holographic binary data storage on microfilm. Proceedings of the American Society for Information Science, vol. 10 (1973): 81-82.

Holland, Roger. CIM: The present and the future. Microdoc, vol. 15 (1976): 52-55.

Hopkins, William L. Microfiche Image Transmission System (MITS). Journal of Micrographics, vol. 11, no. 6 (1977): 83-88.

Hopkins, William L. The Navy's microfiche image transmission system (MITS): Documentation and test. Journal of Micrographics, vol. 15, no. 10 (1982): 17-24.

House, William A. Micrographics and word processing: A practical application in 1978. Proceedings of the Twenty-Seventh Annual Conference and Exposition of the National Micrographics Association, ed. Ellen Meyer. Silver Spring, MD: National Micrographics Association, 1978, pp. 76-78.

Kalow, Samuel J. Interfacing technologies. Journal of Micrographics, vol. 13, no. 1 (1980): 107-10.

Kalthoff, Robert J. Large-scale document automation: The systems integration issue. Videodisc and Optical Disk, vol. 5 (1985): 447-53.

Kneitel, Arnold. Micrographics and the challenge by on-line interactive terminals. Journal of Micrographics, vol. 9, no. 1 (1976): 109-13.

Knudson, D.R. and Marcus, R.S. The design of a microimage storage and transmission capability into an integrated transfer system. Journal of Micrographics, vol. 6, no. 2 (1972): 15-20.

Linden, Alan S. Word processing and micrographics. In Proceedings of the Twenty-Sixth Annual Conference and Exposition of the National Micrographics Association, ed. D.L. Harlow. Silver Spring, MD: National Micrographics Association, 1977, pp. 75-76.

Meyers, W.C. Remote viewing and printing of graphic materials. Journal of Micrographics, vol. 3, no. 3 (1970): 173-78.

Nelson, Kyler F. Electronic image systems for records management. Journal of Information and Image Management, vol. 18, no. 1 (1985): 16-18.

Peck, Ralph. Digital imaging technology at the Federal Energy Regulatory Commission. Journal of Micrographics, vol. 16, no. 3 (1983): 48-56.

Richards, Edwin. Interfacing computers and micrographics for data exchange. Journal of Micrographics, vol. 12, no. 6 (1978): 79-82.

Safdie, Elias. and Jones, T. The scanning solution: Imaging comes alive. INFORM, vol. 1, no. 5 (1987): 24-27.

Saffady, William. Optical Disks for Data and Document Storage. Westport, CT: Meckler Corporation, 1986.

Saffady, William. Optical Disks vs. Micrographics as Document Storage and Retrieval Technologies. Westport, CT: Meckler Corporation, 1988.

Saffady, William. An introduction to microfacsimile: Concepts, technology, and history. Micrographics and Optical Storage Equipment Review, vol. 14 (1989): 103-17.

Slutsky, Joel. The role of the micrographic industry in the office of the future. Journal of Micrographics, vol. 11, no. 5 (1977): 71-74.

Walter, Gerald. Digital conversion of microforms. IMC Journal, vol. 15, no. 2 (1979): 38-41.

Walter, Gerald. Technology overview: Raster image telecommunications. Journal of Micrographics, vol. 15, no. 5 (1982): 30-37.

Walter, Gerald. Redundancy reduction and data compaction technology in microform image transmission systems. Journal of Micrographics, vol. 15, no. 9 (1982): 25-35.

Williams, Robert F. Electronic document management: The coming revolution in records management. IMC Journal, vol. 21, no. 4 (1985): 33-37.

Micrographic Standards

As DISCUSSED IN Chapter One, standards play an important role in the development and use of micrographic products and services. Published standards are indispensible reference tools for the micrographic systems analyst, and familiarity with them is essential to the design, implementation, and operation of effective micrographic systems. As an adjunct to the preceding bibliography of micrographic-related publications, this appendix lists ANSI/AIIM and other micrographic standards, recommended practices, and technical reports that were available at the time this book was written. It also includes selected general photographic and other standards that are significant for micrographic systems analysis. Each citation includes the date when the standard was last revised.

ANSI/AIIM Standards

ANSI/AIIM MS1-1988. Recommended Practice for Alphanumeric Computer Output Microforms—Operational Practices for Inspection and Quality Control.
ANSI/AIIM MS4-1987. Flowchart Symbols and Their Use in Micrographics.
ANSI/AIIM MS5-1985. Microfiche.
ANSI/AIIM MS6-1981. Microfilm Package Labelling.
ANSI/AIIM MS8-1988. Image Mark (Blip) Used in Image Mark Retrieval Systems.
ANSI/AIIM MS9-1987. Method for Measuring Thickness of Buildup Area on Unitized Microfilm Carriers (Aperture, Camera, Copy and Image Cards).
ANSI/AIIM MS10-1987. Method for Determining Adhesion of Protection Sheet to Aperture Adhesive of Unitized Microfilm Carrier (Aperture Card).
ANSI/AIIM MS11-1987. Microfilm Jackets.

[1]Revision in process.
[2]In press.

ANSI/AIIM MS12-1977. Method for Measuring the Screen Luminance, Contrast and Reflectance of Microform Readers.[1]

ANSI/AIIM MS14-1988. Specifications for 16 and 35 mm Microfilms in Roll Form.

ANSI/AIIM MS15-1989. Dimensions and Operational Constraints for Single Core Cartridge for 16 mm Processed Microfilm.

ANSI/AIIM MS16-1981. Dimensions and Operational Constraints for Double Core (Bi-Axial) Cassette for 16 mm Processed Microfilm.

ANSI/AIIM MS17-1983. Test Chart for Rotary Microfilm Cameras.

ANSI/AIIM MS18-1987. Splices for Imaged Film—Dimensions and Operational Constraints.

ANSI/AIIM MS19-1987. Recommended Practice for Identification of Microforms.

ANSI/AIIM MS20-1979. Microfilm Readers.[1]

ANSI/AIIM MS23-1983. Practice for Operational Procedures/Inspection and Quality Control of First-Generation Silver-Gelatin Microfilm of Documents.

ANSI/AIIM MS24-1980. Test Target for Use in Microrecording Engineering Graphics on 35 mm Microfilm.

ANSI/AIIM MS26-1987. 35 mm Planetary Cameras (top light), Test Target and Procedures for Determining Illumination Uniformity.

ANSI/AIIM MS28-1987. Alphanumeric COM Quality Test Slide.

ANSI/AIIM MS29-1987. Cores and Spools for Recording Equipment—Dimensions.

ANSI/AIIM MS32-1987. Microrecording of Engineering Source Documents on 35 mm Microfilm.

ANSI/AIIM MS34. Dimensions for 100 ft. Reels for Conventionally Threaded Processed 16 mm and 35 mm Microfilm.[1]

ANSI/AIIM MS35-1987. Requirements and Characteristics of Original Black-and-White Documents That May Be Microfilmed.

ANSI/AIIM MS36-1987. Reader-Printers.

ANSI/AIIM MS37-1988. Recommended Practice for Microphotography of Cartographic Materials.

ANSI/AIIM MS38-1987. Microrecording of Engineering Graphics—Computer-Output Microfilm.

ANSI/AIIM MS39-1987. Recommended Practice for Operational Procedures, Quality Control and Inspection of Graphic Computer-Output Microforms.

ANSI/AIIM MS40-1987. Microfilm Computer Assisted Retrieval (CAR) Interface Commands.

ANSI/AIIM MS41-1988. Unitized Microfilm Carriers (Aperture, Camera, Copy and Image Cards).

ANSI/AIIM MS42-1989. Recommended Practice for the Expungement, Deletion, Correction, or Amendment of Records on Microforms.

ANSI/AIIM MS43-1988. Recommended Practice for Operational Procedures/ Inspection and Quality Control of Duplicate Microforms of Documents and From COM.

ANSI/AIIM MS44-1989. Recommended Practice for Quality Control of Image Scanners.

ANSI/AIIM MS45-1990. Recommended Practice for Inspection of Stored Microfilm.

ANSI/AIIM MS46-1990. Test Target and Test Method for Determining Output of 35 mm Microfilm Duplicators.[2]

ANSI/AIIM MS111-1987. Recommended Practice for Microfilming Printed Newspapers on 35 mm Roll Microfilm.

[1]Revision in process.
[2]In press.

Other Standards
ANSI Z39.32-1981. Information on Microfiche Headings.
ANSI IT9.1-1989. Imaging Media (Film)—Photographic Processed Films, Plates, and Papers—Filing Enclosures and Storage Containers.
ANSI IT9.2-1989. Imaging Media—Photographic Processed Films, Plates, and Papers—Filing Enclosures and Storage Containers.
ANSI IT9.5-1988. Imaging Media (Film)—Ammonia Processed Diazo Films—Specifications for Stability.
ANSI IT9.7-1989. Imaging Media (Film)—Determination of Brittleness of Photographic Film—Wedge Brittleness Test.
ANSI PH1.25-1984. Photography (Film)—Safety Photographic Film.
ANSI PH1.29-1985. Methods for Determining Curl of Photographic Film.
ANSI PH1.33-1986. Photography (film)—16 mm 100-foot, 16 mm 200-foot, 35 mm 100-foot, and 70 mm 100 foot Spools for Recording Instruments, Microfilms, and Still-Picture Cameras—Dimensions.
ANSI PH1.43-1985. Photography (film)—Processed Safety Film—Storage.
ANSI PH1.51-1983. Photography (film)—Micrographic Sheet and Roll Film Dimensions.
ANSI PH1.52-1986. Engineering Reproduction Films in Sheets and Rolls, Dimensions for.
ANSI PH.1.58-1985. Photography (paper)—Engineering Reproductions—Dimensions of Sheets and Rolls.
ANSI PH1.67-1985. Photography (film)—Processed Vesicular Film—Specifications for Stability.
ANSI PH2.51-1987. Source Document Microfilms—Determination of ASA Speed and Average Gradient.
ANSI PH3.45-1971. Contact Uniformity Test for Photographic Contact Printers.
ANSI PH4.8-1985. Photography (chemicals)—Residual Thiosulfate and Other Chemicals in Films, Plates and Papers—Determination and Measurement.
ANSI/ISO 3334-1989. Microcopying ISO Test Chart No. 2—Description and Use in Photographic Documentary Reproduction.
ANSI Y14.2M-1979 (R1987). Engineering Drawing and Related Documentation Practices—Line Conventions and Lettering.
ISO 3098/1-1974. Technical Drawings—Lettering—Part 1: Currently Used Characters.
ISO 3272/I-1983. Microfilming of Technical Drawings and Other Drawing Office Documents—Part I: Operating Procedures.
ISO 3272/II-1978. Microfilming of Technical Drawings and Other Drawing Office Documents—Part II: Quality Criteria and Control.
ISO 3272/III-1975. Microfilming of Technical Drawings and Other Drawing Office Documents—Part III: Unitized 35 mm Microfilm.
ISO 5475-1980. Technical Drawings—Sizes and Layout of Drawing Sheets.

AIIM Technical Reports
TR1-1988. Guidelines for Metrics.
TR2-1980. Glossary of Micrographics.
TR3-1981. Thermally Processed Silver Microfilm.
TR4-1989. Silver Recovery Techniques.
TR5-1983. COM Input Tape Formats.
TR6-1985. Guidelines for Microfilming Public Records on Silver Halide Film.
TR9-1989. Color Microforms.

[1]Revision in process.
[2]In press.

TR10-1985. Microimage Quality and Method for Measuring Quality in Flow Cameras.

TR11-1987. Microfilm Jacket Formatting and Loading Techniques.

TR12-1989. Bar Coding on Microfilm for Production and Dynamic Distribution Control.

TR13-1988. Care and Handling of Active Microform Files.

TR14-1988. Interchange of Tiled Raster Documents.

TR15. Electronic Image Capture of Documents.[2]

TR16-1989. Recommended Content of Product Specification Sheet for Readers and Reader-printers.

TR17-1989. Facsimile and Its Role in Electronic Imaging.

TR18-1989. Equipment Safety.

TR20-1989. Environmental and Right-to-Know Regulations Affecting Microfilm Processors.

[1]Revision in process.
[2]In press.

Glossary of Micrographic Terms

T HIS GLOSSARY CONTAINS terms and acronyms pertaining to micrographic technology, systems, and applications. It is based on the AIIM Technical Report TR2, *Glossary of Micrographics*, published by the Association for Information and Image Management. Designed as a convenient reference for those who want succinct definitions of specific terms, this listing is intentionally limited to micrographic terms and acronyms discussed in the preceding chapters. Readers should be aware that the TR2 publication, which includes many additional terms and acronyms, remains the definitive reference tool for micrographic systems analysts, records managers, information specialists, librarians, archivists, and others who require a comprehensive treatment of micrographic terminology. Most of the definitions presented here are reproduced exactly as they appear in TR2, although minor grammatical changes have been made in a few cases.

A

accelerated aging — a laboratory method of speeding up the deterioration of a product in order to estimate its long-term storage and use characteristics.

acetate film (acetate base) — safety film with a base composed principally of cellulose acetate or triacetate.

ADSTAR — automated document storage and retrieval.

AIIM — Association for Information and Image Management

alphanumeric — pertaining to a character set that contains letters, numbers, and usually other characters such as punctuation marks and symbols. Synonymous with alphameric.

ambient light — (1) surrounding light. (2) the general room illumination or light level.

ammonia process — the development of diazo materials by immer-

211

sion in a concentrated atmosphere of ammonia. Development is achieved by alkalizing (neutralizing) the acidic stabilizers in the diazo coating.

ammonium thiosulfate — a chemical compound used in the preparation of fixing solutions. Synonymous with hypo.

analog transmission — transmission of electronic signals analogous to tonal variations constituting the content of a document page or any form of original graphics; the representation of visual tonal variations at the input of a scanning system by proportional variations in strength or frequency of a transmitted electrical current.

ANSI — American National Standards Institute.

antihalation undercoat (AHU) — a separate layer of light-absorbing dye located between the emulsion and the base to suppress light reflection. During processing of this film, the dye layer becomes transparent.

aperture card — (1) a card with a rectangular opening(s) specifically prepared for the mounting or insertion of microfilm. (2) a processable card of standard dimensions into which microfilm frames can be inserted.

archival film — a photographic film that is suitable for the preservation of records having permanent value when the film is properly processed and stored under archival storage conditions, provided that the original images are of suitable quality.

archival quality — the ability of a processed print or film to permanently retain its original characteristics. The ability to resist deterioration.

ASCII — American Standard Code for Information Interchange. An American National Standard binary-coding scheme consisting of 128 seven-bit patterns for printable characters and control of equipment functions.

automated retrieval — a microform retrieval system in which the image(s) are displayed automatically. Commonly, the user interrogates an index, which may be manipulated by a computer, to locate the images.

automatic exposure control — a camera component that senses the brightness of an object and adjusts exposure.

automatic threading — the extraction of the leading end of the film and threading of the film by means built into a reader or other device and done without manual manipulation other than the manual operations associated with the actuation or "starting" of a reader, processor, camera, etc.

B

background — the portion of a document, drawing, microfilm, or print that does not include the line work, lettering, or other information.

bar code — an array of rectangular marks and spaces in a predetermined pattern.

bar-code symbol — a machine-generated and readable representation of data (usually numeric) in the form of a printed series of contrasting parallel bars of various widths, spacings, and/or heights.

base — a transparent plastic material, usually of cellulose triacetate or polyester, upon which a photographic emulsion or other material may be coated.

bleed-through — the undesired appearance of information from the back of a document when its front is photographed.

blip — see document mark.

C

camera — a photographic device, employing an optical system, used for exposing light-sensitive material.

camera card — (1) an aperture card containing unexposed and unprocessed microfilm which is to be exposed and processed while in the aperture. (2) the unexposed and unprocessed card input of a processor-camera.

camera head — the portion of a microfilming device that embodies the film, film-advance mechanism, and lens.

camera microfilm — first-generation microfilm; also called the master film.

camera-processor — a device that has both the functions of a processor and a camera.

CAR — computer-assisted retrieval.

cartridge — a container enclosing processed microforms, designed to be inserted into readers, reader-printers and retrieval devices. When applied to roll microfilm, it describes a single-core device.

cassette — (1) a double-core container enclosing processed roll microfilm designed to be inserted into readers, reader-printers and retrieval devices. (2) a lightproof container of rigid metal or plastic containing film for daylight loading in cameras. (3) a container for magnetic tape.

cathode-ray tube recording — the recording of an image created on the phosphor-coated cathode-ray tube via an optical system onto a light-sensitive material.

CCD — charge-coupled device

cellulose triacetate — transparent plastic used widely as a film base because of its transparency and relative nonflammability.

certification — (1) the confirmation or identification that micro-photographs are accurate and complete reproductions of the records. (2) attestation to the accuracy of measuring equipment or standards.

character — one of a set of symbols that may be arranged in ordered groups to express information. The symbols may include the numbers 0 through 9, the letters A through Z, punctuation marks and special characters. The character may be human readable and/or machine readable.

character generator — the electronic device, such as a computer-output microfilmer, which converts digital signals to visible characters.

charge-coupled device — a semi-conductor that can collect, store, and move charges in packets. An imaging charge-coupled device responds to light and provides electrical signals. Synonymous with CCD.

chemical development — the formation of a visible image from a latent image, involving the reduction of the exposed silver-halide grain to silver by a developing agent that is simultaneously oxidized.

chip — a piece of microfilm that is smaller than a microfiche.

chromatic aberration — a lens defect that causes rays of light of different wavelengths to focus in different planes.

CIM — computer-input microfilm.

cine mode — see vertical mode.

clean room — an area from which all dust, down to a certain size particle, has been removed and is prevented from entering, in order to handle delicate materials such as precision photographic film. The size of the dust particle that can be controlled determines the measure of cleanliness.

code — (1) the unique bit configuration describing a symbol or character. (2) a system of symbols representing rules for handling the flow or processing of information.

coding — any identifying information added to or made a part of the microform to enable the selection of a specific unit (microfiche, jacket, aperture card, or a specific frame within a roll or microform).

color microfilm — microfilm that provides a record of and displays with reasonable accuracy the colors in the original document or scene.

color stripe — a color (or colors) placed at the top edge of the heading area of a jacket, aperture card, or microfiche used for identification and retrieval.

column — (1) a vertical series of images on a microfiche or microopaque card. (2) the part of a planetary camera that projects vertically from the base and supports the camera head above the object being photographed.

COM — computer-output microfilm, computer-output microfilmer, or computer-output microfilming.

comic mode — see horizontal mode.

computer-assisted retrieval — the capability to have micrographic images located or identified by commands initiated through a computer terminal.

computer graphics — the methods and techniques for converting data to graphic displays by means of a computer.

computer-input microfilm — the process of reading data contained on microfilm by a scanning device and transforming this data into a form suitable for computer use.

computer-output microfilm — microforms containing data produced by a recorder from computer-generated electrical signals.

computer-output microfilmer — a recorder that converts data from a computer into human-readable language and records it onto microfilm.

computer-output microfilming — a method of converting and recording data from a computer onto microfilm in human-readable language.

condensing lens — a lens or a combination of lenses used to gather light from a source and to converge (condense) it, as upon the aperture of a reader or reader-printer.

contact printing — a method of copying in which the raw stock is held in contact with film bearing the image to be copied.

continuous-tone copy — photographic copy that contains a varying gradation of gray densities between black and white.

contrast — an expression of the relationship between the high and low brightness of a subject or between the high and low density of a photographic image.

control character — a character whose occurrence in a particular context initiates, modifies, or stops an operation, e.g., a character to control line spacing, line skipping, character size, intensity, style, etc.

conventional processing — (1) silver-gelatin films: a series of steps consisting of developing, fixing, washing, and drying. (2) dry-silver films: processing by heat. (3) diazo films: processing in an alkaline environment (e.g., ammonia). (4) vesicular films: processing by heat.

copy — see duplicate.

copyboard — the surface, frame, platform or other device for holding material to be photographed.

core — (1) the center portion of a

reel, spool, cartridge, magazine, or cassette. (2) an unflanged cylindrical form on which film or paper is wound.

corner cut — on aperture cards and microfiche, a diagonal cut at the corner of a card as a means of identification of the photosensitive side of the film.

CPU — central processing unit.

CRT — cathode-ray tube.

D

deformation — in thermoplastic recording, fine ripples on the surface of a plastic layer that scatter light, thereby making images composed of such ripples visible with an appropriate illumination system.

densitometer — a device used to measure the optical density of an image or base by measuring the amount of incident radiant energy (light) reflected or transmitted.

densitometric method (silver) — a testing procedure that produces a yellow stain for density measurement; used for indicating the presence of thiosulfate or other potentially harmful residual chemicals in processed films.

density — the light-absorbing or light-reflecting characteristics of a photographic image, filter, etc. Density is the logarithm to the base 10 of the ratio of the radiant energy (light) falling on a sample and the radiant energy transmitted or reflected. Density is expressed as $D = \log I/T$ where I is the radiant energy that falls on the sample and T is the radiant energy that is transmitted. In practice, there are many types of density depending on the optical system used (geometric) and on the spectral quality (color) of the radiant energy (light).

density, background — the opacity of the noninformation area of a microform.

density, line — the opacity of the line work, letters, or other non-background information of a microform.

depth of field — the distance between the points nearest and farthest from the camera that are acceptably sharp at a given focus and aperture setting.

depth of focus — the allowable tolerance in lens-to-film distance within which an acceptably sharp image of the subject focused on can be obtained at a particular lens aperture setting.

develop — to subject to the action of chemical agents or physical agents (as in electrophotography) for the purpose of bringing into view the invisible or latent image produced by the action of radiant energy on a sensitized surface.

developed image — the reproducible, visible image resulting from the processing of an exposed sensitized material.

developer — (1) a chemical reagent that makes the latent image visible on an exposed photographic emulsion. (2) a physical material, or mixture of physical materials, used to develop a latent electrophotographic image.

diazo — materials (coated films or papers) containing sensitized layers composed of diazonium salts that react with couplers to form azo dye images. The color of the image is determined by the composition of the diazonium compound and the couplers used in the process.

diffused light — radiation that either passes through or is reflected from a surface that causes the light rays to scatter.

digital transmission — the transmission of information in the form of electrical representations of the binary digits (bits) 0 and 1.

dimensional stability — the ability of photographic materials to maintain their original size and shape during and after processing and under various conditions of temperature and humidity.

direct-image film — a film that will retain the same polarity as the previous generation or the original material.

distortion — an aberration of a lens that causes imaging of straight lines as curves usually near the edge of the field of view.

distribution microform — a duplicate microform intended for actual use, as distinct from master and intermediate, whose function is to create distribution microforms.

document — a medium and the data recorded on it for human use, for example, a report sheet, a book.

document mark — an optical mark, usually rectangular, within the recording area below (and/or above) the image on a roll of microfilm; used for counting images or frames automatically.

dot matrix — an array of points of ink, light, or similar image-forming elements that are used to form alphanumeric characters.

dry-silver materials — sensitized film and paper products that are developed by the application of heat rather than by a liquid or viscous process.

duo — (1) a method of recording images on each half of the usable width of the microfilm. Exposures are made first on one half and then continued on the other half in the reverse direction. (2) format on microfilm using the technique described in (1).

duo-duplex — (1) a combination of duo and duplex methods in which, through the use of mirrors or prisms, images of both the front and rear sides of the documents are recorded simultaneously on half of the width of the film (the other film half being masked). When the full length of the film has passed through the camera, it is reloaded so that a second set of images can be photographed on the half previously left unexposed. (2) format on microfilm using the technique described in (1).

duplex — (1) a method of recording on roll microfilm in one exposure the image of the front and back of a document. The micro-images appear side by side across the width of the microfilm. (2) a term applied to any camera capable of performing duplex work as described above. (3) photographic paper having an emulsion coating on both sides. (4) format on microfilm using the technique described in (1).

duplicate — (1) a copy of a microform made by contact printing or by optical means. (2) To make multiple copies of a document or microfilm, usually with the aid of a master or intermediate.

dye-back film — any film having a light-absorbing dye coating on the base side of the film to improve daylight-loading characteristics and to reduce halation. The dye may be removed or made transparent during processing.

E

EBCDIC — Extended Binary Coded Decimal Interchange Code.

edge notching — a system of coding untized microforms for automated retrieval by cutting a pattern of notches along one edge (usually the bottom) or by affixing a prenotched clip to one edge of the microform.

effective reduction — a measure of the number of times an imaginary document would have been reduced to equal the size of a COM-generated microimages.

electrophotography — a process in which the effects of radiation and electricity, usually with the aid of electrophotographic developers, are used to produce a photographic record.

electrostatic process — the formation of a latent electrostatic image on a surface by action of light on a charged photoconducting material. The latent image may be made visible by a number of methods, such as applying charged pigmented powders or particles in a liquid which are attracted to the latent image. The particles either directly or by transfer may be applied and fixed to a suitable medium.

emulsion — a single- or multi-layered coating consisting of light-sensitive materials in a medium carried as a thin layer on a film base.

endorser — a camera accessory that automatically stamps documents as they are filmed. It is used principally by banks to place an endorsement or cancellation on checks.

enlargement — a copy larger than the microimage from which it is made.

enlarger-printer — a device that projects an enlarged image from a microform and develops and fixes the image on suitable material.

exposure — (1) the act of exposing a sensitive material to radiant energy. (2) the time during which a sensitized material is subjected to the action of radiation. (3) the product of radiation intensity and the time during which it acts on the photosensitive material.

F

facsimile — (1) an exact copy of a document. (2) the process or result of the process by which fixed graphic images are scanned, transmitted electronically, and reproduced either locally or remotely.

file — (1) a collection of records; an organized collection of information directed toward some purpose. (2) data stored for later processing by a computer or computer-output microfilmer.

film — any sheet or strip of transparent plastic coated with a light-sensitive emulsion.

film advance — (1) the movement of film across the exposure area of a camera in regular increments for successive frames. (2) the length of film moved after a given exposure.

film channel — the space in a microfilm jacket into which film is inserted.

film gate — a mechanism in cameras, printers, projectors, or similar devices that holds the photographic film in a precise plane and limits the area of illumination at the time of exposure or projection.

film strip — a short strip of processed photographic film, usually 16 or 35 mm, containing a number of frames.

film unit — the part of a microfilm camera which contains the film, film-advance mechanism and, in some microfilm cameras, the lens.

fixed focus — applied to cameras and other photographic and optical equipment for which the position of the lens and film plane are established by the manufacturer and cannot be altered by the user.

fixing — a film processing step that renders the material no longer light sensitive in order to make the developed image stable.

flash card — a target, generally provided with distinctive markings, that is photographed to facilitate indexing of the film. Synonymous with flash indexing and flash target.

flat-bed camera — see planetary camera.

flats — two pieces of glass polished to a high degree of smoothness and evenness used to hold film in cameras, readers, enlargers, etc.

flow camera — see rotary camera.

flow chart — a graphical representation for the definition, analysis, or solution of a problem, in which symbols are used to represent operations, data, flow, equipment, etc.

focal plane — the surface (plane) on which an axial image transmitted by a lens is brought to sharpest focus; the surface where the light-sensitive film in a camera is located.

focus — (1) the plane in which rays of light reflected from a subject converge to form a sharp image after passing through different parts of a lens. (2) to adjust the relative positions of a lens and film to obtain the sharpest possible image.

fog — nonimage photographic density. A defect in film that can be caused by (1) the action of stray light during exposure, (2) improperly compounded processing solutions, or (3) wrongly stored or outdated photographic materials.

form slide — a piece of glass or film that contains a document format, graphics, or other standard information which is superimposed on a frame of computer-output microfilm containing other data.

frame — that area of the film on which radiant energy can fall during a single exposure.

front projection — the process of forming an optical image on a reflective surface for viewing or photographing such that the projector is on the same side of the receiving surface as the viewer or the camera.

G

gelatin — a colloidal protein used as a medium to hold silver halide crystals in suspension in photographic emulsions, as a protective layer over emulsions, as a carrier for dyes in filters, etc.

generation — one of the successive stages of photographic reproduction of an original or master. The first generation is the camera film. Copies made from this generation are second generation, etc.

grid pattern — an array of horizontal and vertical lines (usually imaginary) that divides an area of a microform (usually a microfiche) into spaces called frames. The grid defines the arrangement of rows and columns.

H

halation — a halo or ghost around the desired image on a photographic emulsion caused by the reflection of rays of light from the base to the emulsion or by internal scattering of light within the film.

halide — any compound of chlorine, iodine, bromine, or fluorine and another element. The compounds are called halogens. The silver salts of these halogens are the light-sensitive materials used in silver-halide emulsions.

halide-reversal processing — see partial-reversal processing.

hand viewer — a small, portable magnifying device used for viewing microfilm or transparencies.

hardcopy — (1) an enlarged reproduction from a microform usually on paper. (2) a printed copy of machine output in a readable form, for example, output from a computer printer.

hardware — equipment, as opposed to software.

heading — inscription placed at the top of the microform (microfiche, jacket) to identify its contents. It is readable without magnification.

heading area — an area located at the top edge of the image area of the microform (microfiche, jacket) for the heading. Synonymous with title area and title space.

high contrast — a relationship of image tones in which the light and dark areas are represented by extreme differences in density.

high reduction — reductions above 1:30 up to and inclusive of 1:60.

hood — a part of the structure of a microform reader designed to shield the screen from ambient light.

hopper — in rotary microfilm recorders, the receiving area or tray for documents after they have been microfilmed.

horizontal mode — (1) the arrangement of images on roll microfilm in which the lines of print or writing are parallel to the length of the film for horizontal script and perpendicular for vertical script. (2) the arrangement of images on a microfiche in which the first microimage is in the top left corner of the grid pattern and succeeding microimages appear in sequence from left to right and in rows from top to bottom.

hot spot — an area that appears appreciably lighter than the surrounding area, commonly the result of uneven distribution of light by a reflector or optical system. For example, the central portion of an unevenly illuminated reader screen.

hypo — see ammonium thiosulfate and sodium thiosulfate

hypo elimination — the use of a bath that converts residual hypo into substances that will not react with the silver image and can be easily removed by washing. In a broader sense, hypo elimination also incudes the use of an alkaline or salt bath that increases washing effectiveness without reacting with the sodium thiosulfate or other fixing agents.

I

illumination — the act of providing with light. The process by which a surface receives light.

image — a representation of information produced by radiation. Images are real when they are formed in a plane, as on film in a camera. They are virtual when viewed as in a telescope.

image area — (1) the part of a recording area reserved for the images. (2) the area of a jacket containing film channels for the storage of microfilm images.

image orientation — the arrangement of images with respect to the edges of the film.

image reversing film — a film which when conventionally processed will reverse the polarity and tonal scale of the original material; that is, whites from blacks, blacks from white, negatives from positives, and positives from negatives.

image rotation — the ability to rotate microfilm images in readers in order to allow projection of all images right side up and right reading on the screen.

index frame — usually, the first or last frame of a series of images on a microform that records a table of contents or index to facilitate the location of information within the microform.

in-house — within the organization. Expression applied to work such as microfilming done within an organization, as distinct from work done by a service company. Synonymous with in-plant.

input — (1) the process of entering information into a system, e.g. a computer. (2) the data entered in (1) above.

inserter — see jacket filler.

intermediate — duplicate microform specifically prepared for producing further copies.

ISO — International Standardization Organization.

J

jacket — a flat, transparent, plastic carrier with single or multiple film channels made to hold single or multiple microfilm images.

jacket filler — equipment that cuts microfilm into strips and inserts them into film jackets. Usually equipped with a viewer for frame verification.

L

lap reader — a microform reader that can be placed on a person's lap during use.

laser — a source that produces light that is nearly monochromatic (of only one wavelength) and highly coherent (with waves in phase both temporally and spatially). Acronym for light amplification by stimulated emission of radiation.

latent image — the invisible image produced by action of radiant

energy on a photosensitive material. It may be made visible by the process of development.

leader — (1) a length of film at the beginning of a roll used for protection and for threading into equipment such as cameras, processors, and readers. (2) an unused or blank length of magnetic tape at the beginning of a reel of tape. The leader precedes the text or the recorded data.

leading end of film — the end portion of the film in advance of the first image or, if a separate leader is attached, the precise end portion of this leader.

lead microfiche — the first microfiche in a microfiche set.

LED — a semiconductor device that produces a visible luminescence when a voltage is applied to it. Acronym for light-emitting diode.

lens — the optical instrument or arrange of light-refracting elements designed to collect and distribute rays of light in the formation of an image.

light box — a device for inspecting film that provides diffused illumination evenly dispersed over the viewing area.

light sensitive — materials that undergo changes when exposed to radiant energy (light).

line copy — documents containing only lines and solids with no intermediate tones.

line density — the opacity of line work, letters, or other nonbackground information of an image.

long-term film — film suitable for the preservation of records for a minimum of 100 years when stored under proper conditions, providing the original film was processed correctly.

low contrast — a relationship of image tones in which the light and dark areas are represented by small differences in density.

low reduction — reductions up to and inclusive of 1:15.

luminance — the intensity of light produced or reflected per unit area viewed (the area viewed) by the observer or camera.

M

magazine — lighttight container that facilitates the loading and unloading of sensitized material used in micrographic equipment, e.g., camera, printer, processor.

magnetic tape — a continuous, flexible recording medium which has a base material impregnated or coated with a magnetic material, on which data can be stored by selective polarization of portions of the surface.

magnification — apparent enlargement.

magnification range — the range or span of magnification possible in a given optical system which is usually expressed in diameters or times.

magnification ratio — the expression of the relative degree an object is enlarged by an optical instrument; usually expressed in diameters or times, e.g. 16×, 24×, 30×, etc.

magnifier — a lens or lens system that enlarges an image.

manual retrieval — a microform system in which the user, without the aid of mechanization, extracts the microform from a file by hand, inserts it in a display device, and scans the microform to arrive at the appropriate location. This type of system may or may not be supported by auxiliary indexes to the filmed information.

mask — a device or opaque material to protect specific areas of photosensitive material from exposure.

master — a document or microform from which duplicates or intermediates can be obtained.

master film — any film, but generally the camera microfilm, used to produce further reproductions, such as intermediates or distribution copies.

medium contrast — a relationship of image tones in which the light and dark areas are represented by average or normal differences in density.

medium reduction — reductions above 1:15 up to and inclusive of 1:30.

medium-term film — a photographic film that is suitable for the preservation of records for a minimum of ten years when stored under proper conditions, providing the original film was processed correctly.

methylene blue — a chemical dye formed during the testing of archival permanence of processed microimages using the methylene blue method.

microcopy — a copy obtained by photography in a size too small to be read without magnification.

microdensitometer — an optical instrument that can measure the density of very small image areas on a photographic image.

microfacsimile — the transmission and/or reception of microimages via facsimile communication.

microfiche — a transparent sheet of film with microimages arranged in a grid pattern. A heading or number large enough to be read without magnification normally appears at the top of the microfiche in a space reserved for this purpose.

microfiche frame — an area on the microfiche formed by the grid pattern within which a microimage may be recorded.

microfiche set — two or more microfiche. A lead microfiche followed by one or more additional microfiche.

microfilm — (1) a fine-grain, high-resolution film used to record images reduced in size from the original. (2) a microform consisting of strips of film on rolls that contain multiple microimages. (3) to record microphotographs on film.

microfilm camera — the picture-taking portion of a microfilming mechanism and the lens.

microfilming — the techniques and processes used to record microimages on film.

microform — a form, usually film, which contains microimages.

microform production — the process of creating a microform from documents, from another microform, or by a computer-output microfilm recorder.

micrographics — techniques associated with the production, handling, and use of microforms.

microimage — an image of information too small to read without magnification.

micro-opaque — a very small image on a reflective as opposed to a transparent base, viewed by reflection rather than projection.

microphotography — an application of photographic techniques to produce images smaller than the original material.

micropublishing — to issue new (not previously published) or reformatted information in microform for sale or distribution.

microrepublishing — to issue on a microform material previously or simultaneously published in hardcopy for sale or distribution.

microtransparency — a microimage on a transparent base.

mil — one one-thousandth (0.001) of an inch, often used as a measure of thickness of film base, emulsion coatings, magnetic tape, etc.

mounter — a device that simultaneously cuts, positions, and fastens film frames in aperture cards.

N

negative-appearing image — an image in which the lines and characters appear light against a dark background.

nonimpact printer — a printing device in which the paper is not struck but imaged by other means, e.g., ink jet, electrostatic.

nonunitized microfilm — microforms that contain unrelated information units, e.g., roll microfilm can be nonunitized since it can contain a variety of unrelated information units on the same roll.

notch — a cut-out in either the top or bottom edge of the microform (microfiche, jacket) which is used for indexing, coding, or retrieval.

O

OCR — optical character recognition.

OCR-B — international standard set of characters used in optical character recognition systems.

odometer — instrument for measuring distance traversed. It can be used in microfilm cameras and roll-film retrieval devices for indexing and locating images on roll film.

odometer indexing — a method of image location using the linear location of the images on film.

offline — (1) pertaining to equipment or devices not under direct control of the central processing unit. (2) pertaining to equipment or devices not directly linked to a computer-output microfilmer.

online — (1) pertaining to equipment or devices under direct control of the central processing unit.

(2) pertaining to a user's ability to interact with a computer. (3) pertaining to equipment or devices directly linked to a computer-output microfilmer.

opacity — (1) the ratio of the light level (illuminance) on a sample of film, etc. to the light transmitted by the sample. (2) the characteristic of a material that prevents light from passing through it.

opaque screen — a reader screen of opaque material on which an image is projected.

optical — (1) containing lenses, mirrors, etc. as in optical viewfinder and optical printer. (2) in general, having to do with light and its behavior and control, as in optical properties, optical rotation. (3) pertaining to the science of light and vision.

optical character recognition — a technique by which printed or photographically recorded characters can be rapidly recognized by a combination of scanning techniques and electronic logic and converted to binary digital codes for storage, transmission, etc.

original — a document that may be reproduced.

orthochromatic film — a black and white film coated with an emulsion that is sensitive to ultraviolet, violet, blue, and green radiation. Not being sensitive to red, red objects photographed with orthochromatic film are rendered dark on a print.

output — pertaining to a device, process, or channel that delivers data in any of a variety of media, e.g., hardcopy, cathode-ray tube display, processed film, etc.

P

packing density — the number of useful storage cells per unit of dimension, e.g., the number of bits per inch stored on a magnetic tape.

panchromatic film — a film sensitive to ultraviolet, blue, green, and red radiation.

partial-reversal processing — processing of silver-gelatin emulsions in which an image polarity is obtained which is identical to that of the original. Partial-reversal processing omits the secondary exposure and development. The remaining halide image is not permanent; therefore, the film is not acceptable for achival keeping. Synonymous with halide-reversal processing.

photoconductor — (1) a material which is an electrical insulator in darkness but which becomes electrically conductive when exposed to light to which the material is sensitive. (2) a material that will hold an electrical charge in the dark, but the charge is dissipated when the material is illuminated with light to which the material is sensitive.

photo-optical coding — descriptive data related to documents in photo-optical format on the film. The coding is either adjacent to the document frame or along the edge of the film. It is also possible to encode instructions along with the identification information.

photoplastic film — a polyester-base film with a photoplastic emulsion that is sensitized by an electrostatic change and processed by dry procedures (thermal) with the images recorded as deformations (intaglio) in the film emulsion.

photosensitive — receptive to the action of radiant energy (light).

pixel — a picture element, for example, elements which make up the display on a cathode-ray tube.

planetary camera — a type of

microfilm camera in which the document being photographed and the film remain in a stationary position during the exposure. The document is on a plane surface at the time of filming. Also known as a flatbed camera.

polarity — the change or retention of the dark to light relationship of an image, i.e., a first generation negative to a second generation positive indicates a polarity change, while a first generation negative to a second generation negative indicates the polarity is retained.

polyester — a transparent plastic made from polyesters and used as a film base because of its dimensional stability, strength, resistance to tearing and relative non-inflammability.

portable reader — a microform reader of suitable size and weight such that it can be carried by hand.

positive-appearing image — an image in which the lines and characters appear dark against a light background.

preventive maintenance — upkeep of equipment on a regular basis specifically intended to prevent downtime and to insure trouble-free operation.

print — (1) a reproduction or copy on photographic film or paper. (2) to produce a reproduction or copy on photographic film or paper.

print film — a fine-grain, high-resolution film used primarily for making film copies.

printing — (1) the process used to produce microform copies from the developed microfilm. (2) the process used to produce hardcopy from microforms.

prism — a transparent body with at least two polished plane faces inclined with respect to each other, from which light is reflected or through which light is refracted. Prisms are often used for rotating an image.

processed film — film that has been exposed to suitable radiation and has been treated to produce a fixed or stabilized visible image.

processing — a series of steps involved in the treatment of exposed photographic material to make the latent image visible and ultimately usable, e.g., development, fixing, washing, drying.

processor — any machine that performs the various operations necessary to process photographic material, e.g., development, fixing, washing, etc.

processor-camera — see camera-processor.

projection — (1) formation of an image through optical means on a sensitized surface or a viewing screen, usually in magnified size. (2) an image that is visible after it has been optically projected onto a surface.

pulldown — the distance between the corresponding points on two successive frames.

Q

quality control — the techniques and procedures designed to maintain the repeatability and continuity of sensitometric and physical characteristics of photographic film and/or paper within statistically defined limits during processing.

R

radiant energy — energy in the form of waves of the same or different wavelengths that make up the electromagnetic spectrum, including visible light, invisible "light" (ultraviolet and infrared), heat, x-rays, radio waves, microwaves, and others.

reader — a device that enlarges microimages for viewing; usually consisting of a light source, illuminating optics, microform holder, objective lens, and screen.

reader-printer — a device that enlarges microimages for viewing and also has the capability of producing a hardcopy of the enlarged image.

rear projection — the projection of an image onto a translucent screen from the side opposite to that from which the image is viewed.

records preparation — a series of steps that could include sorting, flattening, removing fasteners (such as staples and paper clips), and index planning preliminary to microfilming.

reduction — the quotient of a linear dimension of an object and the corresponding linear dimension of the image of the same object expressed as $24\times$, $48\times$, etc.

reduction ratio — the relationship (ratio) between the dimensions of the original or master and the corresponding dimensions of the microimage, e.g., reduction ratio is expressed as 24:1, 48:1, etc.

reel — a flanged holder on which processed roll film is wound; designed to be inserted into readers, reader-printers, and retrieval devices.

residual thiosulfate ion — ammonium or sodium thiosulfate (hypo) remaining in film or paper after washing. Synonymous with residual hypo.

resolution — the ability of a photographic system to record fine detail.

resolution test chart — a chart containing a number of increasingly smaller resolution test patterns. The pattern is a set of horizontal and vertical lines of specific size and spacing.

resolving power — the numeric expression of the ability of an optical or photographic system to distinguish or separate two entities spaced closely together. In micrographics, it is the product of the number of the standard test pattern resolved in the image multiplied by the reduction and is expressed in line pairs per millimeter.

retrieval coding — the techniques for retrieving specific images or data from microfilm.

reversal processing — a photographic process used for silver-gelatin film in which an image is produced by secondary development of the silver halide grains that remain after the latent image has been changed to silver by primary development and destroyed by chemical bleach. The process consists of development, bleaching, clearing, reexposure, redevelopment, fixing, washing, and drying. In this process, the polarity of the image is reversed between the first development and the redeveloper. However, the final image has the polarity of the previous generation or the original material: that is, tone for tone, black for black, white for white, negative for negative, positive for positive.

rewind — (1) a support and a device consisting of a spindle geared to a crank, used in pairs to wind film from one reel to another. (2) the act of transferring film from one reel to another.

roll-to-card printer — equipment for producing duplicate, card-mounted microfilm from roll microfilm by contact printing.

roll-to-roll printer — equipment for producing duplicate rolls of microfilm by contact printing.

rotary camera — a type of microfilm camera that photographs documents while they are being moved by some form of transport mechanism. The document transport mechanism is connected to a film-transport mechanism, and the film also moves during exposure so there is no difference in the rate of relative movement between the film and the image of the document.

row — a horizontal series of microimages on a microform.

S

safety film — a comparatively nonflammable film support (base) that meets ANSI requirements for safety film.

scanner — a device that impinges a narrow beam of light on a document or on its microfilmed image and converts the reflected or transmitted light to electrical signals.

scanning — (1) the systematic impingement on an area by a narrow beam of light or other radiation. (2) the movement of an image on a reader screen in a direction perpendicular to the direction of roll film transport.

scanning device — (1) a mechanism found in certain microfilm readers where the entire image does not appear on the screen. The scanning device permits shifting the film or the entire optical system so that different portions of the microfilm frame or reel may be viewed. (2) a device that electrically dissects an image into sequential contiguous lines, within each of which the sequential density variations are converted to electrical variations.

sensitivity — the degree to which an emulsion reacts to radiation or other agents by the formation of a latent image under exposure; especially as this relates to ex-

posure by different wavelengths of light.

sequential indexer — a device that automatically stamps numbers on documents as part of the microfilming operation.

sequential numbering — a technique used for coding and locating images on roll microfilm. The numbers recorded during the filming process can be seen on the reader screen and used to identify and retrieve the image.

service company — an organization that is equipped to provide under contract micrographic and related services. Synonymous with service bureau.

sharpness — (1) the visual sensation (subjective) of the slope of the boundary between a light and a dark area. (2) the degree of (line/edge) clarity.

sheet film — a precut rectangle (not in roll form) of flexible, transparent-base material coated with a photosensitive emulsion.

shelf life — the period of time before deterioration renders a material unusable.

short-term film — microforms that will be needed only for a limited period.

shutter — any device that regulates the time that light is permitted to act on sensitized film or paper.

silver-densitometric method — a method of measuring residual thiosulfate in film.

silver film — a photographic film containing photosensitive silver compounds suspended in a suitable material. When developed, the image consists of metallic silver.

silver halide — a compound of silver and one of the following elements known as halogens: chlorine, bromine, iodine, and fluorine.

silver recovery — the reclamation of silver from spent photographic fixing baths.

simplex — (1) a method of recording images in which a single microimage occupies all or a major portion of the usable width of the microfilm. (2) format on microfilm using the technique in (1).

sodium thiosulfate — a salt used in many fixing solutions. This salt, in water solution, dissolves and removes the silver halides remaining in film after development. Synonymous with hypo.

software — a set of programs, procedures, and documentation concerned with the operation of a data processing system.

source document microfilming — the conversion of documents, usually paper, to microimages.

spacing — the distance between the trailing edge of one frame and the leading edge of the succeeding frame on a microform.

splice — a joint made by cementing, taping, or welding (heat splice) two pieces of film or paper together so they will function as a single piece when passing through a camera, processing machine, viewer, or other apparatus. Cemented splices are called lap splices, since one piece overlaps the other. Most welds are called butt splices, since the two pieces are butted together without any overlap.

spool — a flanged holder on which unprocessed roll film is wound, designed to be inserted into cameras and processors.

stability — the degree to which negatives or prints resist change by the action of light, heat, or atmospheric gasses.

standard — (1) a document that establishes engineering and technical limitations and applications for items, materials, processes, methods, designs, and engineering practices. (2) a fundamental unit or physical constant, e.g., ampere, meter, absolute zero.

step-and-repeat camera — a type of microfilm camera that can expose a series of separate images on an area of film according to a predetermined format, usually in orderly rows and columns, e.g. microfiche.

strip film — any length of film that is too short to be wound on a reel and that is generally housed in a small container or inserted in a jacket or other type of holder.

stroke generator — a method of generating characters using short strokes to draw the alphanumeric character in a manner similar to that used in ordinary handwriting. Some computer-output microfilm devices use this technique to draw the characters on the cathode-ray tube (CRT).

system — an organized collection of people, machines, data, and methods required to accomplish a specific set of functions.

T

target — (1) any document or chart containing identification information, coding, or test charts. (2) an aid to technical or bibliographic control that is photographed on the film preceding or following the document.

TEP — transparent electrophotographic process.

threading — transferring the leading end of the film from the supply spool, cartridge, etc. into photographic or microphotographic equipment, around all idlers, rollers, sprockets, etc., to the take-up device of the equipment.

throat — the entrance used to feed documents into rotary cameras.

toner — the material employed to develop a latent electrostatic image.

trailer — that portion of film beyond the last images recorded.

trailer microfiche — in a set of microfiche, all related microfiche after the first.

translucent screen — a reader screen of treated glass or plastic onto which an image is projected.

transparent photoconductor film — a microfilm that includes a photoconductive layer which, in combination with a special electrostatic imaging system, permits the adding of new images or overprinting of existing images on to an existing photoconductor film.

transport — the moving belt or roller device in a camera that moves documents through the machine.

U

ultrafiche — microfiche with images reduced more than 1:90.

ultrahigh reduction — reductions more than 1:90.

ultrastrip — short lengths of processed microfilm containing material photographed at ultra high reductions. Ultrastrips generally are created in a two-step process that consists of filming the material and then refilming this film at higher reductions.

unitize — (1) to separate a roll of microfilm into individual frames or groups of frames and insert them into a carrier, e.g. aperture cards, jackets. (2) to microfilm on one or more microfiche a unit of information, such as a report, a specification, periodical, etc.

universal camera — a special microfilm camera that can handle 16 mm, 35 mm, and 105 mm film.

updatable microfilm — a microfilm that permits the addition or deletion of images.

updatable microform — a microfilm medium to which additional images can be added at any time.

V

vertical mode — (1) the arrangement of images on roll microfilm in which the lines of print or writing are perpendicular to the length of the film for horizontal script and parallel for vertical script. (2) the arrangement of images on a microfiche in which the first microimage is in the top left-hand corner of the grid pattern and succeeding microimages appear in sequence from top to bottom and in columns from left to right. Synonymous with cine mode.

very high reduction — reductions above 1:60 up to and inclusive of 1:90.

vesicular film — a film in which the light-sensitive component is suspended in a plastic layer. On exposure, the component creates optical vesicles (bubbles) in the layer. These imperfections form the latent image. The latent image becomes visible and permanent by heating the plastic layer and then allowing it to cool.

W

wet processing — processing carried out by using chemicals in liquid or vapor form.

X

xerography — the formation of a latent electrostatic image by action of light on a photoconducting insulating surface. The latent image may be made visual by a number of methods, such as applying charged pigmented powders or liquids that are attracted to the latent image. The particles may be applied either directly or by transfer may be applied and fixed to a suitable medium.

Z

zoom lens — a lens with movable optical elements that can retain an object in focus, while changing the lens focal length. Consequently, the size of the object can be varied, while the camera or reader remains in the same position.

Index

A

Abstract, report, 43

A.B. Dick Record Systems, 37–38, 57

Access speed, data, 36

Acetate, 76

Active system, (Active Records
Management), 7–9, 29, 37, 67,
166–172

active information management,
109

Admissibility of evidence
(in microform), 6

ADSTAR (Automated Document
Storage and Retrieval), 142–143

AIIM (Association for Information
and Image Management), 17,
19–20, 24, 27, 29–31, 33–34,
40, 44, 55, 73–76, 82–83, 99,
102, 104, 114, 117, 118–121, 135,
148, 171, 189

Alkaline, 70

Alphanumerics (versus graphics), 93,
100–102, 115, 146

alphanumeric information, 2, 87

American National Standards Institute
(ANSI), 17, 19–20, 24, 27,
29–30, 31, 33, 34, 40, 41, 44,
55, 73–77, 80, 83, 96, 99, 102,

American National Standards Institute
(continued)
104, 114, 117, 120–121, 135, 148,
171, 191

Ammonia development, 77

Amortization, 4, 168–170, 174

Anti-halation undercoat (AHU), 56

Aperture card (card), 27–28, 42–46,
51, 54–55, 67, 72, 81–82, 85,
90, 110, 116, 119, 129, 150, 180,
188

plotter, 110

enlarger/printer, 128

Applications, 72, 81, 86, 96

characteristics, 116–119

Archival, archives, 56, 75, 77, 79–80,
87, 102, 188, 190

microfilming, 3–7, 14, 109

processing, 76

ASCII, code, 89, 98, 189, 192

Atomic Energy Commission, 31

Automated retrieval, storage,
147–148, 150, 180, 188, 190

Automatic document feeders, 64,
64–67

Automatic duplicators, 75, 81

B

Background density. see Density
Banking, use of in micrographics, 3, 51, 61
Bar code, optical, 104, 143
Beam, laser, 90, 92
Binary code (data transmission), 98, 136, 143, 190
Bits onto film, 181, 183, 187–188
Blip encoding, 135–138, 143, 147, 169
Book pages, microfilming of, 116
"Browsing", 181
Buffer, buffering, 181

C

CAD/CAM (computer-aided design/computer-aided manufacture), 101
Cameras, 1, 10, 27, 37–38, 40, 44, 48, 51–52, 54, 56, 61, 67, 74
  operation of, 38–39, 159–160
  planetary, 58, 61–64, 68–69, 74, 83, 101, 132–133, 147
  rotary, 58–60, 61–64, 67–69, 74, 83, 132, 134–135, 147, 158, 160
  step-and-repeat, 64–65, 68, 69, 139
Camera operator, 131
Camera-processor. see Processor-camera
Capacities, file, 100
CAR (computer-aided retrieval), see Retrieval, computer-aided.
Card, 81
  aperture (see aperture card)
  copy, 46
  duplication/distribution of, 44
  retrieval of, 46
Card jackets, 43–44, 54, 81–83, 116
Card punch, 44
Carrier, transparent (see also Jackets), 123–124, 152
Cartridges, 4, 7, 27–31, 35–37, 48–49, 51, 54–56, 68–69, 71, 83, 98, 100, 124, 127, 130–131, 133, 147, 150, 186, 188
Cassettes, 124

Cathode-ray tube (CRT), 90–92, 103
Cellulose triacetate, 55, 76
Central processing unit (CPU), 183
Checks, microfilming of, 27
Chemicals, processing, 125
CIM.see computer-input microfilm
Cine orientation, 25, 27, 100, 103, 119
Coaxial cable, 180–182
Code, control, 95–96
  digital, 190
Code conversion, electronic, 183
CODE, 40
Coding, retrieval
  binary (discrete), 1
Color
  use of in filing, 36, 42–44, 58, 67, 139
Color microfilm, 56–57, 76, 80, 91, 116
COM, COM device, COM recorder. see Computer-output microfilming.
Comic orientation, 25, 27, 40, 103, 119
Communication channels
  digital, 179
Communication equipment, 179
Compaction, (see also Data compression), 102–103
Component selection, 180, 188
COM-produced images, 2, 10
  versus source document, 21, 31, 33–36
Computer-aided retrieval (CAR).
see Retrieval
  computer-assisted retrieval, 7–9, 130, 137–138, 141–150, 166–167, 169, 177, 179–181, 186
Computer-input microfilm (CIM), 141, 181, 188–190
Computer-output microfilming (COM), 1, 6, 8–12, 17, 21–25, 31, 34, 48, 77, 80–81, 84–108, 117–119, 130, 134–135, 138–140, 147, 172–173, 179–181, 188, 191–192
  graphic, 10
Computer peripherals, 86–87, 104, 189

Computer printouts, filming of, 10,
99, 102, 117
Computer, use of in micrographics,
69, 96–98, 141, 143, 146,
177–178, 182
see also Computer-output
microfilming;
Computer-input microfilming,
Retrieval, computer-aided
Consumption
ammonia, 77
paper, 124
Containers, microform, 77, 150, 160,
180
Contrast, image, 56, 58, 75, 125
Conversion, file, 161–1612 164, 180,
186, 188, 189
Copier, office, 127
Copyboard, camera, 135
Copy card. see Card.
Copy film. see Film, diazo, vesicular
COSATI (Committee on Scientific and
Technical Information), 34, 41
Costs, 155–176
amortization of, 168–170, 173–175
computing of, 178
duplication, 99
equipment, 70, 112, 125–127, 160,
170
floor space, 172
labor, 170–171
loaded, 171
maintenance, 170, 175
preparation, 171
processing, 71
savings in, 7, 36, 41, 96, 105, 173
service bureau, 170–171, 173
CPU. see Central processing unit
CRT. see Cathode-ray tube

D

Data base, 130, 133, 135, 141, 143,
145, 146, 148–150, 178, 182,
185–187, 190
digital, 90, 183
Data compression, 185
Data, digital, 1, 2, 10–11, 15–16, 47,
51, 84, 85–87, 90, 93, 98, 100,

Data, digital (continued)
104, 107, 108, 133, 137,
139–145, 170–172, 178,
184–185, 188, 190, 191, 185
recording of, 21, 87, 89–90, 93,
98, 169, 189
Data processing, 9–11, 85–90, 91, 97,
101, 146, 148, 155, 174,
177–178, 182
Decentralized operation, 180, 182
Decision makers, 162, 165
Defects, film image, 77, 116
Densitometer, 73, 74, 180
Density, image, 70, 73–76, 82,
98–99, 123, 191
Department of Defense (DOD), U.S.,
19
Destruction of images, 146, 158–160,
172
Destruction of records, 6, 160,
170–172
Development, film image. see
Ammonia development, Heat
processing, Processing.
Diazo process, 77–81, 87, 103, 105,
158, 159, 190
Diazo film. see Film, diazo.
Digital data. see Data, digital
Digital representations, 179–180, 183
Digital storage, 180
Direct read after write, 192
Disk, 98, 106–108, 141, 146, 169,
181, 184–185
floppy (diskette), 145, 191
optical, 141, 145, 184–191
Display and reproduction, 35, 109,
111, 145, 170, 187
equipment, 30, 36, 41–42, 46, 69,
77, 79, 109, 112, 121, 129, 135,
141, 146–147, 175
see also Enlarger-printers, Readers,
Reader-printers, Video terminal.
Display, 7–10, 16, 29, 83, 90,
109–111, 113–120, 123–124, 136,
155, 169, 171, 172, 185
CRT, 90–91, 102, 134, 138, 148
see also Video terminal
microimage, 140, 147, 151, 180,
187

Distributed, microform, 3, 8, 12, 16, 48, 77, 87, 103–106, 121, 155, 162, 173, 182, 191
savings in, 173–174
Document size, 16, 20–21, 24, 26, 28, 33–35, 37 40, 42, 46–47, 58, 62–63, 69, 74, 98–99, 102, 106, 117, 119, 129
Documents, rare, preservation of, 1–4, 6–10, 12–17, 19–25, 27–28, 30–31, 33–36, 38–41, 43, 48, 75, 83, 86, 92–93, 101, 108, 112, 116, 124, 127, 141–146, 148–149, 158, 171, 177, 185–186
DOD, 19
Drafting, 20
Drawings, microfilming of, 1, 2, 9–10, 20, 34–35, 40, 42, 44, 46, 51, 56, 62–63, 67, 69, 72–73, 83, 85–86, 98, 101, 109, 116, 118–119, 125–126, 128–129, 145
Duo, duplex formats, roll film, 61, 69, 119
Duplication, microimage, 20, 28, 30, 36, 39, 42, 54–55, 58, 73–75, 77–81, 83, 84, 87, 99, 102–103, 105, 116, 125, 145, 146, 170, 174, 182, 189
automated, 75, 81
demand, 12, 36
production (bulk), 12, 20, 81, 87, 157, 181, 188
Duplicators, 39, 41, 44, 48, 51, 54, 77, 81–82, 87, 90, 104, 109, 111, 144, 167, 190

E

EBCDIC code, 98
EBR (electron beam recording), 90–92
Economic analysis, 161
Economic feasibility, 36, 156
Economics, 11, 105
Edge notching, 43–44
Eight-up image format, 46
Electric accounting machine (EAM), see also Card, EAM, 138
Electrofax, 124, 126–127

Electron beam recording (EBR), 90–92
Electronic data-processing (EDP) equipment, 99, 148
Electronic logic. see Logic
Electronic mail, 179
Electronic microfilming, 183, 186–188
Electronic systems, 178–179
Electrostatic process, 38, 126
Emerging technologies, 190
Emulsion, film, 56, 58, 74–75, 77–80, 99
Encoding, 135–136, 141, 147, 169, 180, 183
Energy, light, distribution of, 31, 38
Engineering drawings. see Drawings
Engineering environment, use of micrographics in, 13, 37, 63, 104, 119–120
Enlargement, microimage, 84, 112, 117, 121, 125–127, 179, 181
Enlarger-printers, 75, 109, 111, 127–128
Environmental factors, 50
Equipment, miscellaneous, 7, 17, 28, 30, 35, 41–44, 51–52, 54–55, 57, 62–64, 70, 73, 77, 83, 87, 89–90, 97, 104, 107, 109, 115, 120–121, 123–125, 129–130, 132, 135, 138, 143, 149–150, 155–156, 158–159, 162, 167, 170, 172–175, 186–188
Equipment, rental, 126–127, 168
Equipment requirements, 53, 114
Equipment selection, 29
Exposure control, automatic, 31, 37–39, 55, 57, 62–63, 64–70, 79–82, 123, 134

F

Facsimile communication (fax), 112, 176, 178–181, 187
analog, 178
digital, 178–180, 185
microfilm, 178–180
Fade, image, 21, 75, 125–126
Fax. see Facsimile communication

Fiche. see Microfiche
File, microform,, 16, 97
  automated. see Retrieval
  basic, 125, 129–130, 169
  duplicate, 146
  location of, 146, 148, 167, 169
  master, 77
  mechanized, (see also Retrieval), 185
  satellite, 9
File access, (see also Access, file), 143, 152
File conversion. see Conversion
File entry, 140–141
File integrity, 3, 8, 9
File organization, 4, 37, 129–130
File security. see Security
File updating. see Purging, updating
Filing, random, 152
Filler, jacket, 83
Film, diazo, 54, 76–82, 103, 105, 116, 159, 171
  direct-duplicating, direct-positive, (silver gelatin), 4, 80, 86, 91, 103, 114, 116
  dry-silver, 38, 57, 76, 77, 86, 91, 103, 114, 124–126
  heat-processed, 91
  roll, 31, 56, 83, 86, 98, 121–123, 128, 170
  silver-halide, 37, 54, 57, 77
  thermoplastic, 79
  vesicular, 54, 76, 77, 80–82, 103, 105, 114
Film chemistry. see Chemistry
Film "chips", 67
Film strips, 39–40, 43, 83, 140
Film technologies, new, 37
Film transport, 112–114, 123–124
Filming, 13, 21, 25, 27, 30, 33, 52, 129, 131, 157
Fixing (of film images), 70, 71, 79
Flash targets, 130–132, 133, 135, 139, 141, 157, 159
Flat-bed camera. see Planetary camera
Floor space, 4, 10, 157, 161–162, 166, 172
  cost of. see Costs

Floppy disk, 191
Flowcharting, flow charts, 17–18, 53, 86, 143, 157
Focus, reader or reader-printer, 121
Fonts, character, 101–102, 106, 189, 192
Format, 31, 33–34, 41, 43, 61–62, 65, 97, 99, 102, 191
  image (roll film), 22–23
Forms, certification, 93
Four-up image format, 46
Forms overlay, forms projection, forms slide, 93–94, 103, 135
Frame size, microform, 27, 33, 61, 95, 100
Fume problems, odor, 126
Fumes, venting of, 77

G

Gas, use of, in micrographics, 77
  ammonia, 77
Generation, microform, (see also Duplication), 20, 55, 73–74, 77–79, 103
Government, use of micrographics in, 3, 12, 14, 19, 31, 34, 85, 142, 156, 182–183, 191
Graphics, 2, 10, 35, 57–58, 74, 83, 84, 87, 90–91, 100–102, 104, 117–119, 190
  color, 57
  tonal, 55, 189
Graphic transfer, graphic transmission. see Communication; Facsimile communication; Retrieval, remote; Transmission, electronic.
Great Britain, museum, 13
Grid, fiche, 30–32, 34, 140
Growth, file, allowing for, 7, 16, 31, 67, 182

H

Halo effect, 120
Hand-held viewer, 112, 119
Handling, special, 28, 47, 69, 71–72, 112

Hardware, micrographic, 2, 149

Header, microfiche, 36, 38–41, 64, 139–140

Heat processing (of film images), 38, 80, 114, 125

Hospitals, use of micrographics in, 7

Host computer, 89–95, 96

Human-computer interaction, 85–87, 189

Human handling (of microforms), see Human interface.

Human interface, human intervention, 120

Humidity, effects of on film, 76

Hybrid systems, 183, 187–189

I

Identification, file user, 15, 36, 38, 40–41, 121, 129, 132, 137, 141, 144, 148, 151, 156

Identifiers, discrete, 144–145, 152

Illumination level, reader, 58, 79, 120, 181

Image management, 36, 180

Image card. see Card

Image data compression, 146

Image fade, 75

Image, latent, 38, 52, 77–80, 105, 126

Image permanence. see Archival Quality

Image quality. see Quality output

Implementation scheduling, 167–169, 172, 181

Improvement, margin for, 111

Inactive system, 155–156, 166

Index formatting, 143

Indexing, 8, 130, 133–135, 137–138, 140–141, 143–146, 148, 149, 169, 172
  computer, 9, 144–145, 149, 178, 183
  microfiche, 97
  odometer, 130, 132–135

Information management, manager, 1, 7–9, 15, 24, 85, 107, 109, 130, 143, 146, 155–156, 167, 168, 176, 177, 181, 182, 187, 188

Information (versus image) retrieval, 17, 20, 36, 38, 41–44, 75, 85–86, 93, 98, 105–106, 108–109, 136, 139–141, 146, 148, 155, 160, 162–163, 171, 172

Information services, 12, 13, 23, 35, 43, 79, 95, 97, 102, 106–107, 115, 162, 190

Information system, 1, 15, 121, 148, 167

Information transfer, 87, 164

Input uniformity, 58, 90, 93

Inspection, film image, 73, 87, 117, 170–172
  equipment for, 77, 82, 90

Insurance industry, use of micrographics in, 1, 7, 37, 52, 137

Integral positional locating, 89, 97, 114

Integrated circuits, 9, 87, 121, 177–179, 192

Integrity, file, 37

"Intelligent" (smart) terminal, 98

International Standards Organization (ISO), 19–20

Investment, recovery of, 161, 164

ISO (International Standards, Organization), 19, 20

J

Jacket filler, 83

Jackets, 23, 27–28, 35, 39–44, 46, 51, 54, 67, 81–84, 112, 119, 129, 138–140, 150

K

Keyboard. see Keystroke input

Keypad, 147

Keypunching, 44

Key-punch reproducer, EAM, 44, 45

Keystroke input, 171, 191

Key-word indexing, 185

Kilobytes, 191

L

Labels, film carton, 114, 131, 133,

Labels, film carton (continued)
135, 159, 160
Labor, 42, 166, 178–179
cost of, 158–160, 168–172, 174
Laboratory notebooks, microfilming
of, 35, 157
Laser efficiency, 92
Laser beam recording, 90, 91, 106
Laser, use of in micrographics, 105,
127
Latent image, 38, 54–55, 80, 87,
103, 105, 126–127
Legal considerations, 6, 48, 84, 178
retention (see also Destruction
Retention), 6, 16, 178
Legibility, (see also Resolution),
20–21, 52–54, 64, 74, 90, 102,
104, 127
individual character, 21, 90–91,
104
Libraries,use of micrographics in, (see
also Book pages, Periodicals), 2,
13–15, 21, 28, 31, 43, 49, 51,
62, 125, 148
Library of Congress, 13
Light box, 52
Light-emitting diode recording,
display, 90, 123, 134, 138
Light, ultraviolet (UV), 80, 82
Light wells, 73
Linear dimension, 20, 21, 117
Loader, cartridge, 114, 137, 148,
185–186
Local area network, 89, 179, 185,
191
Location aids, 100, 114, 121,
129–131, 135, 138, 140–141, 146,
185–187
Logic, electronic, 90, 185

M

Magnetic recording, (see also Disk
Tape), 89–90, 96–98, 141, 145,
169, 180, 183–184, 190
Magnetic storage, efficiency of, 101,
106, 108, 145–146, 188–189
Magnification, 1, 23, 35, 83, 110,
116–119, 121, 128

Mail, electronic, 9
Mailing (of microforms), 2, 105
Mailing costs, 8–9, 15, 105
Mainframe, 11, 12, 87, 89–90, 96,
98, 104, 146, 148–149, 192
Maintenance, 55, 69, 146, 148–149,
157, 168, 170, 174, 177
cost of, 158, 160, 163, 166, 172,
175
space for, 156, 165
Maps in microform, 2, 46, 51–52,
57, 62, 83, 85, 109, 118
Marks, optical, 38, 135
Master, microform, 12, 36, 77–82,
103, 105
Material requirements, 13–15, 19, 21,
58
Mathematical equations in
microform, 20, 168
Memory, computer, 48
Memory devices, 106
Methylene-blue test, 76
Microcard, 49
Microcomputer, 2, 81, 89–90, 97–98,
112, 146, 148–149, 163, 186,
191–192
Microcopy Resolution Test Chart,
NBS, 74
Microfacsimile. see Facsimile communication, microfilm
Microfiche, 1 and forward
Microfilm (see also Microform,
Micrographics, Micrographic
systems), 1 and forward
definition of, 3
destruction of, 6
Microfilmer. see Cameras
Microform, 1 and forward
definition of, 12, 20, 40
multi-image, multicopy, 11
nonstandard, 34
production of, 1, 3, 12, 15–17, 19,
75, 90, 106, 126, 129, 146, 168
selection of, 3, 16, 22, 117, 155
unit, unitized (versus "collective"
or multiimage), 35
nonunitized, 35
Micrographics, 2, 3
definition of, 2

Micrographic system, 8, 11, 15–17, 20, 23, 28–31, 35–37, 49, 54, 56, 83, 89, 109–112, 115, 121, 125, 127, 129, 132, 135, 138, 141–144, 146–147, 149–151, 155–156, 161–162, 166–168, 177–180, 182, 186, 188–189
  active versus inactive, 4, 8
  archival (inactive), 6, 7, 13, 166
  definition of, 1
  flowcharting of, 17–18
  funding of, 19
Microimage, microimaging, 1 and forward
Microimage digitizer. see Computer-input microfilm.
Micro-opaques, 23, 49, 114
Microphotography, 1, 12, 19–23, 37, 48, 51, 77, 99, 177, 179, 190
Microprocessing, microprocessor (see also Logic), 51, 65, 114, 123, 128, 138
Micropublishers, micropublishing, 11–14, 28, 31, 34, 48, 70, 109, 125
Microscope, 52, 73
Microvonics, 38, 57
Microwave communication, 182
Minicomputer, 10, 11, 89, 90, 97, 104, 146, 148, 149, 169, 186, 192
Miscellaneous equipment, 158
Misfiling, 36, 42, 44
3M Company, 29, 31
Motorized advance, (in microimage readers), 112, 121
Mounter, film-to-card, 83
Multiplexing, holographic, 61

N

National Technical Information Service (NTIS), 12
Negative-appearing images, (see also Polarity), 55, 70, 79, 103, 125–126
Negative versus positive images. see Polarity
Newspaper, backfiles, 13

Newspaper pages, microfilming of, 21, 117
  (see also Periodicals)
Nonreversal, nonreversing (defined), 80
"Nuisances" in microfilming, 26

O

Obsolescence, equipment, 43
OCR. see Optical character recognition
OCR-B font, 102, 188
Odometer, 132–133, 141
Office of the future, "paperless office", 9
Online/offline, 9, 10, 28, 89–90, 96–98, 106–108, 112, 144–145, 148, 169, 178, 183, 186, 188, 192
Opaque micorforms, (micro-opaques), 49–50, 114
Opaque marks, 83, 135
Operating space, equipment, 63, 67, 71, 105, 112, 114, 182
Operational considerations, 4, 8, 67–68, 70, 75, 83, 104
Operator, camera, 27, 61–64, 67–68
Optical character recognition (OCR), 179, 189–190
Optical characteristics, 114–116
Optical disk, 185–191
  jukebox, 187
Optical filing system, 185
Optical marks, 83
Optical printing, 48
Optical retrieval, media, 101
  binary (discrete), 143, 190
  blip, image count, 135
Optical scanning, 95
Output formats, 10, 95–97
Output peripherals, 86, 104
Output, system, 11, 89

P

Paper (defined), 6, 10

Paper files, conversion to microform, 6–7, 163–166, 169
(see also Conversion)
Paperless office, 9
Paper, print
characteristics of, 125
oxide-coated, 125, 126
Paper, weight of, 5
PCMI (photochromic microimaging materials), 48, 57
Periodicals in microform, 21, 31, 35, 117
Permanence, image. see Archival quality
Photoplastic film, 38, 76
Photoreceptive, 126–127
Physical planning, 77
Planning, system, 16–18, 98
Plotters, graphic, 101, 110
Plumbing, processor, 71
Polarity, image, 55, 77–79, 103, 123, 125–126
Positive-appearing images, 55, 79, 103, 120, 125–126
(see also Polarity, image)
Preservation of valuable documents, 75
Prices. see Costs
Printers, 101
line, 104–105, 107, 174–175
nonimpact, 104, 106
page, 105–106, 175
Print tape or print file, 95–97
Print processes, 77, 123
dry silver, 76, 86, 92, 103, 124, 125
electrostatic, 126
stabilization, 124
Processing film, 56, 57, 105
cost of, 71
in-house, 157–158, 167
nonchemical, 80
nonreversal, 80
partial reversal, 70
reversal, 55, 70, 72, 80, 125, 139
Processor-camera, 52, 57, 67, 72
Processors, film, 54, 70–71, 86, 103
Processors, operation of, 70
Production, microform. (see Computer-output microfilming,

Production, microform (continued)
Duplication, Filming, Microform, Processing)
Production support equipment, 83, 109
Production volume, 81
Productivity, 3, 8, 56, 63–64, 160
Purging, updating, 53

Q

Quality, archival, 43, 127
Quality control, 61–63, 64–69, 73, 82–83, 104, 105, 159, 171
Quality, output, 1 and forward
(see also Contrast, Legibility, Resolution)

R

Random filing, 140, 152
Reactions, user, 76
Readability. see Legibility
Reader, microform, 27–28, 58, 79, 103, 109–119, 121, 124, 131, 132–133, 135, 138, 145, 147, 150–151, 152, 167, 173–174, 189
card, 83, 112
"lap", 112
large-screen, 112, 119
microfiche jacket, 28, 36, 41, 112, 114, 119, 140, 148, 174
micro-opaque, 114
motorized, 27, 112
multimedia, 116–117
portable, 112, 114, 119
roll-film, 82, 112
screenless (projectors), 110
ultrafiche, 48, 116
Reader-printers, 27–30, 35–36, 39, 41, 58, 75, 79, 103, 109–111, 121–127, 131–133, 135–138, 143, 145, 147–148, 150–151, 152–157, 159, 160, 162–163, 167, 169–170, 179, 187
Real time, 106–108
Records management, 3, 7, 8, 29, 30, 37, 54, 67, 83, 85, 106, 130, 157, 167

Recovery, silver, 71
Reduction, microimage, 3, 20–26, 31,
    33–35, 40, 46–47, 49, 58,
    61–63, 65, 69, 75, 79–80, 83,
    93, 98–100, 102, 103, 117, 118,
    175, 191
Reel, film, 7, 24–25, 27–28, 30,
    54–56, 61, 83, 100, 124, 126,
    127, 129, 132–135, 137–138,
    147, 150, 159, 160, 170
Reference-type systems, 86, 126–127,
    129, 132, 141, 157, 173
Reflectance, 56, 68, 120, 182, 188
Remote access. see Retrieval, remote
Rental equipment, 158, 168
Replenishment, chemical, 103, 126
Report, abstract, 43
Reports in microform, 2, 11, 14, 35,
    42–43, 51, 85, 87–89, 97, 99,
    102–108, 119, 120, 129, 139–141,
    157, 172, 174–175
Reproduction, microimage,, 13–16,
    21–23, 74–75, 93, 179, 181, (see
    also Print processes, Quality)
  full-size versus reduced, 21
Research, use of micrographics in,
    13–14
Residual thiosulfate (hypo), 75–76
  tests for, 76
Resolution, 79, 82, 92, 104, 115–116,
    181, 185, 190
Resolution criteria, 74, 115–116
Resolution test charts, 74, 115
Retention, records, 6, 7, 16
Retrieval, microimage, 1–3, 7–8, 13,
    16–17, 20, 23, 30, 37, 52, 98,
    105, 129–138, 140–146–151, 161,
    167, 169, 172, 175, 178,
    179–180, 182–183, 185–188, 190
    (see also Indexing, Retrieval aids)
  aperture card, 44
  automatic (fully automated), 24,
    30, 135, 142–143, 152
  computer-aided, 1, 7, 9
  microfiche, 31, 130
  optical, 135
  semiautomated, 130, 141
Retrieval aids, 133
Retrieval coding, 69
Retrieval speed, 176

Reversal, reversing (defined), 55, 80,
    139
Reversal processing. see Processing
Rewinds, 73
Roll film. see Film

S

Safety considerations, 56, 114
Savings. see Cost, Labor, Storage
    space
Scanning, 119, 179–181, 182–185,
    190
  optical, 95
Screen, reader, 112, 116–117, 121
  angle of, 115
  size of, 118–119, 121
"Scrolls", 103
Security, file, 3, 42, 69, 87, 145–146
Sequential frame numbering, 135,
    140–141, 144
Service bureau, service vendor, 84,
    89, 96–97, 104, 107, 109, 138,
    146, 149, 157, 159–160, 170–174
Silver densitometric test, 76
Silver film. see Film
Silver recovery, 71
Silver, use of in film production, 21,
    54–55, 57, 70, 77, 86, 91–92,
    103, 124–125
Simplex format, roll film, 58, 69
"Smart" terminal. see "Intelligent"
    terminal
Software, 12, 16, 86, 89, 95–98, 108,
    139, 143, 145, 148–150, 164,
    169, 172, 184, 191
Sorting, high-speed, 46
Source document, 21, 38–39, 177
  definition of, 1
  microfilming, 51–84
  versus COM, 34–36, 104, 117–119,
    140, 155
Space allocation, 112
Space requirements, equipment, 5,
    150
Space saving. see Storage space
Speed, 79
Splicing, roll film, 84
Spool, film, 27–28, 30, 55
Spooling, 97

Stability, image. see Archival quality
Standards, 13
  COM, 99, 102, 104
  EAM aperture card, 44
  flow chart, 17
  micrographic, 17–20, 75–77, 80, 114, 120–121, 135
  microfiche (fiche), 31–34, 119
  national, 75, 83–84
  operational, 29–30, 73, 82
  quality, 73
  roll-film, 27
"Step test", 67–68
Storage capacity, electronic, 148, 178
Storage, microform, 1, 13, 24, 44, 76, 109
  equipment, 150–152, 162
Storage space, savings in, 3–4, 7, 37
Subroutine packages, 96
Symbols, flow-chart, 18
System, active, 8, 28, 37, 166
Systems analysis, analyst, 15–17, 20, 23, 30, 98, 106, 138, 144, 156–157
System, defined, 1, 2, 6, 183
System capacities, 6, 17
System design, 7–8, 18, 23
System output, 10, 97–98
System, updatable, 37–39

T

Tab card, 31, 38, 42–44, 130–131, 150
Tape, 86, 89–90, 96, 98, 173–174, 190, 192
  COM-compatible, 89, 96, 98
  magnetic, 86, 89–90, 96–98, 145, 190
Tape drive, 89
Targets, flash, 104, 115, 130–135, 139, 141, 157, 159
Technicians, use of micrographics by, 12, 70, 74, 109
Telephone dial network, 180
Telephone directories, use of micrographics for, 47
Telephone industry, use of micrographics by, 112, 167, 179, 186

Temperature, equipment, 58, 75–76, 114
TEP (transparent electro-photographic), 44, 57 film
Terminal, interactive, 106–108, 112, 121, 145, 148, 169–171, 188
Terminal-to-line interfaces, 107
Test charts, 74
  density, 73, 76
  legibility, 74
  resolution, 73–74
Tests, quality, 30, 73–75, 103, 115, 157
Theft prevention, 14, 36, 42
Thermoplastic film, 79
Throughput speed, 64–65, 71–72, 104, 158–160, 171–172
  COM, 107
  duplication, 67
Time sharing, 146
Tonality, image. see Polarity
Toner, 38, 105, 126–127
Training, personnel, 16–17, 69
Transmission, electronic, 9, 114, 120, 127, 148, 179–180 182–183, 185, 189, 192 (see also Communication channels)
  telephone, 179, 186
Transmission efficiency, 96–97, 181
Transparent electrophotography (TEP), 38, 114
Transport, film, 9, 58, 61, 64, 69, 86, 112–113, 121, 123–124, 189
Trials, end-use, 83
Trimming, microform, 41
Turnaround speed, 56, 61
Turnkey, 7, 142–143, 146, 149, 169–170, 185

U

Ultrafiche, 21, 47–49, 116
Ultrastrip, 21, 47–49, 116
Ultraviolet (UV) light, use of in micrographics, 77–80, 82
Uniformity, input, 36, 70, 75, 188
Unit, carrier, 83
Unitized microforms, 35, 44, 46, 83

Unitization (see also Microform unit), 42
Universal reader-printers, 124
Updatable systems, 7, 11, 37–40, 42, 57
Updating, file. see Purging
"-up" format (four-up, eight-up), 46
User acceptance, 17, 120
User environment, 13, 17, 19, 115, 120
User reactions, 7, 11–12
UV (ultraviolet) light, 77, 80, 82

V

Vendor, service, 41, 44, 55, 58, 64, 69, 138, 149, 152, 182, 191
Vesicular process, 39, 76, 77–82, 87, 103, 105, 116
Videomicrographic, 180
Video display terminal, 121, 148, 171, 181, 187–188
Volume, production, 23, 56, 69–70, 79–81, 83, 111

W

Warehousing (records microforms), 7, 12
Waste disposal (film processing), 69–70, 124, 160, 182
Wavelength, 92
Weight, 121
Word processing, 9–10, 99, 179, 190–192

X

Xerography, 10, 14, 38, 57, 105, 124, 126–128
X-rays, filming of, 2, 42, 46, 55, 70

Z

Zero bit, 180, 183
Zoom capability, zoom lens, 118